中国古代兵器图鉴

AN APPRECIATION OF CHINESE ANCIENT WEAPONS

于孟晨　刘　磊　编著

西安出版社

图书在版编目（CIP）数据

中国古代兵器图鉴 / 于孟晨, 刘磊编著. — 西安：
西安出版社, 2017.4 (2023.4 重印)
（中国兵器文化研究丛书）
ISBN 978-7-5541-2107-8

Ⅰ.①中…　Ⅱ.①于…②刘…　Ⅲ.①兵器(考古)—
中国—图集　Ⅳ.①K875.82

中国版本图书馆CIP数据核字(2017)第069708号

中国兵器文化研究丛书
Zhongguo Bingqi Wenhua Yanjiu Congshu
中国古代兵器图鉴
Zhongguo Gudai Bingqi Tujian

编　　著：于孟晨　刘　磊
责任编辑：张增兰
装帧设计：纸尚图文设计
出版发行：西安出版社
社　　址：西安市雁塔区雁南五路1868号曲江影视大厦11层
电　　话：（029）85253740
邮政编码：710061
印　　刷：天津图文方嘉印刷有限公司
开　　本：787mm×1092mm　1/16
印　　张：20.25
字　　数：137千
版　　次：2017年4月第1版
　　　　　2023年4月第3次印刷
书　　号：ISBN 978-7-5541-2107-8
定　　价：72.00元

图书在版编目（CIP）数据

中国古代兵器图鉴 / 于孟晨, 刘磊编著. — 西安：
西安出版社，2017.4（2023.4 重印）

（中国兵器文化研究丛书）

ISBN 978-7-5541-2107-8

Ⅰ.①中⋯ Ⅱ.①于⋯②刘⋯ Ⅲ.①兵器(考古) —
中国 —图集 Ⅳ.①K875.82

中国版本图书馆CIP数据核字(2017)第069708号

中国兵器文化研究丛书
Zhongguo Bingqi Wenhua Yanjiu Congshu
中国古代兵器图鉴
Zhongguo Gudai Bingqi Tujian

编　　著：于孟晨　刘　磊
责任编辑：张增兰
装帧设计：纸尚图文设计
出版发行：西安出版社
社　　址：西安市雁塔区雁南五路1868号曲江影视大厦11层
电　　话：（029）85253740
邮政编码：710061
印　　刷：天津图文方嘉印刷有限公司
开　　本：787mm×1092mm　1/16
印　　张：20.25
字　　数：137千
版　　次：2017年4月第1版
　　　　　2023年4月第3次印刷
书　　号：ISBN 978-7-5541-2107-8
定　　价：72.00元

△ 读者购书、书店添货或如发现本书印装质量问题，请寄回调换。

中国古代兵器图鉴

AN APPRECIATION OF CHINESE ANCIENT WEAPONS

于孟晨　刘　磊　编著

西安出版社

总 序

20世纪六七十年代，我时常骑着自行车从灞桥到城里听课或者办事，要路过现在的金花北路，至今清楚地记得那里有个大学，门口挂着的木牌子上写的是西安工业学院。

我没有上过大学，所以一直对这所大学心有神往，心里头默默地想，要是自己哪一天能进到这个大学该是多好的事情。大概是九十年代，西安工业学院办了个作家培训班，请我做过报告，有幸第一次进到了这个学校，但是一直与之无有深入的交集，也就常为无缘成为其中一员而深感遗憾。直到2005年，西安工业学院有意成立以我的名字命名的当代文学研究中心，聘请我做客座教授，才圆了我的一个梦，我终于成为了其中的一员。

现在西安工业大学的前身就是西安工业学院，虽然是一所以研究兵器为主的工科学校，却有着近六十年的人文积淀，享誉书坛的"关中四老"中的刘自椟和陈泽秦两位老先生就曾任教于这里一直到终老。陈忠实当代文学研究中心成立以后，在校方的大力支持下，尤其是国平和希哲的具体组织努力下，学校的文学研究方面取得了不少成果，给这个学校带来了新的品质和内涵，实在是可喜的事情。我虽然挂着中心主任的头衔，但是实在没有多少精力顾得上过问，只是遇到大的文学研讨活动、校庆等事情的时候露个面，说说文学方面的感受，或者以尽作为西安工业大学一员应尽的责任和义务。倘若时间和精力允许的话，我时或会给爱好文学的学生讲讲课，也因此常常深受感动，竟然有那么多的工科学生喜欢着文学。最让我记忆深刻的是学生曾专门办过我的作品研讨会，一个个稚嫩的面孔，一个个新颖的见解，吸引我从头听到尾。我当时很是吃惊，《白鹿原》的故事和历史场景已经距离他们很远了，或者说几乎是隔陌的，但他们认真地读作品，又发表着不同的见解，的确让我感慨万千，真正体悟到"文学依然神圣"的内在必然性，也着实为文学事业的未来希望而高兴！

前些日子，研究中心的负责人给我说，学校新成立的中国兵器文化研究中心组织青年学者和博士们编撰了一套《中国兵器文化研究丛书》，包括《中国古代兵器图鉴》《中国兵器文化概要》《＜武经总要＞注》等，作为第一辑的成果集体推出，要我写个序。近些年，精气神大不如前，眼力也不好使，我已不应允作序一类的事，为表达歉意，常用题写书名代替。但是这次我得写点话，终究我是西安工业大学的一员，我深为这些年轻人非凡的才华和渊博的学识而敬佩，也为学校能从文化层面来总结我们历史的传统而欢舞，能把器转化为道，又从道中传承民族精粹是多么富有意义的事情，无论放置在急功近利普泛的当下，还是展眼中国历史脉源的承继，或者对学生的浸染，都是功德无量的大事一桩！可惜的是，我涉猎有限，知之寥寥，加之身体欠佳，读书稿无有精力支撑，实在不敢为序，只能借助文字鼓励他们，也向读者朋友推介他们的大作，因为他们值得信任，他们是我的同事。

说起兵器，实际上自人类产生以来，为了生存需要就已经产生，那个时候估计多是用木头改造或者用石头打磨出来的。后来随着社会发展和科技进步，慢慢先有青铜的，后有钢铁的，到后来还有了火药，一步一步走过来。距离我家不远的秦始皇兵马俑就展列着不少的出土兵器。在参观一些出土遗物时，总会多多少少有一些兵器。令人惊奇的是，一些古时候的兵器至今还在劳动生产中应用，比如《白鹿原》里，杀死田小娥的鹿三用的梭镖，实际上是过去农村人常用来抵御野兽侵袭的，现在野兽少了，用这些家什的也就稀罕了。《白鹿原》里头写冷先生进城给亲戚看了病去三意社看戏，看的是宋得民的《滚钉板》，那个滚钉板想来在古代也是在战场上使用的，如今却出现在舞台上。

　　总之，如同茶米油盐，兵器的存在与制造也是人类必不可少的，只不过一个为了生活，一个为了安全，性质不同，目标应该是确切的一致——为了安全地生存。因之兵器里渗透了太多人的大聪明大智慧。在我看来，研究兵器文化与研制兵器一样重要。没有文化的民族是可怕的，缺少文化的民族也是不经折腾的。但愿这些年轻人的学术理想能为中华民族文化的复壮贡献自己的绵薄之力，我愿为他们的事业鼓与呼！

陈忠实

2015年5月27日

目录

CONTENTS

中国古代兵器源远流长。在绵延数千年的古代战争中，中华民族发明出了种类繁多、工艺先进、杀伤力强的兵器，在历史上写下了辉煌灿烂的篇章。这些兵器是古代中国人勇敢、智慧、创造力的结晶，也凝聚了当时的科技、审美、社会、历史等多方面元素，因此，古代兵器能够成为我们了解古代战争、兵制、科技、历史、审美、社会发展的一个重要的窗口和断面。

中国古代兵器由远古的狩猎工具演变而来，大致经历了石兵器、青铜兵器、铁兵器与古代火器等发展阶段，前三个阶段为冷兵器阶段，后一个阶段则为冷热并用阶段。古代兵器发展的方向是朝着结构更为复杂、使用更便捷灵活、性能更优良、杀伤力更强大迈进。中国古代兵器的发展给世界兵器乃至世界文明带来了深远的影响，火药和火药兵器的西传引起了世界兵器划时代的革新。历史也给中华民族留下了深刻的教训，故步自封和闭关自守窒息了这个民族的活力和创造力，鸦片战争后，西方更为先进的坚船利炮进入中国，逐渐结束了中国古代兵器的辉煌历史。

中国古代兵器种类和数量非常多，先秦有"五兵"之说，南宋时期的兵书《翠微北征录》则首次提到了"十八般武艺"，元以后"十八般武艺"一说流传甚广，但到底是哪"十八般"在典籍中没有详细记述。明谢肇淛的博物学著作《五杂俎》和朱国祯的笔记小说《涌幢小品》明确了"十八般武艺"为：弓、弩、枪、刀、剑、矛、盾、斧、钺、戟、鞭、锏、挝、殳、叉、耙、绵绳套索、白打。其中，前十七种为兵器，白打则是散打搏击。同为明代人的施耐庵在其《水浒传》中却有不同说法，认为"十八般武艺"为十八种兵器的使用，它们是：矛锤弓弩铳，鞭简剑链挝，斧钺戈戟，牌棒与枪杈。现在我们说"十八般武艺"一般是指刀、枪、剑、戟、斧、钺、钩、叉、鞭、锏、锤、抓、镗、棍、槊、棒、拐、流星锤。

其实，中国古代的兵器从种类上远不止这十八种，加上火器、大型攻守城器械、战车、战船等，其总数不下百种。对于兵器的分类，较为科学的方法就是根据它在实战中的用途来划分。本书中我们将古代兵器大致分为长兵器、短兵器、远射兵器、软兵器、暗器、防护具、火器、战车、战船、攻守城器械等几大类，这些分类基本构成了中国古代兵器的框架。

古人留下的关涉兵器的典籍相当丰富，多是对古代兵器形制、用法、工艺等的文字性介绍和说明，也有部分典籍用了较为直观和形象的图片。北宋官修的军事类书《武经总要》、明天启年间茅元仪编成的《武备志》、抗倭名将戚继光所著《练兵实纪》和《纪效新书》等记录了当时军队所用的兵器和装备，特别是《武经总要》和《武备志》有大量的兵器图片。随着火器的大规模使用，出现了一些图文结合的介绍军队使用火器的相关著作，最重要的有明赵士桢于万历年间写成的《神器谱》、刊印于崇祯五年(1632)孙元化的《西法神机》、崇祯十六年(1643)刊印的焦勖的《火攻挈要》。

在这些典籍和前人对古代兵器的研究基础上，本书详细地回顾了各类兵器的发展历程，选取那些具有典型性和较大文化价值的兵器予以展示和描述，力图做到资料翔实、重点突出、形象直观、文字精准、图文并茂、通俗易懂，让读者在了解古代兵器和兵器文化、获得更多的历史知识的同时，增强国防观念和民族自豪感。

长兵器

长兵器是古代较长的手持格斗兵器的统称，是相较于较短的手持格斗兵器而言的。古代长兵器与短兵器的划分没有严格的尺寸标准，一般将等于或超过身长、多用双手操持的冷兵器列为长兵器，主要种类有戈、矛、枪、大刀、戟、长斧、钺、棍、殳、铍，等等，其材质从石质、青铜到铁、钢逐步变化，而其种类、形制及用途也随着不同时代作战方式的演变与制造技术的发展相应而变。

长兵器以刺为主要攻击方式，与短兵器相比，具有时效性强、可先发制人的优点，是历代军队中不可或缺的兵器装备，更是以战车作战为主的年代必不可少的重要兵器。

第1节

戈

　　戈是古代重要的长兵器之一，可以横击、啄刺或钩拉敌人。一般认为戈由镰刀类工具演化而来，盛行于商周至战国时期。

　　戈主要由三部分构成：戈头、戈柲和镈。戈头位于顶端，标准形态包括援、内、胡。"援"是戈最具杀伤力的部分，上下有刃、前有尖锋；"内"位于援的后部，内上有孔，称为"穿"，供装戈柲时系结所用；援的下部延长成"胡"，胡上也有刃，和援的下刃连接成弧形。为了防止钩啄时戈头脱落，常在援、内之间设"阑"。戈柲为竹木所制，柲的下端是套筒状的青铜镈。

河南偃师二里头遗址中发现的青铜戈距今约 3500 年，是目前发现的最早的青铜戈。二里头文化时期，青铜戈形制比较简单，有直内戈和曲内戈之分。直内戈像一把稍宽的剑，整体作长条形，援狭长，无上下阑，内的后部呈齿状，便于用索固定在戈柲上；曲内戈的基本形制如直内戈，援狭长，上侧略有弧度，只是内稍向下弯曲。

商代中期，陕西汉中地区出现了一种戈，它的援部较宽短，呈三角形。商代晚期是戈发展的重要时期，青铜戈的形制最多，有直内、曲内、銎内、三角援、条形短胡戈等。西周戈继承了商代晚期直内戈的形制并有所发展，特点表现在两个方面：一是援与阑的夹角由直角扩大到小于100 度的钝角；二是胡延长加穿，更多地使用了中胡戈。

春秋时期戈的形式较多，如短援阔内戈、狭援长胡戈、圭援戈。圭援戈上刃较平直，甚至向外侧稍凸起，下刃向内一侧微凹，整个援部给人以中间鼓、两头稍低的紧绷感，更有杀伤力。此时胡也比早期长，而且有继续加长的趋势。从战国初开始，戈援和内发生了较大的变化，援由平直变成弧曲状，并在下刃和胡上做出刺，这样就增强了钩杀的功能；戈内上翘，并有锐利的边刃，缚柲的内可用来击敌。战国时期，由于冶铁业的发展，铁兵器的使用逐渐增多，青铜戈也开始逐渐被铁戟取代。

秦戈沿袭了战国铜戈的形态，其基本特点为：长胡、三穿或四穿、曲援、内上翘，除了援有锋利的刃外，内和胡上也磨有利刃，增强了钩杀和啄击的效果。到东汉时期，戈作为实战兵器已经在战场上销声匿迹。

除用于战场杀敌，青铜戈、玉戈亦作为礼器使用，如用作祭祀用品、仪仗用品。

图 1-1

嵌绿松石青铜戈[①]（商）
Bronze Dagger-axe embedded with turquoise
（Shang Dynasty）

图 1-2

宽援戈（商）
Dagger-axe with a broad blade
（Shang Dynasty）

① 嵌绿松石青铜戈：商王武丁时期，河南安阳殷墟妇好墓出土。

Bronze Dagger-axe embedded with turquoise：It was made in the Period of King Wuding in Shang Dynasty and was unearthed from the Fuhao Tomb of Yin ruins in Anyang City, Henan Province.

图 1-3

有阑直内铜戈（商早期）
Bronze Dagger-axe with a tang and straight
symmetrical blade（Early Stage of Shang Dynasty）

图 1-4

銎内戈（商）
Dagger-axe with a tang and rectangular rear blade
（Shang Dynasty）

图 1-5

曲内戈（商）
Dagger-axe with curved blade（Shang Dynasty）

图 1-6

连柄铜戈①（商中期）
Bronze Dagger-axe with a shaft
（Middle Stage of Shang Dynasty）

① 连柄铜戈：商代中期东胡人所用，辽宁凌海市水手营子村出土，秘长 80.2 厘米。

Bronze Dagger-axe with a shaft：It was used by Donghu People (an ethnic group living in the Northeast of Kingdom Yan) in the middle stage of Shang Dynasty, and was unearthed from Shuishou Yingzi Village in Linghai City of Liaoning Province. Its handle was 80.2 cm long.

图 1-7　　**直内短胡一穿戈**^①（**西周早期**）

Dagger-axe with a straight, short blade containing a fixing hole and tang (The Early Stage of Western Zhou Dynasty)

图 1-8　　**龙纹四穿戈（西周）**

Dagger-axe with Dragon Design and four mounting holes (Western Zhou Dynasty)

①西周早期，胡与穿的出现使戈捆绑得更牢固，增强了铜戈的杀伤力。

　　In the early stage of Western Zhou Dynasty, the emergence of short rear blade and holes could help the dagger-axe be fixed firmly to the shaft and strengthen its lethality.

| 图 1-9 | **斜刃戈（西周早期）**
Dagger-axe with angled blade
(The Early Stage of Western Zhou Dynasty) |

| 图 1-10 | **"宋公栾"青铜戈**[①]**（春秋时期）**
" Song Gongluan's " Bronze Dagger-axe
(The Spring and Autumn Period) |

---

① 宋公栾即春秋时期宋国国君宋景公。
Song Gongluan refers to Song Jinggong, the emperor of State of Song in the Spring and Autumn Period.

图 1-11   "滕侯夨"青铜戈^①（春秋时期）
" Teng Houze ' s " Bronze Dagger-axe
（The Spring and Autumn Period）

图 1-12   圭援铜戈（春秋时期）
Bronze Dagger-axe with narrow rear blade
（The Spring and Autumn Period）

---

    ① "滕侯夨（zè）"青铜戈：春秋时期古滕国滕侯夨所造，山东滕县出土。

    "Teng Houze ' s " Bronze Dagger-axe: It was made by Teng Houze in State of Teng in the Spring and Autumn Period, and was unearthed in Teng County of Shandong Province.

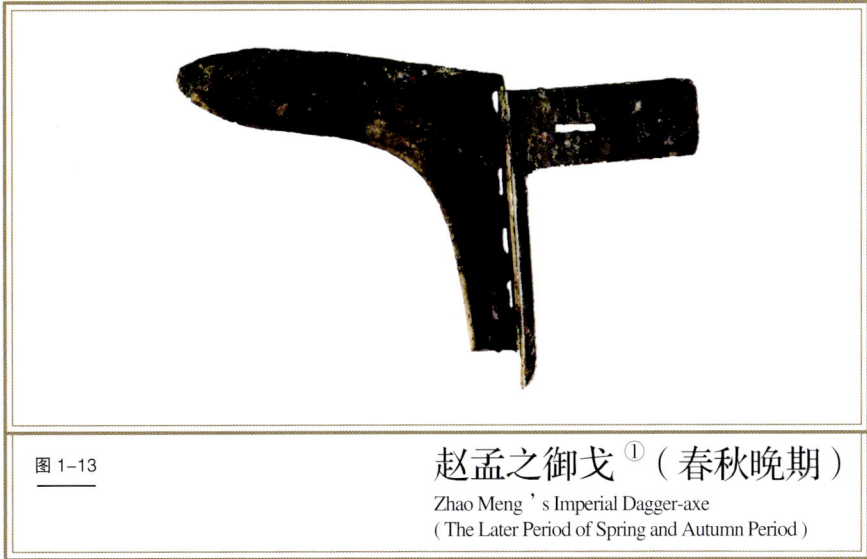

图 1-13

赵孟之御戈 ①（春秋晚期）
Zhao Meng's Imperial Dagger-axe
(The Later Period of Spring and Autumn Period)

① 赵孟之御戈：出土于山西太原金胜村，为春秋晚期晋国所造，其形制就是春秋中期流行的长胡多穿戈，也称为"普通型方内戈"。此戈援部较直，上仰，仰角达104度，援锋收成尖叶形。援中偏上起脊棱，横截面呈上下不对称的菱形。下刃与上刃保持平行，至中段弧转而下，延伸为胡部，胡底平折。援后上角设一长方形穿，胡内侧设三个长方形穿，共四穿。援、胡部后侧起阑，阑末凸出胡底之下为下齿。长方形直内平伸，内中设一长方形穿，内前端两角方正。戈头通长20.7厘米，援长13厘米，内长7.5厘米、宽3厘米，胡长6.8厘米、宽2.3厘米，阑高12.1厘米，重260克。胡部正面有线刻铭文一行五字："赵孟之御戈"。赵孟，即赵鞅、赵简子，春秋后期晋国卿大夫。

Zhao Mengzhi's Imperial Dagger-axe: It was unearthed at Jinsheng Village in Taiyuan of Shanxi Province. It was made in State of Jin in Spring and Autumn Period, and its shape and structure followed the Dagger-axe with long dagger base and multi-holes that was popular in the middle stage of Spring and Autumn Period, which was also called Ordinary-type Dagger-axe with Square rear blade. Its dagger was straight and tilted upward at an angle of 104°. The edge of dagger blade was shaped like a leaf-tip, and the upper edge in the middle of the dagger blade raised as ridge so that its cross section looked like an asymmetrical rhombus. The lower and upper blade would keep parallel, which came to the middle part to turn downward with a curve which was extended to lower base. One rectangle hole was designed at the bottom of dagger blade and three rectangle holes were on the inner side of lower base. The rear side of dagger and base had a bar with the end stretching out the bottom of the base. The straight rectangle rear blade was extending horizontally with a rectangle hole and both square front ends. Its head had a length of 20.7cm. Its dagger blade was 13cm in length, and its rear blade was 7.5cm in length and 3cm in width. Its base extension was 6.8cm in length and 2.3cm in width. The extension bar was 12.1cm in height and 260 grams in weight. The front side of dagger base was inscribed with 5 characters in a line, which read "Zhao Mengzhi's Imperial Dagger-axe." Zhao Mengzhi referred to Zhao Yang or Zhao Jianzi, who was the minister of State of Jin in the later stage of Spring and Autumn Period.

图 1-14

锦纹青铜戈（战国时期）
Bronze Dagger-axe with brocade
（The Warring States Period）

图 1-15

"二年"刻铭铜戈 [①]（战国时期）
Bronze Dagger-axe with inscription of "Two Years"
（The Warring States Period）

---

① "二年"刻铭铜戈：目前所发现的战国时期中山国唯一的一件刻铭实用兵器。

Bronze Dagger–axe with the inscription of "Two Years"：It was the only discovered practical weapon with an inscription made in the State of Zhongshan in Warring States Period.

| 图 1-16 | 燕王职戈 ① （战国晚期）
Bronze Dagger-axe of Emperor in State of Yan
(The Later Stage of Warring States Period) |

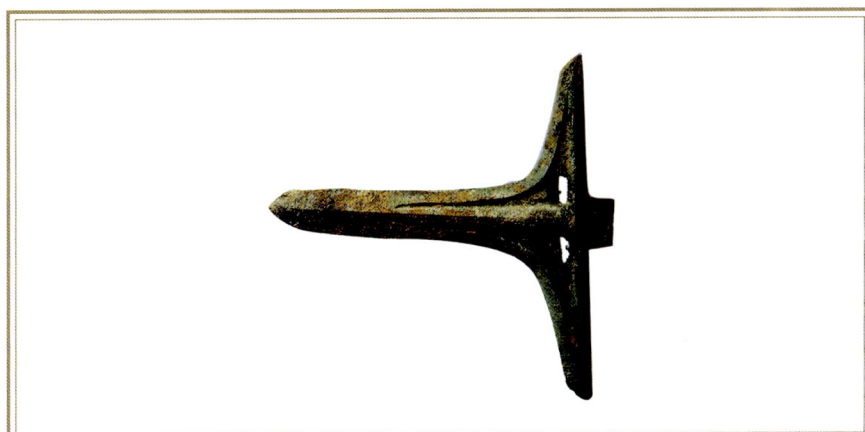

| 图 1-17 | 双胡戈 ② （战国时期）
Dagger-axe with double dagger base
(The Warring States Period) |

① 燕王职戈：通长 27.2 厘米，形体大，中部有隆起的脊，脊旁有凹形血槽，胡为三弧线，阑内三穿，内铸虎纹，胡上铸铭文。

Bronze Dagger-axe of Emperor in State of Yan：It was 27.2cm in length with a large shape. Its middle part raised a ridge with concave blood groove on its side. Its dagger base was designed in three arcs, and there were three holes in the base and tang. There was tiger design on the rear blade and an inscription on the base of the dagger.

② 双胡戈：辽宁建昌东大杖子墓地出土，长 17 厘米，高 16.5 厘米，类似形制多见于西南地区，罕见于东北。

Dagger-axe with a double dagger base：It was unearthed at the Da Zhangzi tomb of the east of Jianchang in Liaoning province. It was 16.5cm in length. This type of dagger-axe was popular in the Southwest region and rarely found in the Northeast region.

图 1-18

镏金鸳鸯铜戈 ① （西汉）

Gilding Bronze Dagger-axe with the design of a Mandarin
Duck （The Western Han Dynasty）

图 1-19

M 形内宽体鸟啄援戈 ② （西汉）

Dagger-axe with M-shape rear blade and the tip of broad dagger
shaped like a bird-pecking （Western Han Dynasty）

---

① 镏金鸳鸯铜戈：山东省淄博市临淄区出土。长 22.5 厘米，长胡三穿，援微曲，形制与战国时期的相仿。内上靠近胡处贯穿一筒形金帽，顶部装饰有一只回首鸳鸯，堪称西汉铜戈的精品。这一类铜戈可能主要用于宫廷仪卫。

Gilding Bronze Dagger-axe with the Design of a Mandarin Duck：It was unearthed at Linzi District of Zibo City in the Shandong Province. It was 22.5cm in length and had a slight curving dagger. There were three holes in the base of the dagger. Its shape and structure was similar to the one in the Warring States Period. There was a shape of gilded barrel near the base, on whose top laid a mandarin duck looking back. It could be regarded as the boutique of the bronze dagger-axe in the Western Han Dynasty. This type of dagger was mainly used by the honour guard in a Parade.

② M 形内宽体鸟啄援戈：西汉时期西南夷夜郎国造，贵州兴义马岭出土，通长 22.2 厘米。

Dagger-axe with M-shape rear blade and the tip of broad dagger like a bird-pecking：It was made in the State of Yelang in Southwest areas of Western Han Dynasty. It was unearthed at Ma Ling of Xingyi City in Gui Zhou Province, and had a length of 22.2cm.

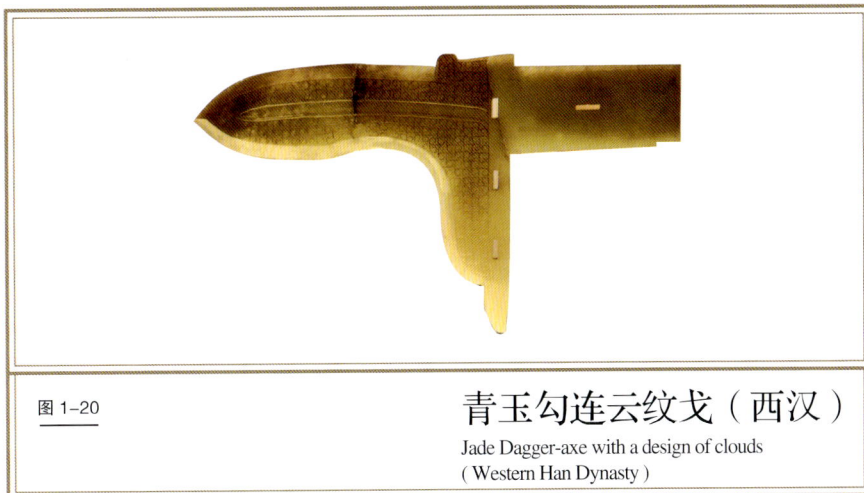

图 1–20

青玉勾连云纹戈（西汉）

Jade Dagger-axe with a design of clouds
（Western Han Dynasty）

第 **2** 节

矛

　　矛是一种用于直刺和挑扎的长兵器，由矛头和矛柄组成。矛头分为"身"和"骹（qiāo）"两部分。矛身顶尖为"锋"，中部为"脊"，脊左右两边展开为带刃的矛叶；骹是用来连接脊的直筒，用于插柄。有的矛头两边铸有环或孔，可将绳穿过把矛头牢牢绑缚在柄上，以免拔矛时矛头脱落，也可系缨。矛柄也称为"柲"，一般为木质或竹质，末端装有铜、铁等金属制成的镈（zūn），尖锐或平整，使矛平稳立置。

　　矛的雏形是原始社会人类狩猎所用的前端削尖的竹木棒。随着复合工具的发明，人类开始在竹木棒的一端安上石头或兽骨制成的矛头，矛的基本形态就形成了。在新石器时代，人们开始在矛的基部钻孔，更利于绑缚矛柄。

商代出现了青铜制的矛头，阔叶，呈三角形或亚腰形，中有凸脊。当时制造的青铜矛数量已经很大，是仅次于戈的兵器。西周矛的形制已逐步由阔叶向窄叶发展，至春秋晚期出现了形制成熟的窄体矛。窄体矛的基本特点是窄体、直刃、骹部有孔或双钮。战国中晚期矛进一步演变，形成了一种新形制——脊线上有两个凸起的刃，使矛身上形成了血槽，称"饮血"，在矛头刺入人体时出血进气，杀伤力更强。

秦代的矛刃体趋向宽而直，变短并附孔以固骹，通体长度稳定在15厘米左右。据《考工记》所载，最长的夷矛不过三寻，约合今5.54米，而出土的步兵秦矛有的长达6.3米，这是因为步兵用矛远比车兵便利，所以出现了特殊的长矛。

矛是汉代最重要的长柄格斗兵器，材质以钢铁为主。相较于铜矛，铁矛的形体更大，矛头逐渐加重加长。东晋十六国和南北朝时期，重装骑兵是军队的主力，长矛"稍"成为骑兵的主要格斗兵器，一直延续到隋唐，之后逐渐被枪取代。

图 1-21

石矛头 ① （旧石器时代晚期）
Stone Spear-head（The Later Stage of Paleolithic Age）

图 1-22

石矛 ② （新石器时代）
Stone Spear（The Neolithic Age）

---

① 石矛头：籍箕滩遗址出土，旧石器时代晚期细石器遗存物。

Stone Spear-head：It was unearthed from the relics of Jiqi Tan, and was used in the later period of the Paleolithic Age.

② 石矛：屈家岭遗址出土，距今 5000—4600 年。

Stone Spear：It was unearthed at the relics of Qu Jialing, which had a long history of 4600 to 5000 years.

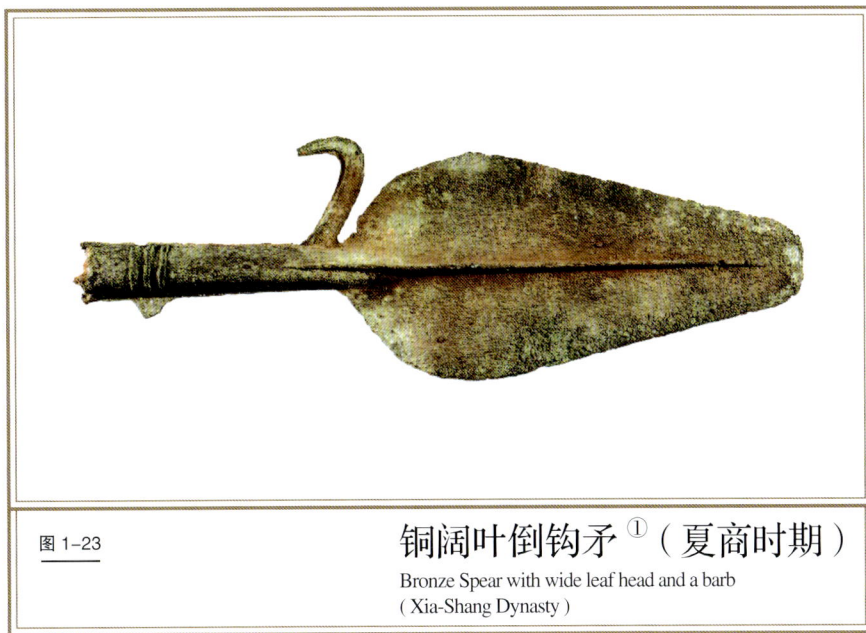

| 图 1-23 | 铜阔叶倒钩矛 ① （夏商时期）
Bronze Spear with wide leaf head and a barb
（ Xia-Shang Dynasty ） |

① 铜阔叶倒钩矛：夏商时期齐家文化至卡约文化（前 20 世纪—前 11 世纪）遗存物，青海省西宁市马坊乡小桥村沈那遗址出土。高 61.5 厘米，矛叶甚宽，形似柳叶，前锋圆钝。骹呈圆筒形，也很长大。骹下端有数道凸棱，侧面有一钮，上端有一凸棱直达矛锋，在矛叶与骹相交处，斜出一倒钩。

Bronze Spear with wide leaf head and a barb：It was a representative of Xia-Shang Dynasty, Qijia Culture (the culture of the Neolithic Age in Gansu Province) and Kayue Culture(it referred to the culture of Bronze Age) (20th century B.C–11th century B.C). It was unearthed at Shenna's tomb of Xiaoqiao Village in Mafang County, Xining City, Qinghai Province. It had a height of 61.5cm, whose leaf was wide. It looked like willow leaf with round top. The part of pastern had a big shape of cylinder. There were several ridges on the lower part, and a knob at its side face. There was a ridge extending to the top of the spear, and there was a barb on the joint of the spear leaf and tang.

图 1-24

铜矛（商）
Bronze Spear（Shang Dynasty）

图 1-25

长骹单系铜矛（商）
Bronze Spear with single hole and long pastern
（Shang Dynasty）

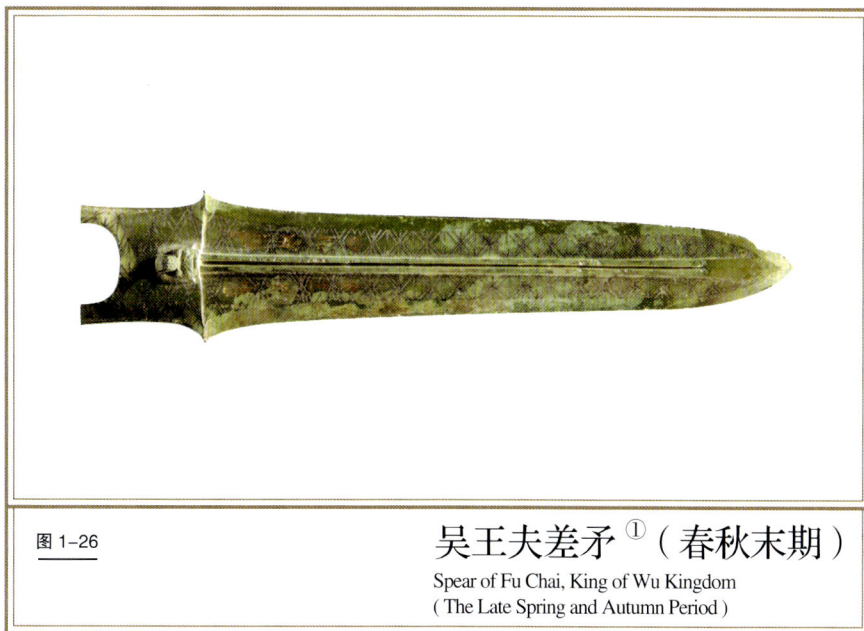

图 1-26

吴王夫差矛 ①（春秋末期）
Spear of Fu Chai, King of Wu Kingdom
(The Late Spring and Autumn Period)

① 吴王夫差矛：中国春秋末期吴王夫差使用的一把青铜矛，湖北省江陵县马山 5 号墓出土，仅存矛头，现藏于湖北省博物馆。矛头为青铜铸造，长 29.5 厘米，宽约 5 厘米，中部纵向突起脊棱，并有血槽。骹（筒）部较短，下部铸成燕尾形。矛骹的断面呈椭圆形，骹孔直达锋尖。在矛骹上部两面各铸有一个精美的兽面形钮。矛的通身铸饰菱格形暗纹。矛叶的正面在靠近骹部的地方，有铭文八字："吴王夫差，自乍（作）用剑。"字口错金，至今仍光亮如新，为春秋同类兵器之最。

Spear of Fu Chai, King of Wu Kingdom：It was one of the bronze spears used by Fu Chai, King of Wu Kingdom in the late Spring and Autumn Period in China, which was unearthed from the No.5 Tomb of Mashan in Jiangling County, Hubei Province. The spear-head, the only remaining part, was kept in Hubei Provincial Museum. It was made of bronze, and was 29.5cm in length and about 5cm in width. Its middle part raised a ridge vertically so that a blood flute was formed. Its pastern was short and its lower part was cast into the shape of swallow-tail. The section of its pastern took the shape of oval and the opening of its pastern spread to the sharp top. There were two elegant knobs with the shape of animal face on each side of its pastern. On the whole body of this spear was decorated with dark fringes of diamond shape. There were inscription of 8 characters on the front side of Spear-leaf near the pastern, which meant "(Belonging to) Fu Chai, King of Wu Kingdom, made for his personal use". These characters were inlaid gold so that they were still shining. Therefore, it was regarded as the superior example compared with the other weapons of the same kind in the Spring and Autumn Period.

图 1-27

吊人青铜矛（西汉）
Bronze Spear with two hanging men
（Western Han Dynasty）

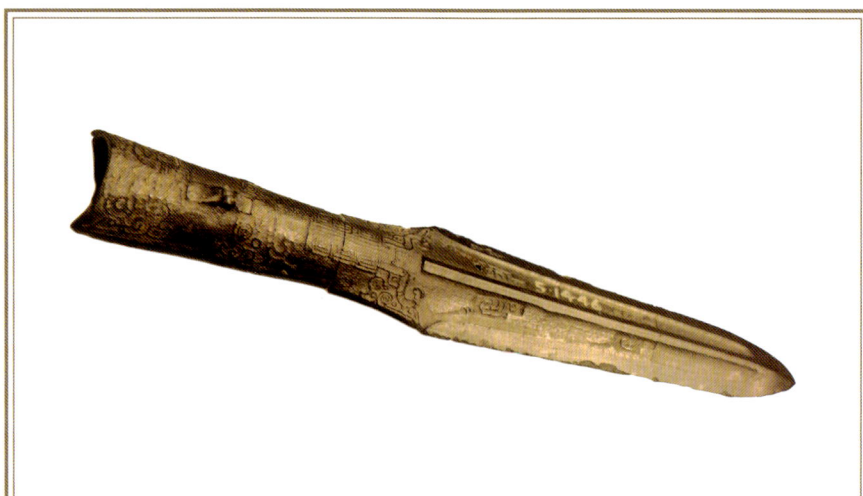

图 1-28

兽面纹矛（战国时期）
Spear with animal-face design
（The Warring States Period）

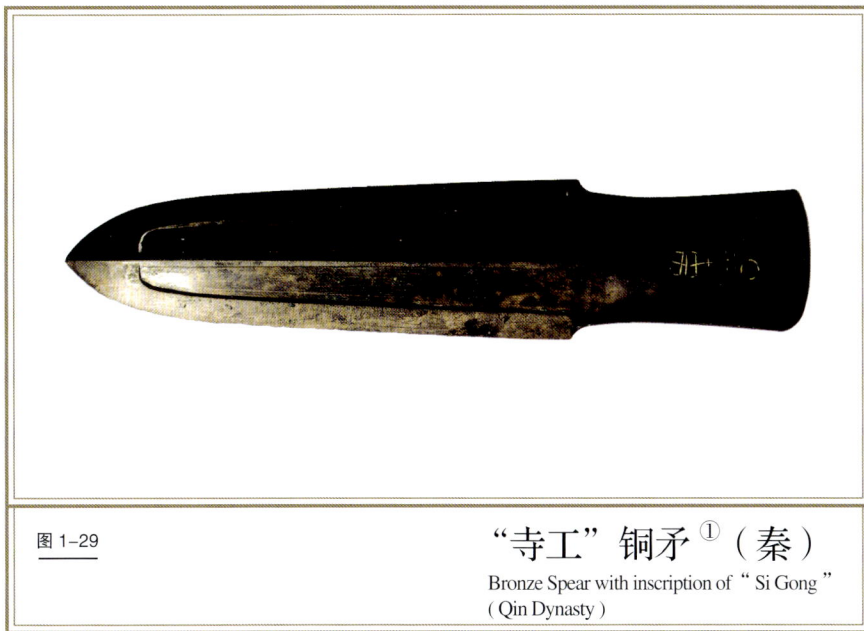

图 1-29	"寺工"铜矛 ① （秦） Bronze Spear with inscription of "Si Gong" (Qin Dynasty)

① "寺工"铜矛：出土于陕西临潼秦始皇陵兵马俑一号坑。矛头前锋收成尖叶形，两刃直而外斜，延伸至叶末，最宽处即为叶、骹结合部；叶中起棱，叶部中空，空腔上抵前锋附近，下与骹部相通，矛叶上开血槽；骹部较短，筒口呈椭圆形，由骹口至骹末均匀地过渡为宽扁喇叭形，与叶末相续，叶、骹浑然一体，可概括为"叶骹融合体"。骹部有对穿钉孔，与中脊线大体相对。通长 17.6 厘米，叶长 11.6 厘米、宽 3.6 厘米，骹长 6 厘米，骹筒为椭圆口，口径 3 厘米 ×2.4 厘米。骹部钉孔之上有刻划铭文一行二字，自上而下依次为"寺工"。"寺"是秦国青铜兵器的主要生产机构。

Bronze Spear with inscription of "Si Gong"：It was found at Pit One in Mausoleum of the First Qin Emperor in Lintong of Shaanxi Province. The front edge of its spearhead was shaped like a leaf tip, and both blades were straight and sloping outward which extending to the end of spear point.The widest part was the joint of its leaf and shaft. A ridge in the middle of the leaf with a hollow inside stretched upward to the top and linked with the shaft. There was a blood flute on the spear–leaf. Its shaft was slightly short with an oval–shaped mouth, which was changed into a wide and flat bell gradually to the end of the tang. The leaf and tang integrated into a whole, which could be generalized into a "Fusion of Leaf and Tang". There was a hole on tang which was opposite to the middle ridge. It was 17.6cm in whole length. Its leaf was 11.6cm in length and 3.6cm in width. The tang had a length of 6cm with an oval shape, whose caliber was 3cm × 2.4cm. There was inscription with 2 characters in a line laid above the hole, which read from the top to the bottom as "Si Gong". "Si" was a facility in charge of manufacturing bronze weapons in Qin Dynasty. "Gong" meant crafts.

图 1-30

铁铤^①（西汉）
Iron "Chan" (Spear)
(Western Han Dynasty)

图 1-31

蛙形矛^②（西汉）
Spear in the shape of a frog
(Western Han Dynasty)

① 铁铤（chán）：铁柄的矛。其较一般矛头稍微细长，矛身扁平，两侧有刃，下有铁柄，柄较短，流行于西汉，适用于在林莽地带作战。

Iron "Chan" (Spear)：It was a spear with iron handle, which was slightly narrower and longer than the ordinary spear-heads. Its body was flat, and there were blades on both sides. The bottom of the spear was a short iron handle. It was popular in Western Han Dynasty and was suitable to fight in forests.

② 蛙形矛：云南晋宁石寨山出土。通长 17 厘米，矛叶宽肥，近似等边三角形。两刃略弧，前锋圆钝。整体造型像一只青蛙伏在矛上，前足抱住骹口，后腿托住矛叶。

Spear in the shape of frog：It was unearthed from the old tombs of Shi Zhaishan in Jinning county, Yunnan Province. It was 17cm in whole length, and its leaf was wide and fat, which looked like an equilateral triangle. Its two blades had a light arc and the top was round and dull. The whole shape looked like a frog lying on the top with two forelegs clasping the mouth of the pastern and two back legs holding the spear leaf.

图 1-32

铁矛 ① （唐）
Iron Spear（Tang Dynasty）

图 1-33

三宝公铁矛 ② （明）
Iron Spear of the Revered San Bao
（Ming Dynasty）

① 铁矛：唐代渤海国造，黑龙江宁安虹鳟鱼场渤海墓地出土。通长 28 厘米，锻制品，矛身略呈柳叶形，尖锋，中脊起棱，截面呈菱形，骹与矛身分界不明显，骹后呈燕尾形。

Iron Spear: It was made in Kingdom of Halhae in Tang Dynasty and unearthed from Balhae Tombs in Ning'an, Hei Longjiang Province. It was 28cm in length and was forged into willow-leaf-shaped body. Its top was sharp and its mid-ridge raised edge, so its section was in the shape of rhombus. There was no exact distinctive division between its pastern and body. And the bottom of the pastern took the shape of swallow tail.

② 三宝公铁矛：两面分别凸铸 "三宝公" 和 "三宝大人" 铭文，是印度尼西亚民间纪念三宝太监郑和的祭典之器。

Iron Spear of the Revered San Bao：It was inscribed on both sides with "The revered San Bao" and "Officer San Bao", which was used as the sacrificial weapon by the Indonesian folks to commemorate the eunuch San Bao, also known as Zheng He.

第 **3** 节

戟

　　戟是一种融合戈与矛两种兵器功能的兵器，主要由锋、援、胡、内、穿等五个部分组成，可以前刺，亦可横击与钩杀。

　　目前我国发现最早的戟出现于商代晚期，其戈、矛是分别铸造的。西周时期出现了通体合铸的"十"字形青铜戟，一种是以矛为主，侧面出援，秘装在矛体的銎部；另一种是以戈为主，适当加宽阑和锋，但因戟头质轻体薄，实战效果并不突出，于西周末被淘汰。

　　春秋战国时期戟是重要的车战兵器，它的戈头和矛头分别铸制，然后再联装在秘上。在江淮流域的楚、蔡等国出现了一种装有多重戟援的

"多果（戈）戟"，在一根秘上联装 2 个或 3 个戟援，秘长均为 3 米左右，杀伤力大大提高，如湖北随州市曾侯乙墓出土的长柄三戈戟。战国晚期，冶铁技术的发展催生了钢铁铸造的戟，其形体也有所改进，通体合铸，援由宽钝变为窄尖，取消了内，用胡来缚秘，整体造型由"十"字形进化为"卜"字形，称为"卜字铁戟"。

西汉以后，戟的援由平直变为弧曲上翘形成钩刺，前刺的杀伤力进一步增强，因而戟成为当时军队的常备兵器。三国时期，戟的种类增多，有长戟、手戟、双戟。手戟柄短体轻，可刺可掷，是性能优良的防身自卫兵器；长戟、双戟柄长体重，杀伤力大。到了唐代，戟退出了军用兵器行列，成为一种表示身份等级的礼兵器，叫"稍戟"。

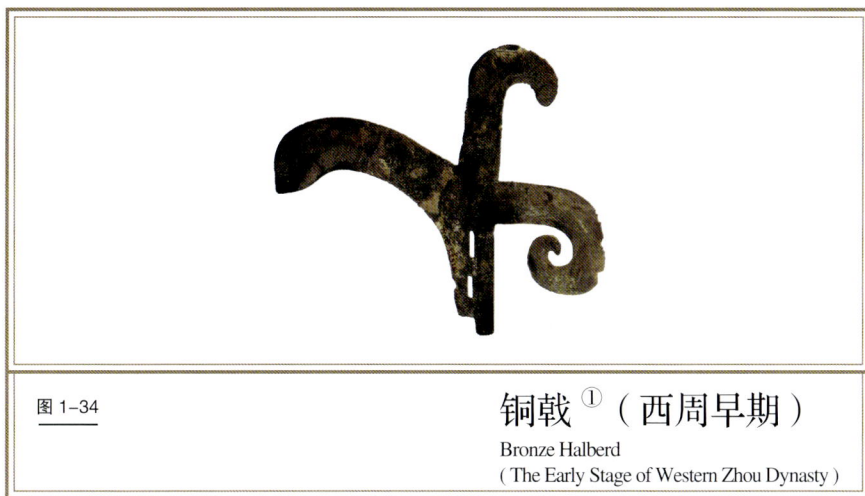

图 1-34

铜戟① （西周早期）
Bronze Halberd
（The Early Stage of Western Zhou Dynasty）

---

① 铜戟：戟兼有戈之钩杀、矛之刺击两种功能。此戟前端并非矛形，可能是戈、刀合体，也可能是没有实用功能的仪仗器。

Bronze Halberd: It had the dual function of a dagger's stabbing and a spear's impaling ability. Its front end didn't take the shape of spear, which might be the combination of the dagger and the sabre, or which might be a ritual utensil without any offensive function.

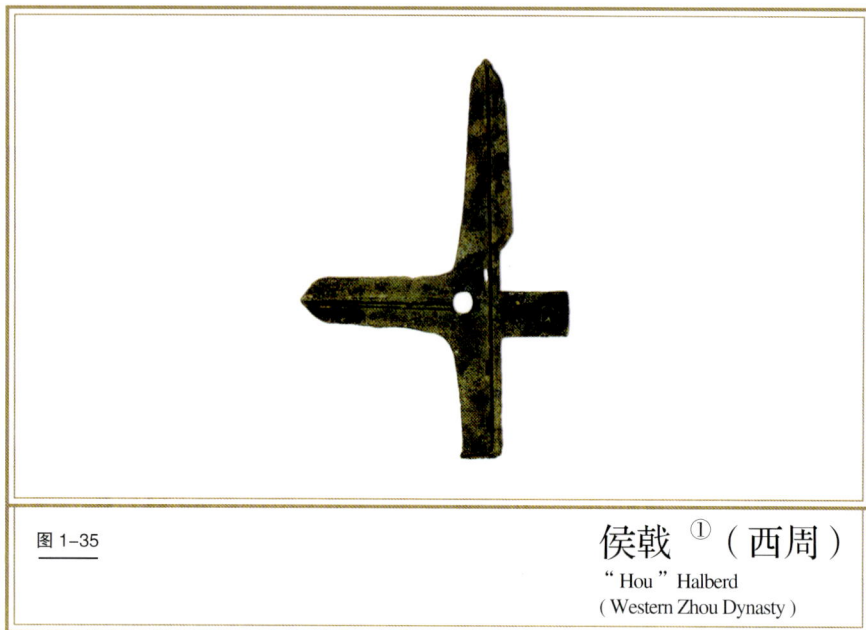

图 1-35

侯戟 ① （西周）
"Hou" Halberd
(Western Zhou Dynasty)

---

① 侯戟：河南浚县辛村出土，通长 27.5 厘米。上端为扁形刺，中段为戈形，有脊，下连长胡，三穿，直内较短，器内部铸铭文"侯"，是西周早中期的典型式样。

"Hou" Halberd: It was unearthed at Xin Village in Xun county, Henan Province. It was 27.5cm in length, with the top fitted with a flat thorn and mid-part in the shape of dagger with a ridge. The bottom was linked with long dagger base. There were three "holes" on it, and the straight rear blade was slightly short. It was inscribed with a Chinese character "Hou". The halberd was the typical style of the early and middle stage of Western Zhou Dynasty.

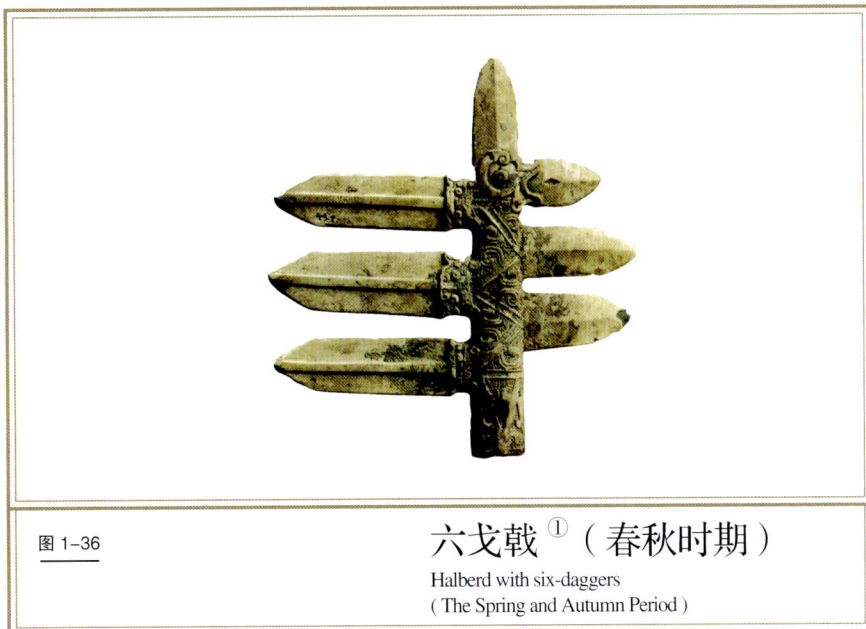

图 1-36

六戈戟 ① （春秋时期）

Halberd with six-daggers
(The Spring and Autumn Period)

---

① 六戈戟：河南省叶县旧县乡 4 号墓出土，青铜材质，戟首长 23.3 厘米、宽 22.3 厘米。此戟銎较长，銎口呈卵圆形，上面装饰有花形；銎顶出短剑形戟刺；銎左右参差平出六枚戈头，一边较长，一边较短。长的三枚形状尺寸相同，中脊粗壮，前锋呈三角形；短的三枚中最上的一枚最短，中、下两枚尺寸相当，断面呈菱形。较长的三枚戈头及銎上端铸有兽面纹，兽面张口衔住戈头。銎中部饰有两对四条蜷体蛇纹并加饰折带纹，下段饰三角纹。这件戟形制少见，与同时代其他戟大相径庭。

Halberd with six-daggers: It was unearthed from the No.4 tombs at Jiuxian Village of Ye county in Henan province. It was made of bronze with a length of 23.3cm and a width of 22.3cm. The halberd had a slightly long hole, whose mouth was egg-shaped with flower-designed decoration. A short sword extended from the top of the tang, which was like the thorn of halberd. There were three paralleled rows which totaled six dagger-heads on the right and left side of the tube respectively. The heads on one side were longer than the ones on the other side. The longer heads were in the same size and their mid-ridge was strong. Their cutting edges took triangle shape. The upper one among the shorter heads was the shortest, and the other two were in the same size, whose sections were rhombus-shaped. There was a beast-face design on the longer three heads and the tube. There were four curled snakes design with a folded rope design on the mid-part of the tang. The lower part was decorated with a triangle design. The shape and structure of this halberd was rare, and different from other halberds.

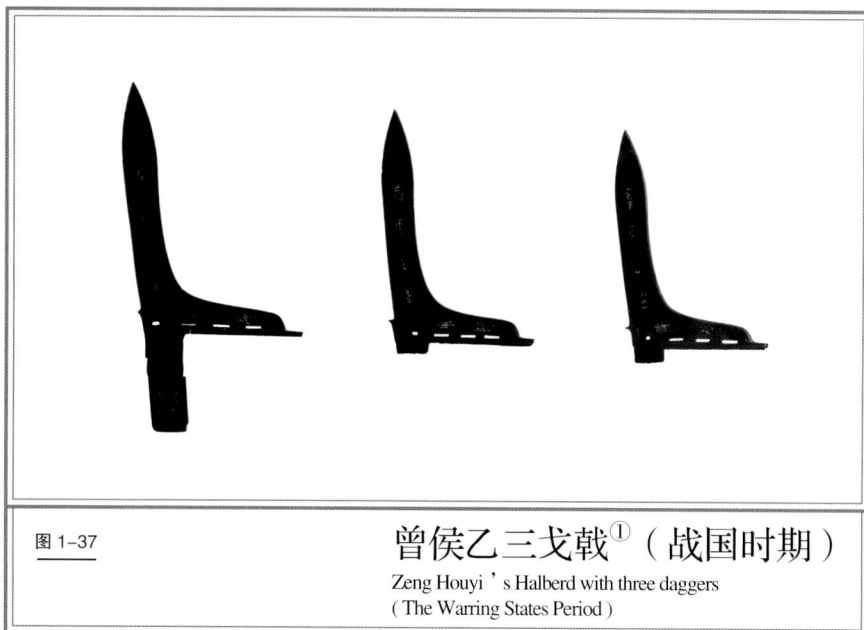

图 1-37

曾侯乙三戈戟^①（战国时期）
Zeng Houyi' s Halberd with three daggers
(The Warring States Period)

① 曾侯乙三戈戟：湖北省随县擂鼓墩 1 号墓出土，长 3.43 米，有"曾侯乙之用戟"六字铭文，戈内后部阴刻由龙与兽组成的"曾"字徽记。此戟顶端装铜矛头和有内铜戈，往下 4.7 厘米处又装一无内铜戈，再往下 5 厘米处再装一无内铜戈，一矛三戈同秘，当是战车上使用的长兵器。这种兵器在中国是首次发现。

Zeng Houyi' s Halberd with three daggers: It was unearthed from Pit 1 at Relics of Leigu Dun in Sui County of Hubei Province. It was 3.43m in length, and was inscribed with 6 characters (which read "Zeng Houyi' s Halberd"). There was a logo of Chinese character "Zeng" formed by a dragon and a beast carved on the back side of rear blade. The top of this halberd was fixed with bronze spear-head and bronze dagger with rear blade which curved downward. 4.7cm below was a bronze dagger without a rear blade. At a further 5cm below, another a bronze dagger, without a rear blade, was mounted. The spear and three daggers were bound onto one handle. At that time the halberd was called a Long Weapon and was used on chariots.

图 1-38

楚王孙渔戟（战国时期）

Halberd of Sunyu, the King of Chu Kingdom
（The Warring States Period）

图 1-39

中山国铜戟（战国时期）

Bronze Halberd in Zhongshan Kingdom
（The Warring States Period）

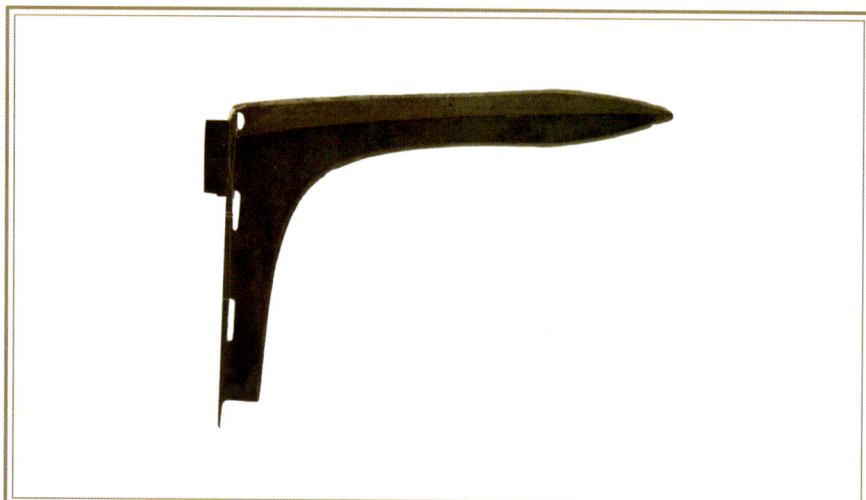

图 1-40

铜戟（战国时期）
Bronze Halberd
（The Warring States Period）

图 1-41

剑形铜戟（战国时期）
Bronze Halberd in the shape of sword
（The Warring States Period）

图 1-42

铁戟 ① （西汉）
Iron Halberd
（Western Han Dynasty）

图 1-43

铁戟（西汉）
Iron Halberd
（Western Han Dynasty）

① 铁戟：1956 年河南省陕县后川出土，长 33.7 厘米。此戟呈"卜"字形，是汉代最常见的戟形。戟身扁平，前端直刺呈尖锋，后端微钝，戟身中部横出一直刃，亦为尖锋。

Iron Halberd：In 1956, it was unearthed from Houchuan in Shan County, Henan Province, and had a length of 33.7cm. It looked like the Chinese character of "卜" (pronounced Bu). Its body was flat, and its top was sharp. The lower end was slightly dull. There was a straight blade with a sharp edge protruded from the middle of its body. It was quite frequently used in Han Dynasty.

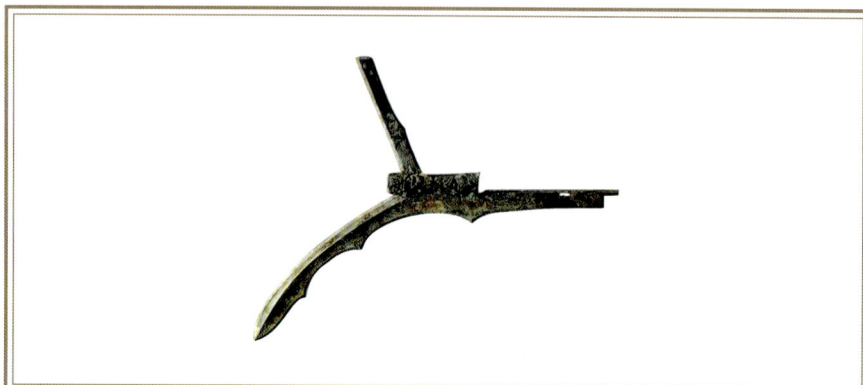

图 1-44

铜鸡鸣戟 ①（西汉早期）
Bronze Halberd in the shape of crowing rooster
（The Early Stage of Western Han Dynasty）

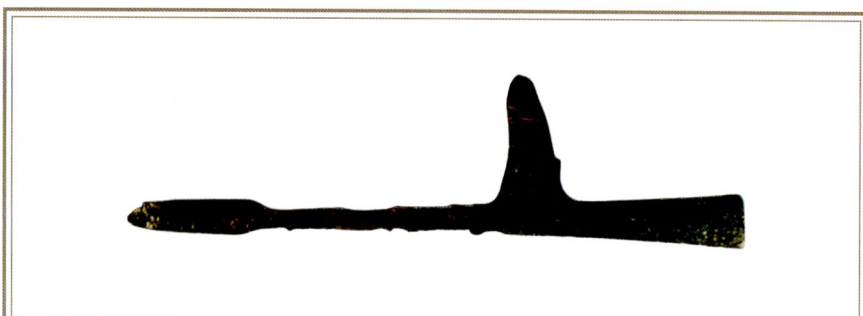

图 1-45

铜骹铁戟 ②（西汉中期）
Iron Halberd with bronze tang
（The Middle Stage of Western Han Dynasty）

---

① 铜鸡鸣戟：江苏徐州狮子山西汉楚王陵墓出土，通长 53 厘米。

Bronze Halberd in the shape of crowing rooster：It was unearthed from Tomb of King of Chu Kingdom in Western Han Dynasty on the Shizi Mountain of Xuzhou city, Jiangsu Province, and was 53cm long.

② 铜骹铁戟：云南江川李家山出土。"卜"字形，通高 28 厘米，刺刃长 6.9 厘米，枝长 5.7 厘米，骹径 2.3 厘米。西汉中期西南夷滇国所造。

Iron Halberd with bronze tang：It was found on Lijia Mountain of Jiangchuan county, Yunnan Province, and was made in Ancient Dian Kingdom of Southwest Tribes in the mid-stage of Western Han Dynasty. It looked like the Chinese character "卜"（bu），and was 28cm long. Its spear blade was 6.9cm long. Its barb blade was 5.7cm in length, and the diameter of the tang was 2.3cm.

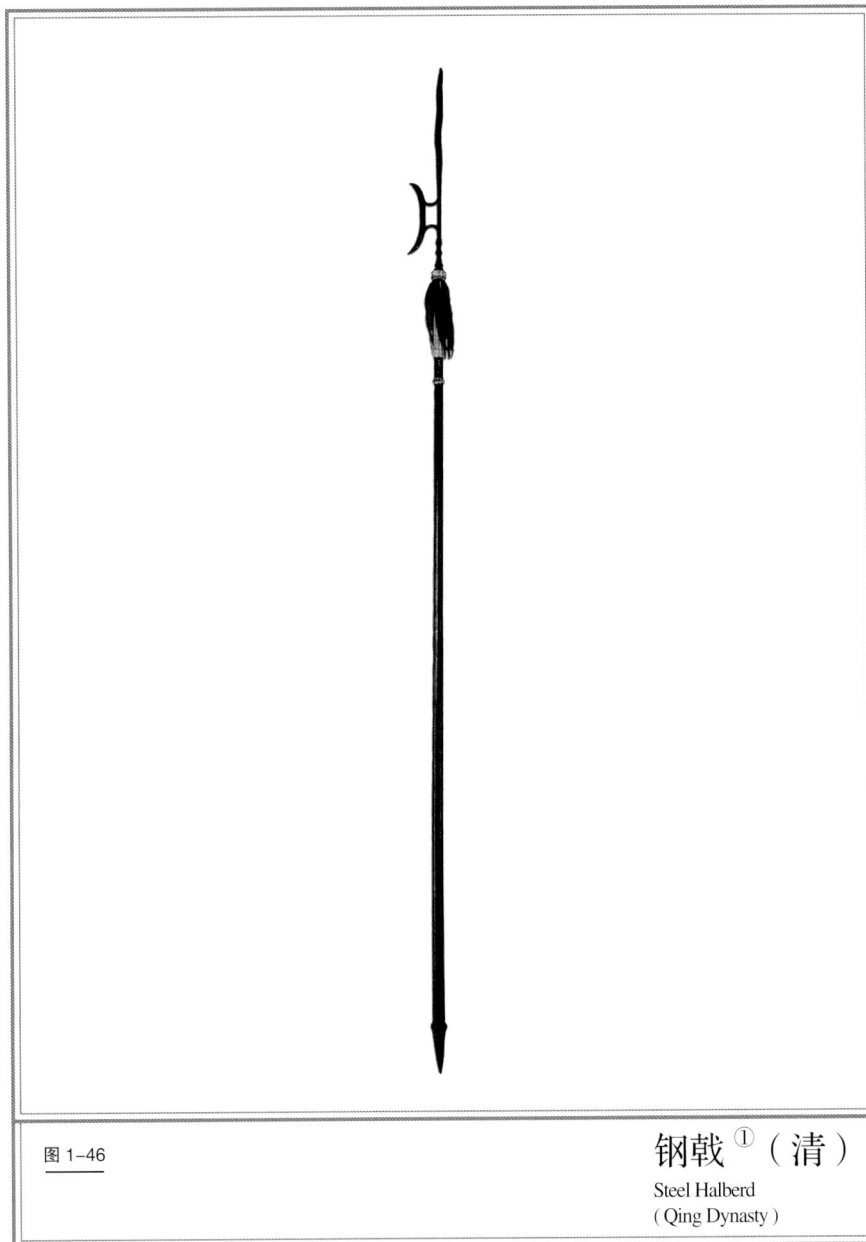

图 1-46

钢戟 [①]（清）
Steel Halberd
（Qing Dynasty）

① 钢戟：长 2.65 米，木柄，骹部镶铜镀金缕如意云饰件，系红缨，底镶铁镈。

Steel Halberd：It had a length of 2.65m with a wooden shaft. Its tang was inlaid with bronze and gold in the design of clouds, and tied with a red-tassel. The base of the shaft was attached to a forged iron queue.

第**4**节

枪

枪被称为"百兵之王"，由传统的矛演变而来。枪包括金属枪头、枪缨、枪杆三部分。《周礼·考工记》里规定：枪的长度以不超过使枪人身高的三倍为限。虽然枪越长越容易刺到敌人，但是枪杆过长就会发生弯曲，反而降低了兵器的威力，因此必须长短合适。枪杆的粗细根据使用者性别、年龄而异。枪缨的长度不短于 20 厘米。

最早作为兵器的枪是三国时代蜀国诸葛亮发明的。到了晋代，枪逐步流行起来，与矛相比，其形制趋于短而尖。到了唐代，矛与枪才被分为两种不同的兵器。唐中叶以后长枪取代了长矛（矟）。

　　宋代军队作战也以枪为主，其形制种类较多，《武经总要》中就记录了宋代枪的常见类型，称为"枪九色"。此外还出现了枪与火器相结合的一种兵器，即"花枪"，又名"梨花枪"，因药筒中喷出之药像梨花飘落而得名。它在原有枪的红缨部位绑上一个喷火筒，交战时先用火药烧灼敌人，药尽再以枪头刺杀。

　　明清时虽然以火器为主，但枪仍然是近战的主要兵器之一。明代枪的形制较宋代更简化。清代的枪有长枪、虎枪、钩镰枪、双钩镰枪、虎牙枪等，这些枪是八旗、绿营的常规武器。其中长枪使用最普遍，钩镰枪随挨牌使用，钉枪用在战船上。到清末，经战争的淘汰，种类繁多的长枪趋于单一化，枪头大多扁平、圆底，筒外加数个铜箍，其外形接近矛头。

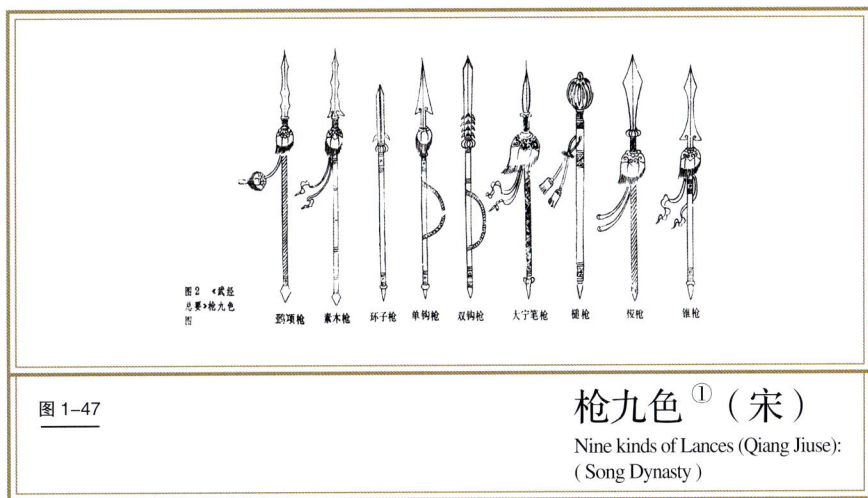

图2 《武经总要》枪九色图

鸦项枪　素木枪　环子枪　单钩枪　双钩枪　太宁笔枪　锤枪　梭枪　锥枪

| 图1-47 | 枪九色 ① （宋）
Nine kinds of Lances (Qiang Jiuse):
(Song Dynasty) |

　　① 枪九色：图源自《武经总要》，从右至左依次为：锥枪、梭枪、槌枪、太宁笔枪、双钩枪、单钩枪、环子枪、素木枪、鸦项枪。

　　Nine kinds of Lances(Qiang Jiuse): According to *Wujing Zongyao* (Complete Essentials for the Military Classics), they were named from the right to the left as an awl-shaped lance, a pike-shaped lance, a hammer lance, a pen-tip lance, a double-hook lance, a single-hook lance, a lance with rings (Huanzi Qiang), a lance with a horse-neck head and curved blade (Sumu Qiang),and a lance with crow-neck head.

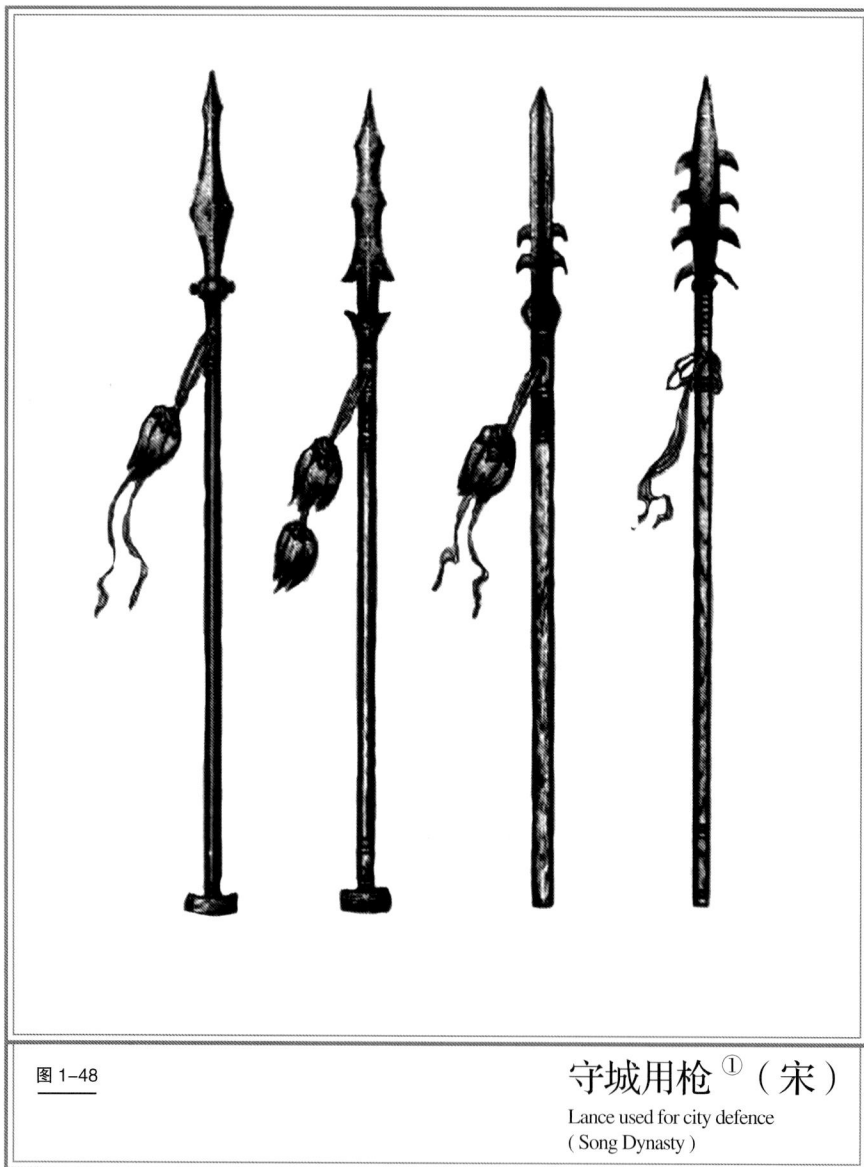

图 1-48　　　　　　　　　　　　　**守城用枪**^①（宋）
Lance used for city defence
（Song Dynasty）

①守城用枪：从左至右依次为拐突枪、拐刃枪、抓枪、钩竿，枪杆长二丈五尺左右（约合7.68 米）。

Lance used for city defence: They were named， from the left to the right， as a Crutch–like lance with wheat–ear head, a Crutch–like lance with sharp blade and three fillisters on its head, a hand–grabbing lance and a hook lance. Their shafts were about 7.68m long.

图 1-49 钩镰枪（宋）
A lance with a single barb (Goulian Qiang)
(Song Dynasty)

图 1-50 双钩镰枪（清）
A lance with double barbs and sickles
(Shuang Goulian Qiang) (Qing Dynasty)

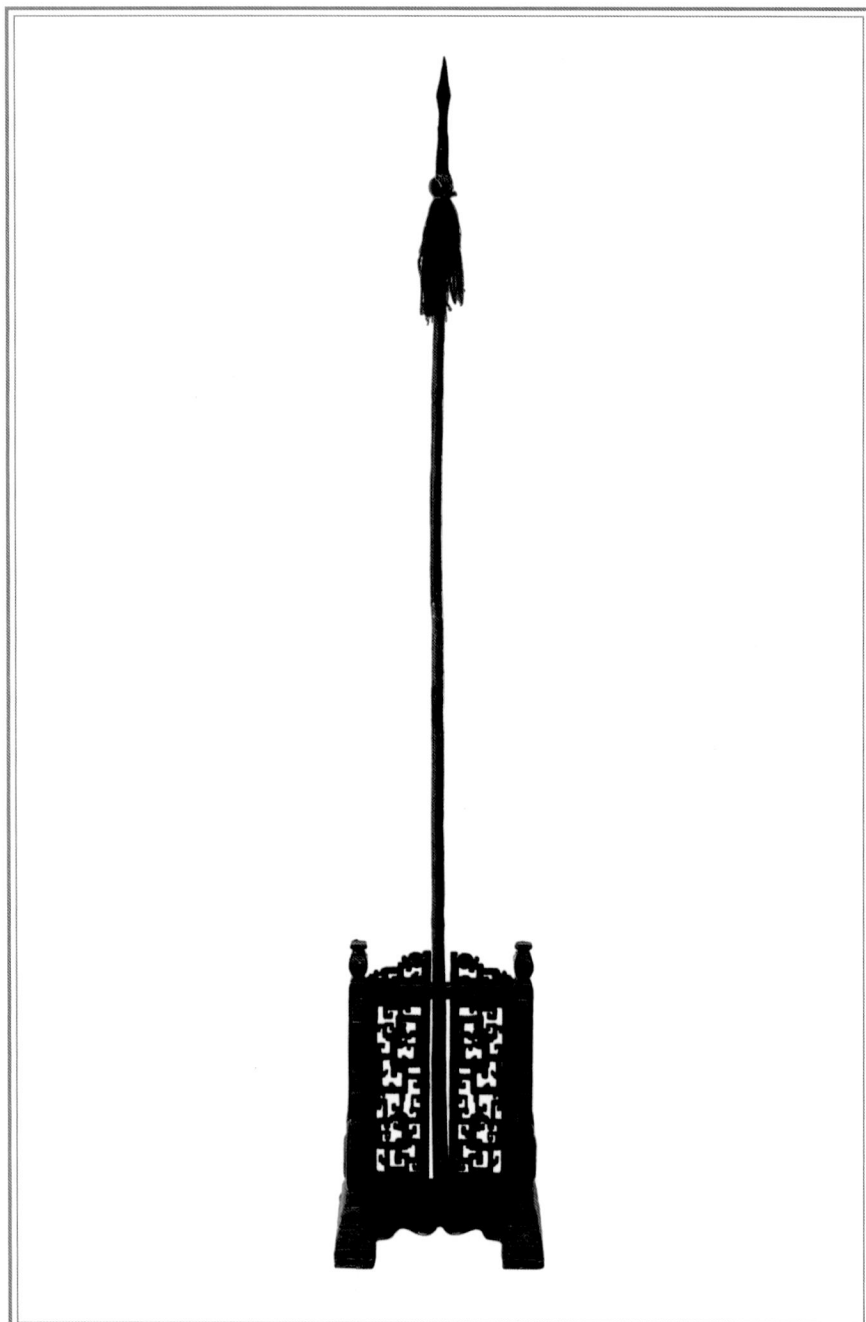

图 1-51

长钢枪（清）
Long steel lance (Qing Dynasty)

第 **5** 节

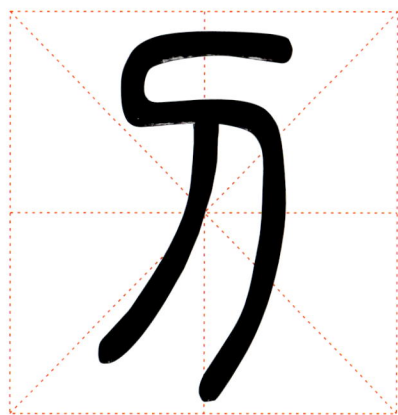

大刀

刀是一种用于劈砍的兵器，由刀身和刀柄构成。《释名》解释："刀，到也，以斩伐到其所乃击之也。"刀一般按照长度可分为长刀和短刀。大刀即长刀，是一种砍杀类长柄兵器，将刀安装在木质长柄上，柄长，刃锋利，砍杀有力。

在原始社会，人们就用石头、蚌壳、兽骨打磨成各种形状的刀，既做劳动工具，也是防身武器。在新石器时代遗址中常见的长方形多孔石刀，据推测是装在长柄上使用的。

到了商代，军事力量已具有相当规模，战争规模也空前扩大，同时青铜冶铸技术大大提高，这些都为兵器的发展提供了条件。于是铜刀大量出现，但形体一般较小，多做工具或护身兵器，而用于劈砍的大刀则成为战车的武器装备之一，至西周时期仍有使用。此外还出现了一种波状刃的青铜砍杀兵器。商代的长柄大刀刀体狭长，直刃平背，刀头向后弯曲，覆盖刀柄顶端。

在汉代，随着冶铁和锻钢工艺的进步，"百炼钢""淬火"等技术使得钢铁兵器迅速发展，铁刀和钢刀逐步取代铜刀。到了魏晋南北朝时期，出现了可安装长柄的铁刀，预示着隋唐以后刀的发展趋势。唐代出现了长柄的大刀，即陌刀，两面有刃，长达3米，重15斤。《唐六典·武库令》注："陌刀，长刀也，步兵所持。"

宋代是大刀发展的兴盛时期。此时的长柄刀形制多样，刀刃前锐后斜，柄为木制，安有铁镈，是宋代军队常用兵器之一。《武经总要》中记载的宋代长柄刀有掉刀、屈刀、偃月刀、戟刀、眉尖刀、凤嘴刀和笔刀，被列入"刀八色"之中。明代的长柄刀沿袭了宋代的传统，但是形制简化，主要有偃月刀、钩镰刀、夹刀棍等。清代的大刀并无多少创新，绿营里虽保留有长柄刀，但已不是主要兵器。

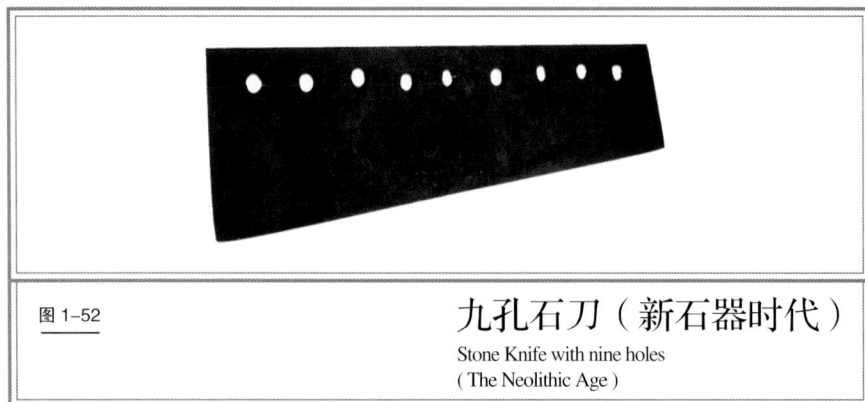

图 1-52

九孔石刀（新石器时代）
Stone Knife with nine holes
(The Neolithic Age)

图 1-53

三銎刀（商）

Sabre with three tubes
(Shang Dynasty)

图 1-54

铜大刀^①（商后期）

Bronze Sabre
(The Later Stage of Shang Dynasty)

① 铜大刀：河南省安阳殷墟妇好墓出土。通长45.7厘米，柄长7.6厘米。刀身宽大，单面刃，根部平直，中段内凹，往前渐宽弧收。刀背较厚，前端翘起，脊背上有一条脊棱。刀柄呈窄条形，略下弯。

Bronze Sabre：It was unearthed from Fuhao Tomb of Yin ruins in Anyang Henan Province. It was 45.7cm long and its handle was 7.6cm long. The body of the sabre was broad with single blade. Its bottom was flat and straight. The mid of the blade was concave with an arc to the tip. The back of the blade was slightly thick with the tip upward, where there was a ridge. Its handle was a narrow strip with a slightly bend.

图 1-55 乳钉纹三銎刀 [1]（西周早期）
Sabre with three tubes and small rivet design
(The Early Stage of Western Zhou Dynasty)

图 1-56 卷首铜刀（西周）
Bronze Sabre with a curved blade tip
(Western Zhou Dynasty)

---

[1] 乳钉纹三銎刀：此刀背上有三銎孔，銎穿长木柄纵贯整个刀背。这种刀背装柄的铜刀后来被末端装柄的刀所取代。

Sabre with three tubes and small rivet design：There were three tubes on the back of its blade to let the wooden handle pass through the whole back. This kind of sabre was replaced by the sabre with the handle passing toward the top end.

图 1-57 铜刀 ① （战国时期）
Bronze Sabre
(The Warring States Period)

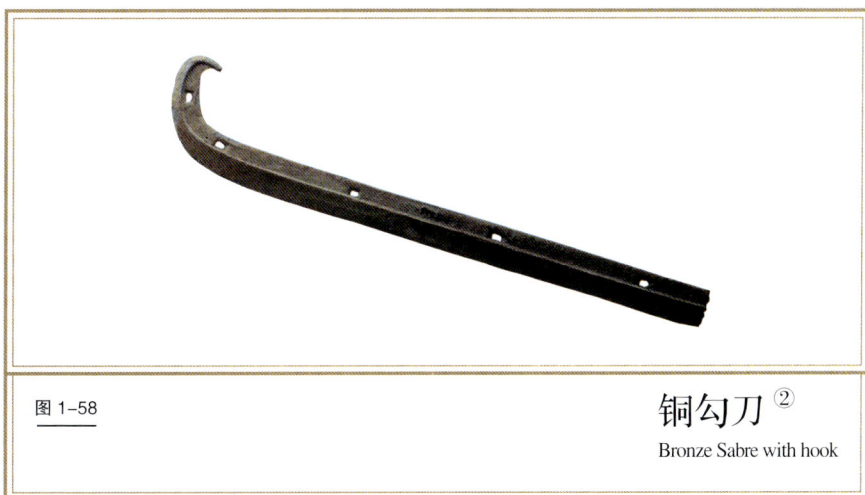

图 1-58 铜勾刀 ②
Bronze Sabre with hook

① 铜刀：云南省昌宁达丙营盘山出土。长 40 厘米，刃宽 8 厘米。刀身长而向上方弯曲，如弯月，下部较宽。銎呈筒形，上细下粗。近銎口部饰竖平行短线纹，上有两个连弧纹和圆圈纹。其形制较为少见，有古代滇文化特色。

Bronze Sabre：It was unearthed from Yingpan Mountain of Dabing, Changning County, Yunnan Province. It had a length of 40cm and its blade was 8cm in width. Its body was long and its top was bending backward, which looked like a crescent. Its bottom was a little wider. The tang for installing a handle was cone shaped. The entrance to the tang was decorated with double joint arcs and circles design. Its shape and structure were rare, and exhibited the cultural features of Ancient Dian Kingdom.

② 铜勾刀：刀身为长条状、双面刃、中间起脊，脊上五穿供捆扎之用。

Bronze Sabre with hook：Its body took the shape of strip, and had cutting edges on both sides. In the middle raised a ridge was fitted five holes for fixing the shaft.

046

图 1-59

青龙偃月刀（清）
The Black Dragon Lower Moon Sabre fitter to
a wooden shaft (Qing Dynasty)

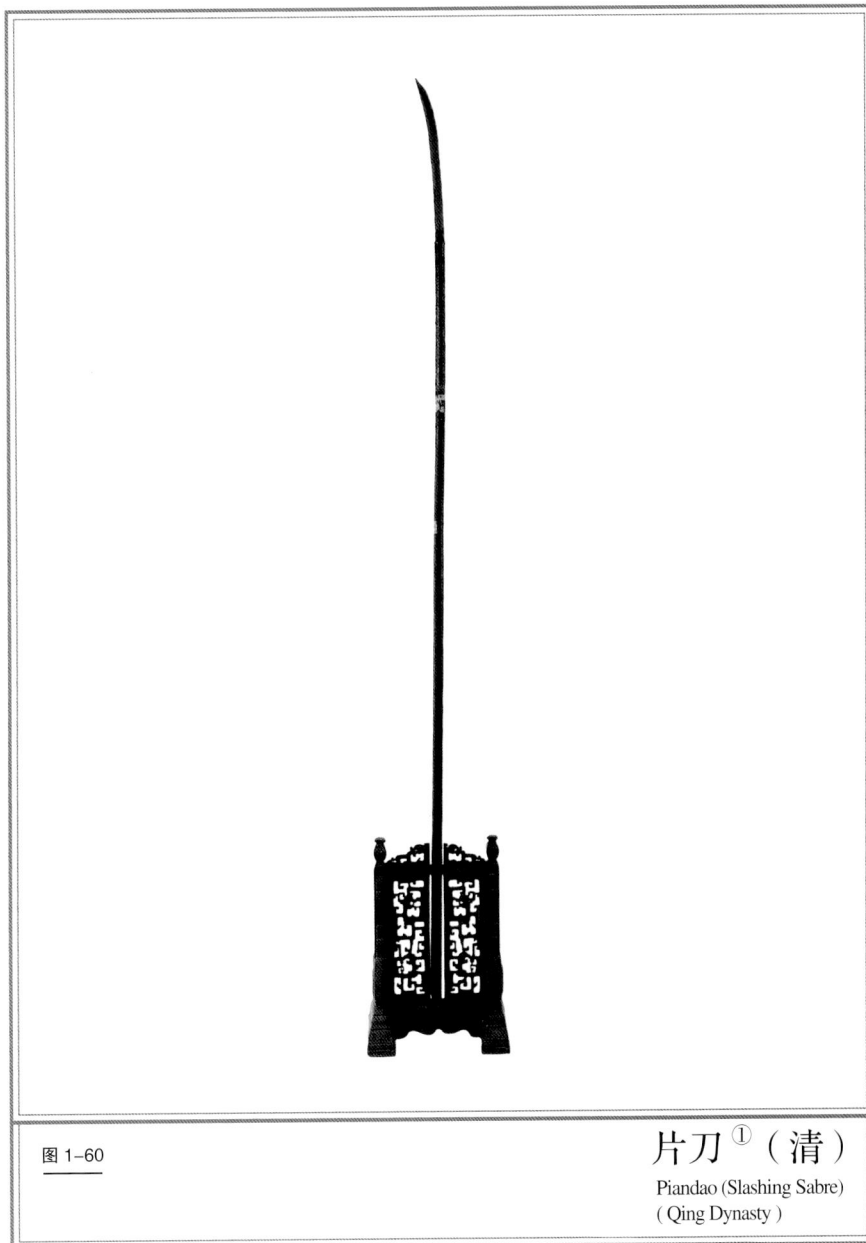

图 1-60

片刀 [1]（清）
Piandao (Slashing Sabre)
(Qing Dynasty)

① 片刀：清代钢刀，长 2.57 米，木柄，柄头髹黑漆，洒螺钿。

Piandao (Slashing Sabre): It was made in Qing Dynasty with a length of 2.57m. It had a wooden handle, with the top painted black and inlaid with mother-of-pearl.

第6节

长斧

　　长斧是一种用来劈砍的长兵器，基本构造有斧头、柄、镈三部分。斧头一面平直，一面为斧刃，下有銎，用于安装斧柄。

　　斧起源于石器时代，初为石制，随着青铜铸造业的出现而改用铜制。军队中的斧还可以用来筑城、构筑营地、挖坑道等。商周时期，斧与钺常联称"斧钺"，多作为礼器，是权力的象征。

　　南宋时期，为了有效抗击装甲骑兵，出现了用大刀、大斧和铠甲装备起来的装甲步兵，上砍骑兵，下砍马蹄。侵宋金军元帅完颜兀术曾评价说："宋军武器之中，最好、最厉害的就是神臂弓，其次就是大斧，除

此之外，就没有什么可怕的兵器了。"后来随着火器的流行，大斧逐渐
失去了昔日的优势。

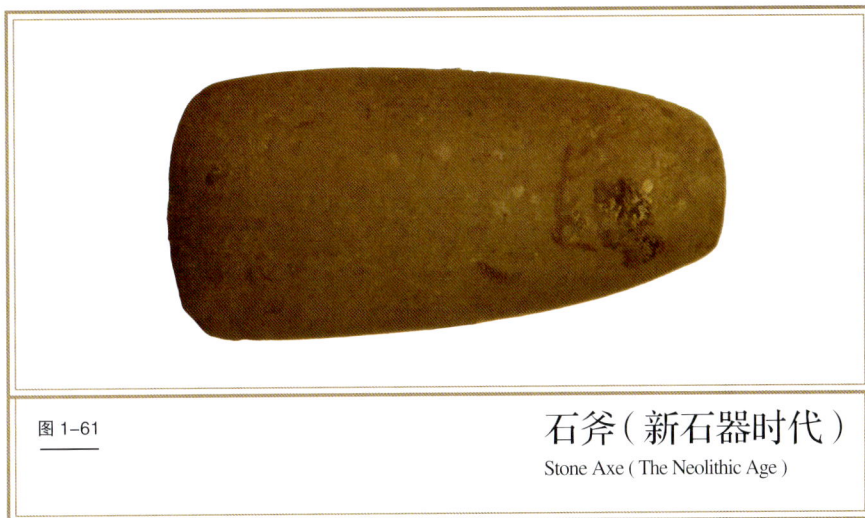

图 1-61

石斧（新石器时代）
Stone Axe (The Neolithic Age)

图 1-62

直线纹斧（商）
Axe with straight-line design
(Shang Dynasty)

图 1-63

大铜斧（春秋时期）
Large Bronze Axe
（The Spring and Autumn Period）

图 1-64

铜斧（春秋时期）
Bronze Axe
（The Spring and Autumn Period）

图 1-65

铜斧（春秋时期）
Bronze Axe
(The Spring and Autumn Period)

图 1-66

鎏银鱼龙纹铁斧（宋）
Iron Axe with silver gilding and with fish and
dragon design (Song Dynasty)

图 1-67

长柄斧 [①]（清）
Axe with long handle
(Qing Dynasty)

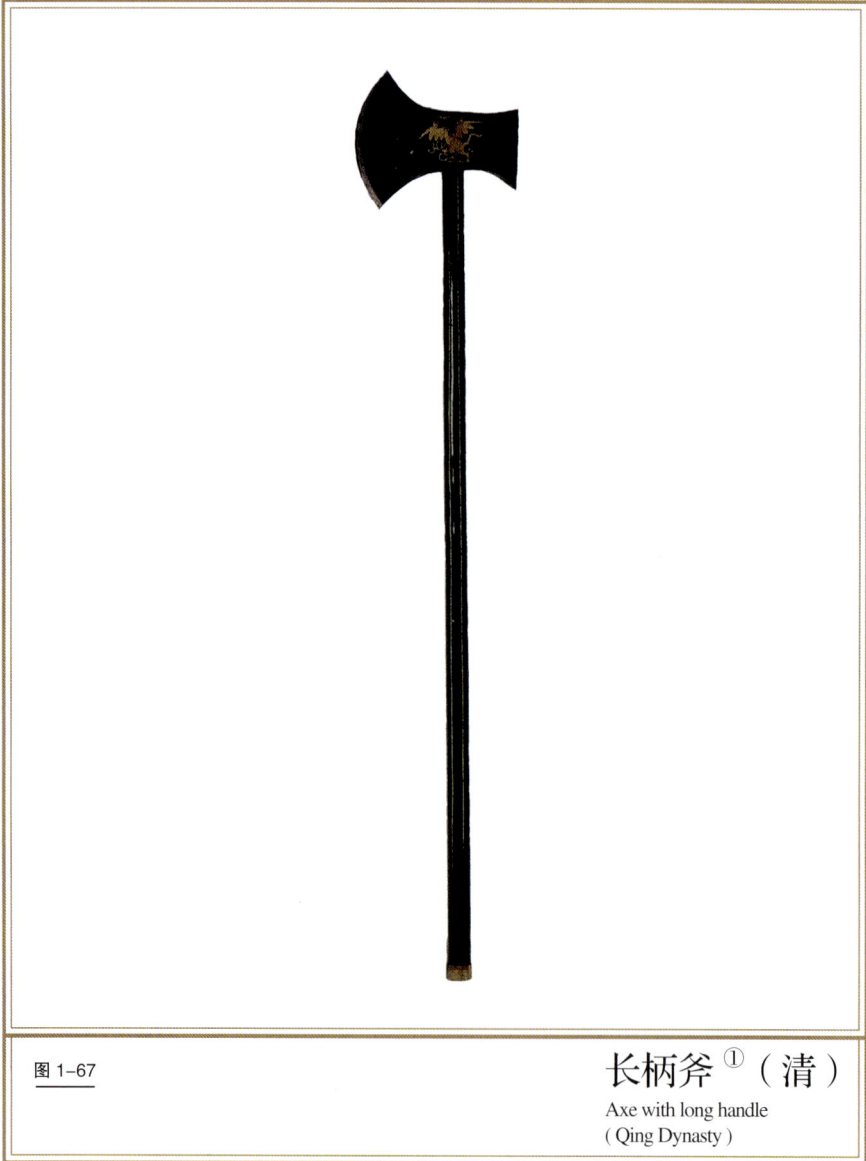

① 长柄斧：钢斧，长 1.36 米，斧面中部双面镀金飞虎火焰纹，黑漆木柄，底帽为铜镀金饰件。

Axe with long handle：It was a steel axe with a handle length of 1.36m. The middle part of the axe-body was covered with a flying tiger and flame design and gilded with gold on both sides. The handle was painted black and its base end was covered with a bronze sheath gilded with gold.

第 **7** 节

钺

钺也是以劈砍为主的长兵器 ，由石斧演化而来，主要流行于商和西周。钺与斧形制相近，由钺身和木柲组成；装柲方式与戈相似，区别在于钺刃宽大。其主要形制为圆刃长柄；也有直刃的，称为"方钺"。

早在新石器时代就出现了精细磨制的石钺。商代出现了青铜铸造的钺，用作兵器、刑具以及典礼和仪仗用具等。商初时钺身多素面，仅有一穿，后来出现了两穿或三穿钺，内加长，钺身中部开始出现圆孔，并饰以夔纹、雷纹等图案。商代中期钺身与内之间出现了阑，使钺身与柲结合得更加牢固。商代后期开始出现大型钺，如安阳殷墟妇好墓出土的铜钺，其刃部宽37.5～38.5厘米，重8.5～9公斤，是权力的象征。此时铜钺的图案、制作技法及装饰物也更加多样，样式精美。

西周时期的青铜钺依然主要是一种象征杀伐之权的仪仗兵器。东周时期，青铜钺在中原地区使用减少，但北方草原地区的游牧民族仍然广泛使用。

汉代出现了似戟似钺的兵器"钺戟"，由钺和刺两部分构成，前端为刺，形若短剑，刺茎插入钺的銎内，呈现出"十"字形。钺呈扁平体，刃端宽而薄，装有长柄，多为熟铁锻造，是汉代独具特色的兵器。

宋以后，钺基本上退出战争兵器序列，作为一种象征意义，只在祭祀等特定的场合还有所保留，或者作为一种刑具少量使用。

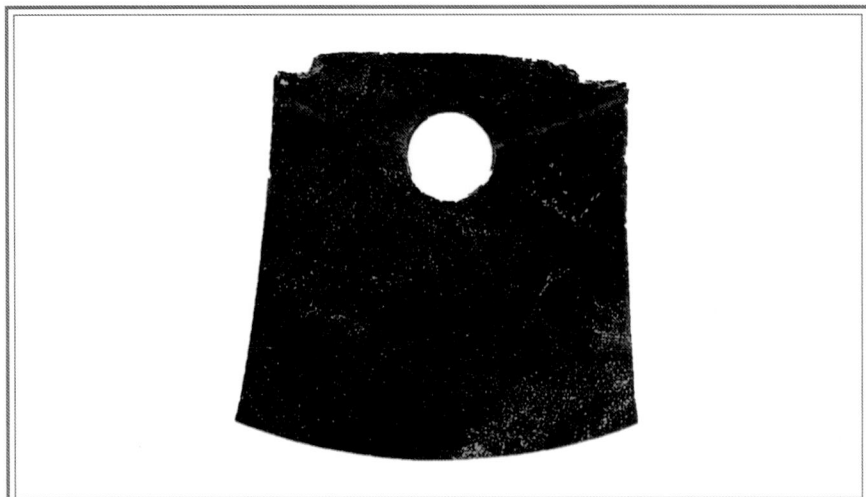

图 1-68　　　石钺 [1]（新石器时代晚期）
Stone Tomahawk
(The Later Stage of the Neolithic Age)

---

[1] 石钺：宽体有肩弧刃，辉绿岩质地，通长17.3厘米。

Stone Tomahawk：It had wide body and shoulder with a curved blade. It was made of stone with a length of 17.3cm.

图 1-69

玉钺 ① （二里头文化时期）
Jade Tomahawk
（Period of Erlitou Culture）

图 1-70

直边弧刃铜钺（商前期）
Bronze Tomahawk with straight edges and curved blade
（The Early Stage of Shang Dynasty）

① 玉钺：用作仪仗礼器。
Jade Tomahawk：It was used in ritual ceremonies.

图 1-71

兽面纹铜钺（商）
Bronze Tomahawk with animal face design
on the blade (Shang Dynasty)

图 1-72

夔龙纹铜钺（商）
Bronze Tomahawk with dragon design
(Shang Dynasty)

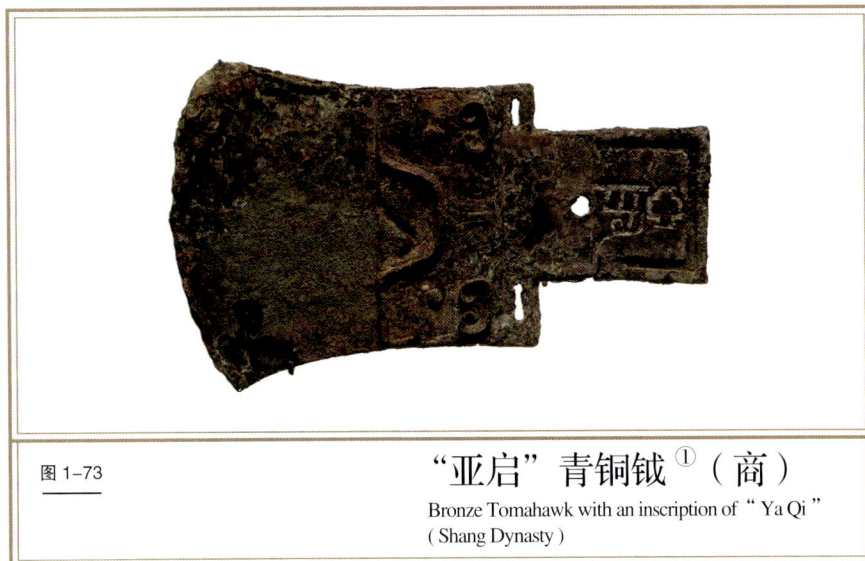

图 1-73

"亚启"青铜钺[1]**（商）**
Bronze Tomahawk with an inscription of "Ya Qi"
（Shang Dynasty）

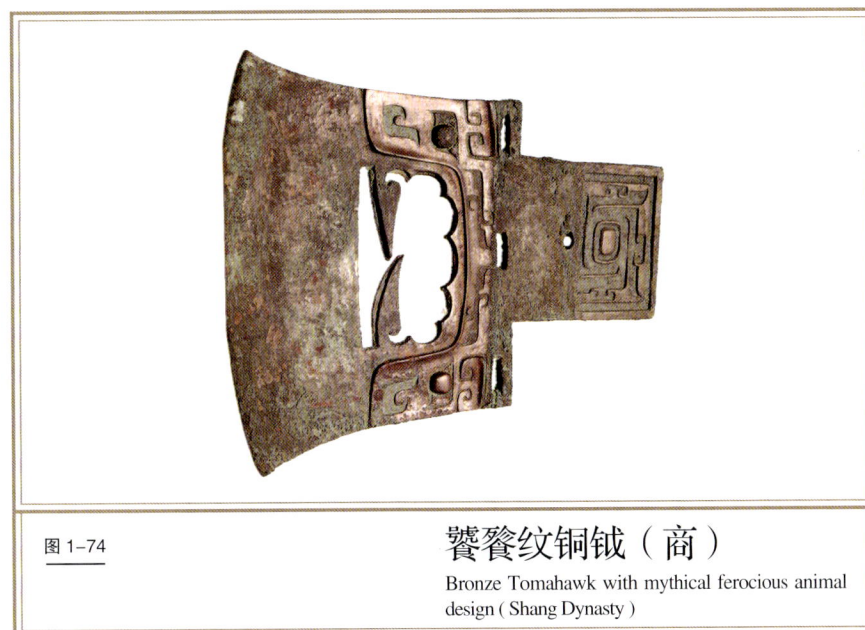

图 1-74

饕餮纹铜钺（商）
Bronze Tomahawk with mythical ferocious animal
design（Shang Dynasty）

---

[1] "亚启"青铜钺：制作于商王武丁时期，河南省安阳殷墟妇好墓出土，器内铸铭文"亚启"。
Bronze Tomahawk with an inscription of "Ya Qi"：It was made in the period of Wuding, the King of Shang Kingdom and was excavated from Fuhao Tomb of Yin Ruins in Anyang, Henan Province. On the blade were inscribed the 2 characters of "Ya Qi".

图 1-75	双饕餮噬人头纹钺 [①]（商后期）
	Tomahawk with the design of mythical animal seizing a man's head（The Late Stage of Shang Dynasty）

① 双饕餮噬人头纹钺：1976 年在河南安阳殷墟妇好墓出土。长 39.5 厘米，刃宽 37.5 厘米，重约 9 千克。钺身宽大，平肩弧刃，两侧铸出扉棱；刃角外侈，靠肩部开有两个长条形穿；钺身上部铸饰双饕餮噬人头主纹，云雷纹为衬，饕餮大头小身，张巨口，人头纹凸出，摄人心魄；纹饰下部正中铸有"妇好"二字铭文；内部方折，较粗短，素面。

Tomahawk with the design of mythical animal seizing a man's head：In 1976 it was unearthed from the Fuhao Tomb of Yin Ruins in Anyang, Henan Province. It was 39.5cm long and its blade was 37.5cm in width and over 9 kilograms in weight. Its body was broad, and it has square shoulder and curved blade with raised strips on both sides. The tips of the blade stretched outward. There were two rectangular holes on the top of shoulder. On its body was there the design of double mystical animal biting a man's head, behind which was the design of winding lines. The animal had a big head and small body with the mouth widely opened. The design of the man's head was raised on the blade. In the middle part below the ornament was inscribed "Fuhao" (the name of a wife of King Wuding in Shang Dynasty). The blade was in the shape of square, with a short, thick and plain appearance.

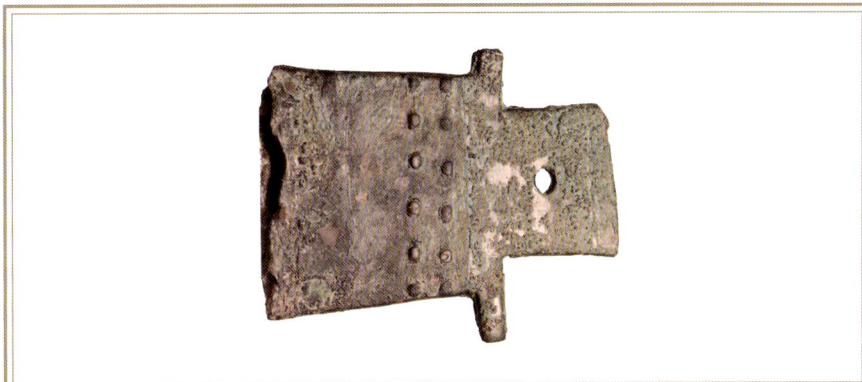

图 1-76

铁刃铜钺 [1]（商中期）
Bronze Tomahawk with iron blade
(The Middle Stage of Shang Dynasty)

图 1-77

双孔夹内钺 [2]（商晚期至西周）
Tomahawk with double holes and curved blade
(the Later Stage of Shang Dynasty to Western Zhou)

[1] 铁刃铜钺：此器刃部用经过锻造成形的陨铁，钺身用锡青铜，是中国最早的铜铁复合器物。装饰华丽，推测为仪仗之用。

Bronze Tomahawk with iron blade：Its blade was forged from aerosiderite, and its body was forged from tin bronze. It was the earliest fusion of bronze and iron in China. It had beautiful decorations and it was thought to be used in ritual ceremonies.

[2] 双孔夹内钺：商代晚期至西周时期东夷系统所用，辽宁法库弯柳街遗址出土，通长 17.7 厘米，刃宽 16.2 厘米。

Tomahawk with double holes and curved blade：It was used by the Easterners in Ancient China from the later stage of Shang Dynasty to Western Zhou Dynasty, and found among the Relics of Wanliu Street in Faku, Liaoning Province. It was 17.7cm long and its blade was 16.2cm in width.

图 1-78　三孔卷刃管銎钺 [1]（商晚期）
Tomahawk with three holes, rolled blade and cone-shaped handle
receptacle (The Later Stage of Shang Dynasty)

图 1-79　涡纹管銎钺（西周）
Tomahawk with spiral lines and cone-shaped handle
receptacle (Western Zhou Dynasty)

[1] 三孔卷刃管銎钺：商代晚期北狄林胡人所用，通长 18 厘米，宽 14 厘米。
Tomahawk with three holes, rolled blade and cone-shaped handle receptacle：It was applied by the
Northern barbarian tribes in the later stage of Shang Dynasty. It was 18cm long and 14cm wide.

图 1-80

七孔曲刃钺（西周早期）

Tomahawk with seven holes and curved blade
（The Early Stage of Western Zhou Dynasty）

图 1-81

凹口竖銎钺[1]（西周晚期至春秋早期）

Tomahawk with a notch in the handle receptacle（The Later Stage of
Western Zhou Dynasty to the Early Stage of Spring and Autumn Period）

[1] 凹口竖銎钺：西周晚期至春秋早期巴蜀地区所用，纵长 34 厘米，刃宽 19.5 厘米。

Tomahawk with a notch in the handle receptacle：It was used in the Bashu District (two ancient cities in Sichuan) from the later stage of Western Zhou Dynasty to the early stage of Spring and Autumn period. It was 34cm long and its blade was 19.5cm wide.

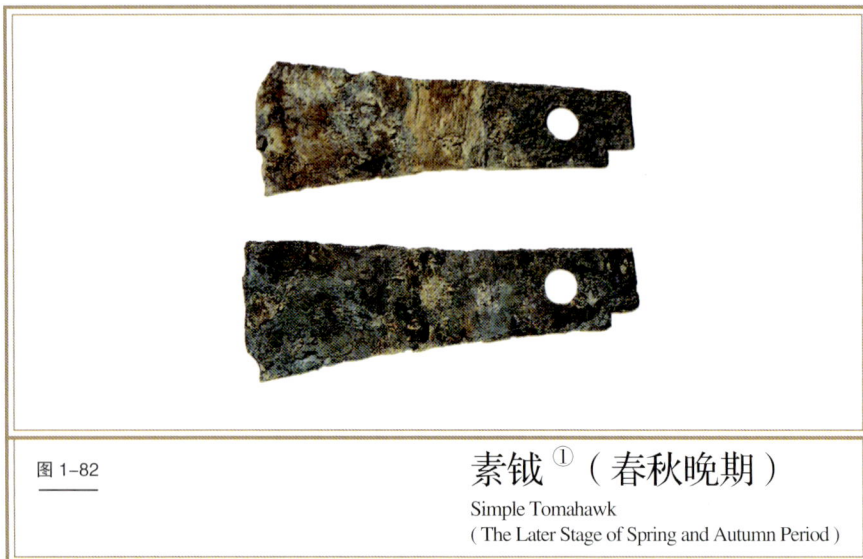

图 1-82

素钺^①（春秋晚期）
Simple Tomahawk
(The Later Stage of Spring and Autumn Period)

图 1-83

靴形青铜钺（战国时期）
Boot-shaped Bronze Tomahawk
(The Warring States Period)

① 素钺：春秋晚期晋国造。此器共两件，通长皆为 19.3 厘米。

Simple Tomahawk：It was made in Jin Kingdom in the later stage of the Spring and Autumn period. It was composed of two parts, and was 19.3cm in length.

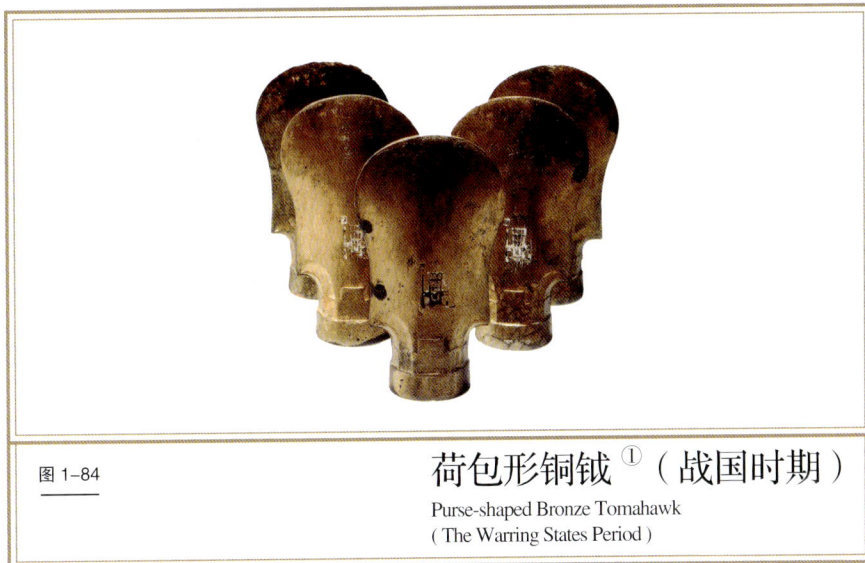

图 1-84 荷包形铜钺 ① （战国时期）
Purse-shaped Bronze Tomahawk
(The Warring States Period)

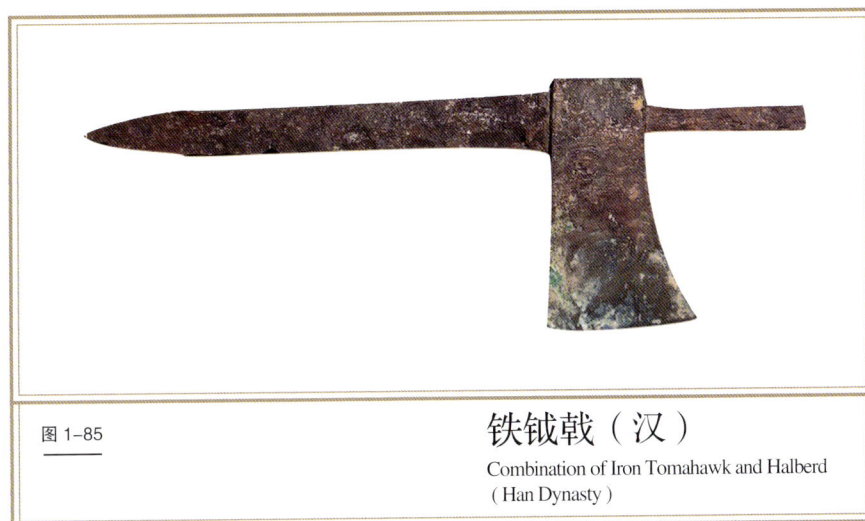

图 1-85 铁钺戟（汉）
Combination of Iron Tomahawk and Halberd
(Han Dynasty)

① 荷包形铜钺：五件铜钺形制大小完全相同，且出于一处。钺平肩，刃圆弧。钺身后接铸短銎，銎口外部有凸棱，钺身上刻有特殊的巴蜀符号，是巴蜀兵器的典型制式。

Purse-shaped Bronze Tomahawk：These five tomahawks were same in size and shape, and found in the same place. They had square shoulders and curved blades. Above the tomahawk casted a short handle cone supporting the shaped blade. Some special signs of Bashu (two ancient cities in Sichuan) were carved in the body of the tomahawk, which was in the typical shape of Bashu's weapon.

图 1-86

鱼鹰钮钺[1]（西汉）
Tomahawk with an osprey-shaped figure
（Western Han Dynasty）

图 1-87

铜龙吞铁钺[2]（清）
Iron Tomahawk in the mouth of bronze dragon
（Qing Dynasty）

[1] 鱼鹰钮钺：西汉时期西南夷滇国造，云南晋宁石寨山出土，通高 11.3 厘米。

Tomahawk with an osprey-shaped figure：It was made in the Kingdom of Dian (where lived the ancient ethnic groups in southwest part of China in Western Han Dynasty). It was unearthed from Shizhai Mountain in Jinning county, Yunnan Province. It had a height of 11.3cm.

[2] 铜龙吞铁钺：铁钺以铜镀金龙衔之，前端有突出的矛头，长 73 厘米，宽 23 厘米。

Iron Tomahawk in the mouth of bronze dragon：The iron tomahawk was held in the mouth of a gilded dragon. There was a protruding spearhead mounted above the blade. It was 73cm long and 23cm wide.

第**8**节

殳

　　殳是原始社会主要生产工具之一，也是最早用于战争的武器之一。殳由原始社会中狩猎用的竹木棍棒发展而来。《尚书·武成》中有"血流漂杵"，"杵"就是商代士兵所使用的殳，那时的殳一般用一根坚实的木棒制成。周朝把殳列入"车之五兵"之一，是用于实战的兵器。《周礼》曰："殳以积竹、八觚，长丈二尺，建于兵车。"

　　关于殳的形制与尺寸，据《考工记》记载，"殳长寻有四尺"，东汉人郑玄注曰"八尺曰寻"，由此可见殳的长度为一丈二尺，即约3米。1978年曾侯乙墓出土了多件带铭文的实战与礼仪用的殳，包括锐殳7件、晋殳 14 件。其中 3 件锐殳刃部较长，顶端有锋，呈三棱矛状，并在锋后装有带尖刺的铜镦，一侧刃上铸篆书"曾侯越之用殳"，是中国迄今为止唯一一次出土自铭为"殳"的兵器，真正解开了殳的形制之谜。

秦殳形制简单，是一个铜圆筒，顶部呈三棱锥形，无利刃，长约 10.5 厘米，直径 2.3~3 厘米，深 8.9 厘米，下接长柄，主要作为仪仗队的礼仪兵器。从秦始皇兵马俑坑中出土的殳来看，全都是青铜圆筒套头、无锋刃的仪仗器。汉承秦制，汉代的礼仪用殳被称作"金吾"，金吾也为铜制套头，两头镀金，御史大夫、司隶校尉等常常"执金吾"夹侍、拱卫皇帝。

殳这种实战兵器之后并未消亡，而是继续演化为棒或杖在历代广泛传承与使用。三国时代，殳称为"白棓"，宋代称为棍棒。

图 1-88

"必戈"铭铜殳首 ① （西周）
Bronze Head of the Long Pole with an inscription of "Bige"
(Western Zhou Dynasty)

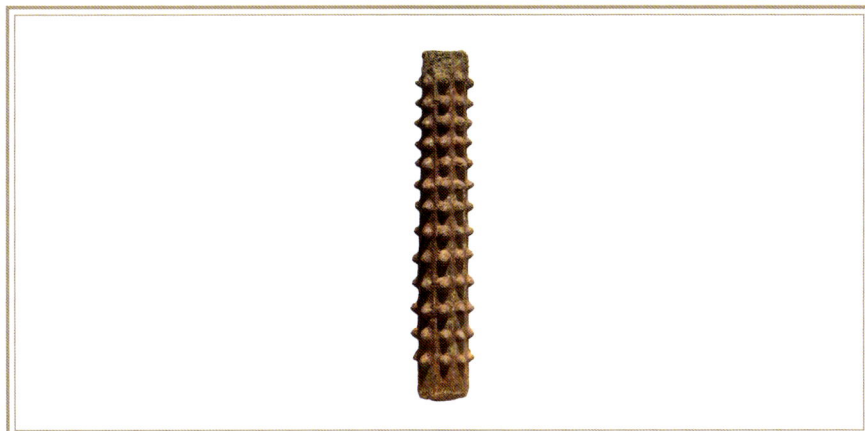

图 1-89

铜殳首（春秋时期）
Bronze Head of the Long Pole
(The Spring and Autumn Period)

① "必戈"铜铜殳首：通高 11 厘米，口径 4 厘米，腹围 25.6 厘米，直口，口沿有两圈弦纹，高颈，鼓腹。器口内侧有"必戈"两字铭文，通体光洁。

Bronze Head of the Long Pole with an inscription of "Bige": It was 11cm wide and its diameter of its mouth was 4cm, and its diameter of its body was 25.6 cm. The tube was upright, and there were bow string pattern on the mouth. It had a long neck and round belly. Inside the mouth was incised with two character of "Biding". Its external surface was smooth and clean.

图 1-90

铜殳首 ① （春秋中期）
Bronze Head of the Long Pole
(The Middle Stage of Spring and Autumn Period)

图 1-91

殳（战国时期）
Long Pole
(The Warring States Period)

———————

① 铜殳首：河南省淅川县和尚岭一号墓出土。残长 10.8 厘米，筒口径 3.2 厘米。形体较短，身呈三棱锥形，向上聚成尖锋，棱体每面都有血槽，下部铸饰兽面纹，骹筒几乎与殳身等粗，出三排乳钉，筒口铸箍棱，其上有一方形钉乳。

Bronze Head of the Long Pole: It was unearthed from the No. 1 tomb of Heshangling in Xichuan County, Henan Province. The relic was 10.8 cm long and its diameter was 3.2cm. It was slightly short in the shape of triangular pyramid with a sharpened top. There was a blood flute on each side of prism. The design of the animal face was cast in the lower part. The tube of the tang was as thick as its body with the cover of three rows of little nails. On its mouth was there a round arris with a little square nail above.

图 1-92　　**铜头木皮铁芯柄殳**[1]（战国中晚期）

A Long Pole with Bronze Head and a handle with wood cover and iron core（The Middle and Later Stage of the Warring States Period）

图 1-93　　**刺球箍三棱殳首**[2]（战国早期）

The Head of a Long Pole in the shape of three prisms and carrying balls covered with thorns（The Early Stage of the Warring States Period）

---

①　铜头木皮铁芯柄殳：河北省平山县三汲镇中山王墓出土。通长 1.59 米，殳头铜铸而成，呈八棱筒形，外表用金银错出折线三角纹，内衬卷云文。殳镦呈圆筒形，底部大于殳镦筒。殳柄铁制，外面用整条木皮拼贴其上。

A Long Pole with Bronze Head and a handle with wood cover and iron core: It was excavated from the Tomb of Zhongshan King at Sanji Town in Pingshan County, Hebei Province. It was 1.59m long and the head was made of bronze in a tube-shape with eight prisms. The surface was incised with triangle design in gold and silver underneath which was carved clouds pattern. Its bottom was in tube-shape and bigger than its tamg. The handle of Long Pole was made of iron with a wooden cover.

②　刺球箍三棱殳首：湖北曾侯乙墓出土。连柲全长 3.3 米，上箍顶部置三棱矛，周围刺粗而疏，其下另设一箍，刺细而密。

The Head of a Long Pole in the shape of three prisms and carrying balls covered with thorns: It was found in the Tomb of Marquis Yi of the State of Zeng in Hubei Province. It was 3.3m long with its handle. There was a triangular prism spear installed on the top, and a hoop under the spear scattered with thick barbs. There was another hoop near the bottom covered with thin barbs.

| 图 1-94 | 曾侯邸（越）殳首①（战国早期）
The Head of Long Pole with the Tomahawk of Marquis in State Zeng（The Early Stage of the Warring States Period） |

| 图 1-95 | 蟠虺纹殳首②（战国晚期）
The Head of a Long Pole with a snake pattern
（The Later Stage of the Warring States Period） |

①曾侯邸（越）殳首：湖北曾侯乙墓出土，通长 17.9 厘米，銎径 3 厘米。殳头呈三棱刮刀形，骹部饰有浮雕龙纹，该兵器自名为"殳"，首次解开了殳形制的谜团。

The Head of Long Pole with the Tomahawk of Marquis in State Zeng: It was found in the Tomb of Marquis Yi of State Zeng in Hubei Province. It was 17.9cm in length and the diameter of its shaft receptacle was 3cm. The head was in the shape of cant scraper, and the dragon pattern was embossed on its pastern. The weapon was incised with the character "Long Pole" to manifest the shape and structure of Long Pole for the first time.

②蟠虺（huǐ）纹殳首：安徽淮南蔡家岗出土，通长 14.7 厘米。

The Head of a Long Pole with a snake pattern: It was unearthed from Caijiagang in Huainan city, Anhui Province. It was 14.7cm long.

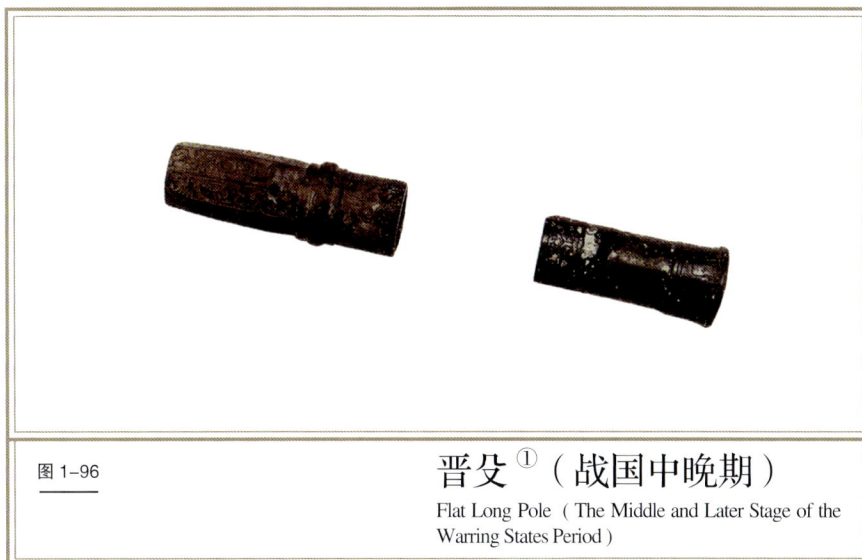

图 1-96

晋殳 [1]（战国中晚期）
Flat Long Pole（The Middle and Later Stage of the Warring States Period）

图 1-97

铜殳首（秦）
Bronze Head of the Long Pole(Qin Dynasty)

① 晋殳：殳首长 8.4 厘米，直径 2.2 厘米；镦长 7 厘米，直径 2.8 厘米。

Flat Long Pole：The head was 8.4cm long, and its diameter was 2.2cm. Its lower tube was 7cm long and its diameter was 2.8cm.

第 **9** 节

铍

铜铍自西周晚期萌芽，最早记载见于《左传·襄公十七年》："贼六人以铍杀诸卢门。"战国中期逐渐成熟、定型，战国晚期达到鼎盛。

铍头形制和短剑相似，长 30~35 厘米，尖锋平脊两刃；铍身断面为六边形，后端为扁平或矩形的茎，用以装柄；一般在茎的近端处开有圆孔，以便穿钉固定在长柄上；后装长约 3~3.5 米的积竹柄或木柄，是一种极其锐利的刺杀兵器。铜铍一般分为銎骹铜铍和扁茎铜铍，还有少量特殊形制。目前发现的銎骹铜铍数目少于扁茎铜铍，且年代较早，基本属于春秋至战国中期，是较为原始的类型。扁茎铜铍是铜铍的主要形态，也是成熟形态。

西汉初期，铁铍逐渐开始取代铜铍。此时铍头比秦代显著加长，击刺的效能增强。铍头颈部有尖齿状铜箍，使铍头与柲结合得更加牢固，柲末端有铜镦。西汉中期以后，铍逐渐从战场上消失。

图 1-98

铜铍 ①
Bronze Bayonet

---

① 铜铍：湖北武汉盘龙城遗址出土。前锋呈三角状，骹作长条状，锋末端有阑。此铍为现存最早的铜铍。

Bronze Bayonet: It was found at the Ruins of Panlongcheng in Wuhan City, Hubei Province. The edge of blade was in triangle shape, and its tang was an extended base. There was a guard at the bottom of blade. It was the earliest bronze bayonet ever detected in China.

图 1-99

铜铍 ①
Bronze Bayonet

图 1-100

铜铍 ②（春秋晚期）
Bronze Bayonet（The Later Stage of
Spring and Autumn Period）

① 铜铍：湖北武汉盘龙城文化遗址王家嘴 6 号灰坑出土。

Bronze Bayonet: It was unearthed from the Pit 6 of Wangjiazui in the Ruins of Panlongcheng in Wuhan City, Hubei Province.

② 铜铍：长 24.5 厘米，宽 3.5 厘米。铍身如剑，中间纵起中脊，脊两侧下凹形成血槽，末端斜收后外展形成短茎，茎端有节，形制少见。

Bronze Bayonet: It was 24.5cm long and 3.5cm wide. Its body was like a sword with a vertical ridge in the middle along with a blood flute on both sides. Then it was inclined to form a thin bottom with a slightly flat and very short stem with a knot. This kind of shape was quite rare.

图 1-101　　铜铍^①（春秋晚期）
Bronze Bayonet（The Later Stage of
Spring and Autumn Period）

图 1-102　　有銎铜铍^②（春秋晚期）
Bronze Bayonet with shaft tang（The Later Stage of
Spring and Autumn Period）

① 铜铍：长 24.2 厘米，宽 3.2 厘米。铍身窄如剑，中间纵起脊棱，末端收窄成短茎，茎两侧各有一齿状突棱。

Bronze Bayonet：It was 24.2cm long and 3.2cm wide. Its body was narrow like a sword with a vertical ridge in the middle. It became narrower to form a short stem, on both sides of which there was a tooth-shaped ridge.

② 有銎铜铍：春秋晚期晋国所制，山西太原金胜村赵国赵卿墓出土，通长 53 厘米。

Bronze Bayonet with shaft tang：It was made in Kingdom Jin in the later stage of Spring and Autumn Period. It was excavated from a minister's tomb in zhao state of Jinsheng Village in Taiyuan City, Shanxi Province and was 53cm long.

图 1-103 　　"卅三年郑令"铜铍 [①]（战国晚期）
Bronze Bayonet with an inscription of "Thirty-three Years Zhengling"
（The Later Stage of the Warring States Period）

图 1-104 　　铜铍 [②]（战国）
Bronze Bayonet
（The Warring States Period）

---

① "卅三年郑令"铜铍：战国晚期韩国所造。通长 31.8 厘米，刃宽 3.5 厘米，有铭文两行二十一字。

Bronze Bayonet with an inscription of "Thirty-three Years Zhengling"：It was made in State Han of the later stage of Warring States Period. It was 31.8cm long and its blade was 3.5cm wide. There is an inscription of 21 characters in two lines.

② 铜铍：陕西省旬阳县战国楚墓出土。扁圆形銎，近銎处有一周凸棱；两侧朝刃面起弧，形成对称的三连弧刃，与两侧直刃相接；刃面较宽，断面呈四棱形；通长 42.4 厘米，中宽 4.2 厘米。

Bronze Bayonet：It was found in the tomb of State Chu of the Warring States Period that was located in Xunyi County of Shaanxi Province. It had an oblate receptacle with a ridge around its end. Up to the top of receptacle there was the arc to form the blade so as to make symmetric curved triple-blades which was jointed with the straight blades on both sides. The blade surface was slightly wider and its cross-section was in quad-prismatic shape. It was 42.4cm in length and 4.2cm wide in the middle.

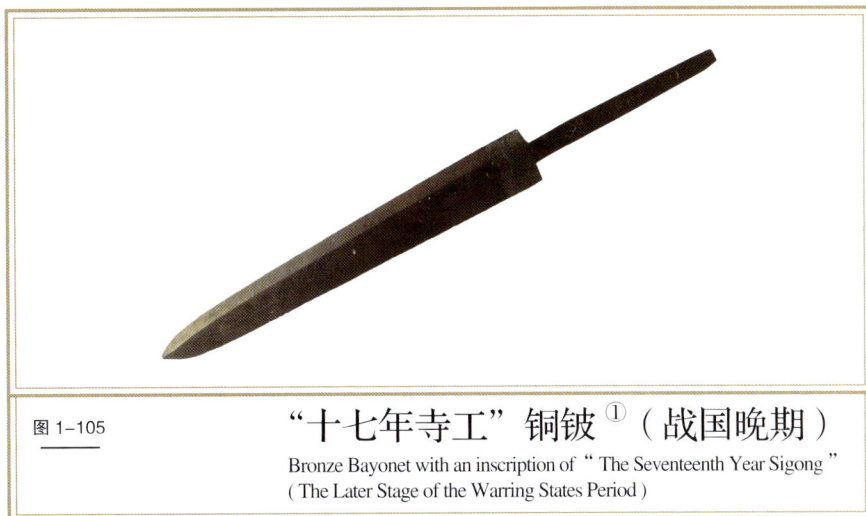

| 图 1-105 | "十七年寺工"铜铍 ①（战国晚期）
Bronze Bayonet with an inscription of "The Seventeenth Year Sigong"
(The Later Stage of the Warring States Period) |

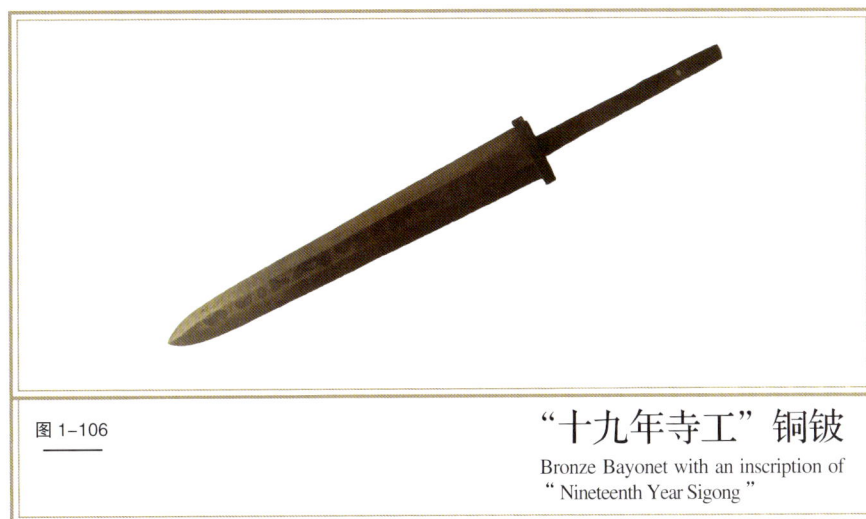

| 图 1-106 | "十九年寺工"铜铍
Bronze Bayonet with an inscription of
"Nineteenth Year Sigong" |

① "十七年寺工"铜铍：秦王政十七年造，陕西西安临潼区秦俑一号坑出土。铍头形如扁平短剑，刃两侧共六面，前锐后宽，刃口为直线，前收为锋。茎部装一字形格，茎体扁平，截面呈长方形，茎下部有孔。茎与身一次铸成。

Bronze Bayonet with an inscription of "The Seventeenth Year Sigong": It was made in the 17th year of Emperor of Yingzheng in Qin Dynasty, and unearthed from Pit 1 of Terracotta Warriors and Horses in Xi'an City. The head of bayonet was similar to a half-sword. It was a flat object with six faces. It had a sharp top and broad downward. The blades were straight upward to the tip. The body and stem was cast in one. The stem was in-line shape and flat with a rectangular cross-section. There was a hole at the lower part of the stem.

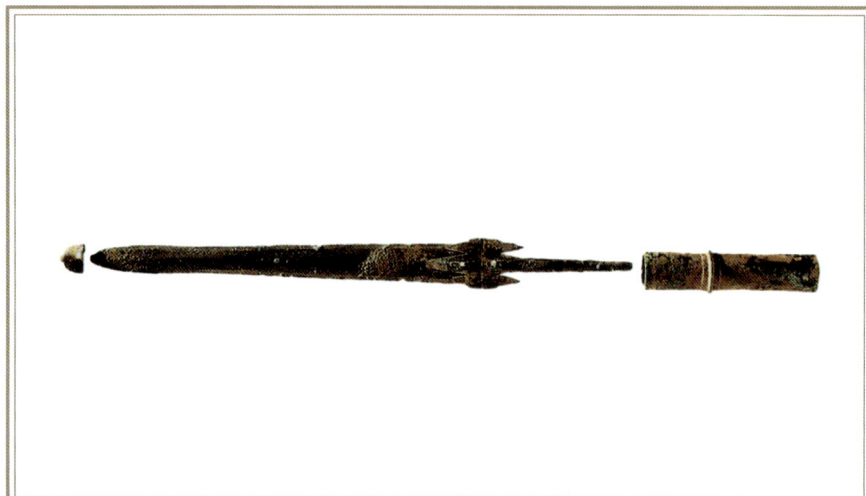

图 1-107

有镡（xín）铜铍（西汉）
Bronze Bayonet with protruding parts between the body and
the handle of the bayonet（Western Han Dynasty）

第 10 节

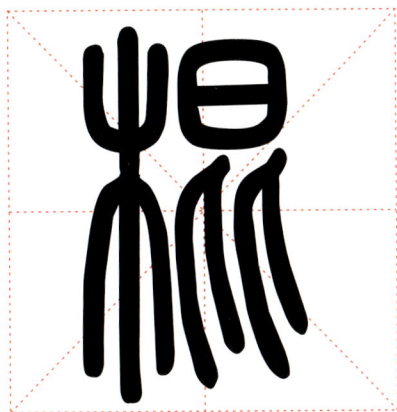

棍

棍，亦被称作"棒"，属于无刃兵器、打击兵器，素有"百兵之首"之称。棍历史悠久，是原始社会主要生产工具之一，也是最早用于战争的武器之一。后来为了提高使用性能，将棍进行加工，称为"殳"。汉代至唐代期间，把经过加工的棍棒称为白棓。宋代的棍棒种类较多，记录于《武经总要》的共有七种，其中有最简单的一般棍棒，如杆棒、白棒；也有经过加工的强化棍棒，如诃藜棒、钩棒、杵棒、抓子棒、狼牙棒。

棍棒有木制和金属制两种，以木棍最常见。棍的长度约为 1.3~2.6 米，也有的长达 4 米，截面一般为圆形，粗细以单手能够把握为准。棍是近战搏斗兵器，它的攻击范围大于刀、枪，自古有"棍扫一大片"的说法。但是棍棒主要是造成钝器伤和瘀伤，其杀伤力比刀、枪等要小。火器出现以后，棍棒逐渐成为武术运动的器械，退出了军事舞台。

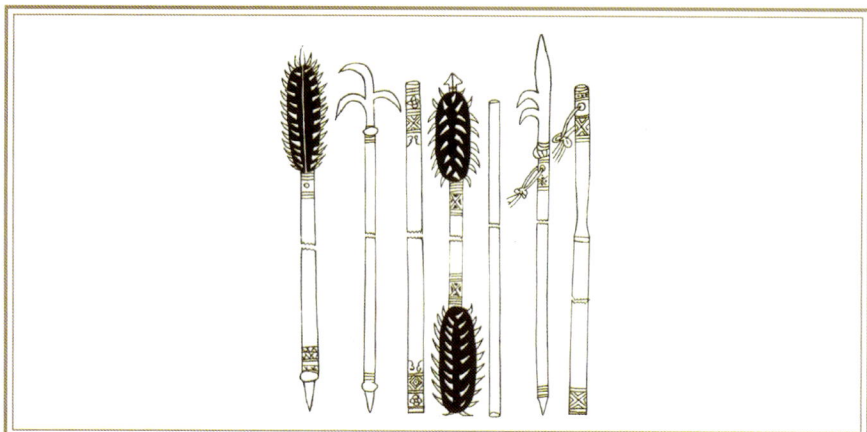

图 1-108　　《武经总要》中的七种棍棒 ①

The Seven Kinds of Staff described in the book *Wujing Zongyao*

---

①《武经总要》中的七种棍棒：从右至左依次为诃藜棒、钩棒、杆棒、杵棒、白棒、抓子棒、狼牙棒。诃藜棒，铁包棒首；钩棒，头有锐刃，下有双钩；杆棒，长约六尺，粗可盈把，以白蜡杆或带有韧性之木制成；杵棒，长五尺，尖长一寸二分，棒头的两端各长一尺五寸，上端植有小刺 48 个，下端植有小刺 50 个，小刺长五分，状如狼牙，具有刺、枪、劈、戳、撩、锯、扫等用法；抓子棒，头尾安有钩和镈；狼牙棒，长约六尺（1.7~1.9 米），棒头为蛋形圆木，上植许多铁钉，形如狼牙，故名，狼牙棒重而笨，一般为骑战所用。

The Seven Kinds of Staff described in *Wujing Zongyao* were named from the right to the left as Heli staff, hooked staff, pole staff, pestle, plain staff, clawed staff and wolf's fangs staff. Heli staff was named because of the iron cover on the top; Hooked staff was named because of the sharp blade on the top and double hooks beneath it; Pole staff was in length of about 6 chi(a unit of length, about 1/3 meter). It was made of Bailagan (a kind of plant) or the ductile wood and could be held in a hand; Pestle was in length of 5 chi with a sharp top of a length of 1.2 cun (a unit of length, about 1/3 decimeter) . On the both ends which were about 1.5 chi long were covered some thorns. There were 48 thorns on the top and 50 thorns on the bottom. These thorns were in a length of 150 centimeters like wolf's fangs. Thus it could be used for thrusting, chopping, poking, lifting, cutting and sweeping, etc.. Clawed staff was named owing to the claw-shaped blades on the top and a sharp set on the bottom; Wolf's fangs staff was in a length of about 1.7 to 1.9 meters. Its head was an egg-shaped wood with many embedded iron nails, which looked like wolf's fangs. It was heavy and used for fighting by a person riding on the horse.

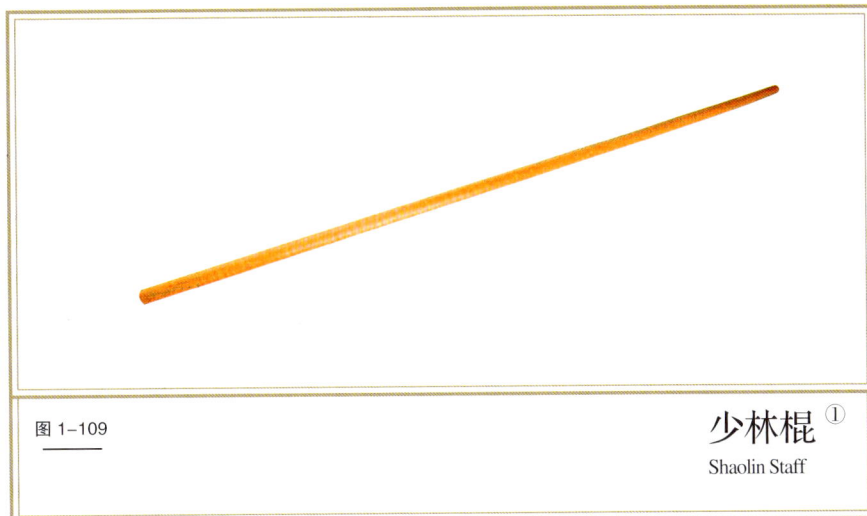

| 图 1-109 | 少林棍 ①
Shaolin Staff |

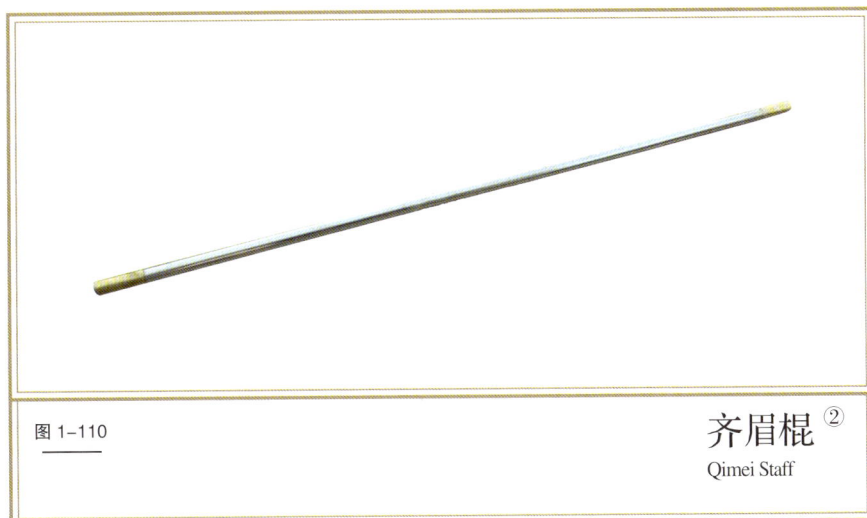

| 图 1-110 | 齐眉棍 ②
Qimei Staff |

① 少林棍：木制，长八尺至八尺五寸，通体粗细一致。

Shaolin Staff：It was made of wood and in a length of 2.67 to 2.83 meters. There was no change for its thickness between the two ends.

② 齐眉棍：常以白蜡杆制成，粗有盈把，因棍竖直与人眉高度相近得名。

Qimei Staff：It was often made of Bailagan (a kind of plant), and suitable to be held by a hand. The upright height was equal in height to a person's eyebrow.

图 1-111　**带矛狼牙棒** ① （战国时期）
Wolf's Fangs Staff with a spear
(The Warring States Period)

图 1-112　**虎噬牛狼牙棒** ② （战国时期）
Wolf's Fangs Staff with a model of tiger biting a bull
(The Warring States Period)

① 带矛狼牙棒：云南省江川县李家山滇墓出土。通长 32 厘米，矛长 12 厘米，棒头呈八棱柱状，外表遍布狼牙状锥刺。下部束收，中空为銎，以装木柄。顶部呈圆盘形，上铸一矛头，矛叶较宽。

Wolf's Fangs staff with a spear: It was unearthed from the Dian Tomb at Lijia Mountain in Jiangchuan County, Yunnan Province. It was 32cm in overall length and its spear was 12cm long. Its head was in eight prisms shape covered with thorns like wolf's fangs. The lower part became narrow with a tube-shaped receptacle to be fitted with a wood shaft. A spear was cast on a disc-shaped top, and its leaf was wide.

② 虎噬牛狼牙棒：云南省江川县李家山滇墓出土。通长 30.7 厘米，最粗处直径为 4.6 厘米，棒头较粗长，断面呈八棱形。下部束收，密布短刺。平顶，上铸一虎一牛，虎伏于牛的后臀上，前爪抱住牛的后腿，正欲咬噬。

Wolf's Fangs Staff with a model of tiger biting a bull: It was unearthed from the Dian Tomb at Lijia Mountain in Jiangchuan County, Yunnan Province. It was 30.7cm in overall length and its diameter was 4.6cm in the thickest part. Its head was slightly long and thick, and its cross-section was in eight prisms shape. The lower part became narrow. It was densely covered with short thorns.

第 11 节

槊

　　槊，同"矟"，常指马槊，《释名·释兵》说："矛长丈八曰矟，马上所持。"可见槊的长度约为 4 米。槊分槊锋与槊杆两部分，槊锋刃长达 50~60 厘米，为多棱状，有的头上装有铁钉若干，比矛要厚重，能够承受马飞奔时的高速冲击力。

　　槊产生于东汉晚期，魏晋南北朝时期达到鼎盛。当时重装骑兵是军队的主力，槊取代戟成为骑兵的主要格斗兵器。隋唐五代时期，槊仍是最重要的长柄格斗兵器，唐代以后多称为枪。《唐六典》记载，唐代的枪有四种：漆枪、木枪、白干枪、朴头枪，其中漆枪为骑兵所用，即槊。

火器出现后，矟也随着装甲骑兵的消失退出了古战场。

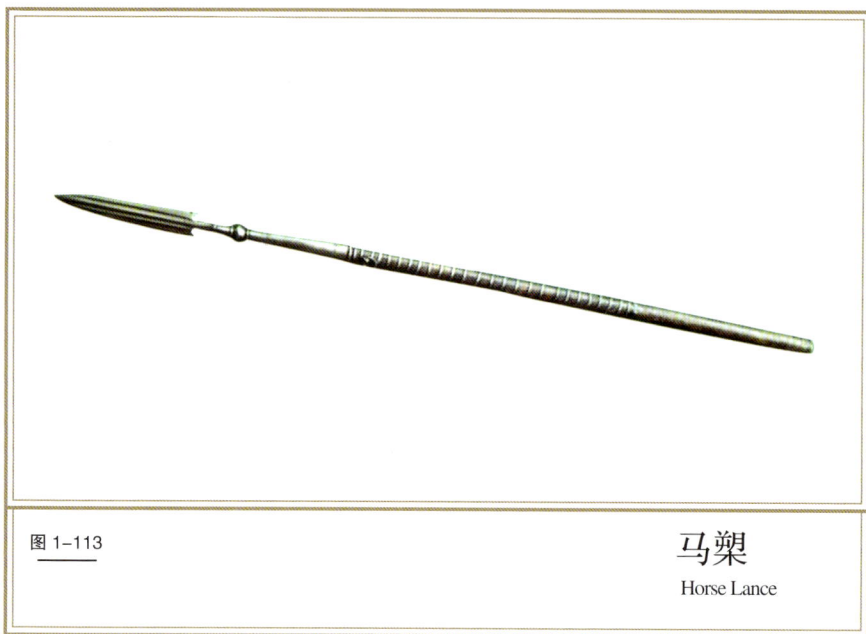

图 1-113

马矟
Horse Lance

第 **12** 节

长锤

锤是一种较为古老的兵器，属于打击类冷兵器。最早出自春秋战国时期，但很长时期内都作为仪仗所用，并未用于实战。汉代以后，特别是五代十国至宋，由于装甲骑兵的出现和发展，锤的功用在战争中不断凸显出来。

锤由锤头和柄组成，锤头有石质、铜质、铁质，形状有球形、瓜形、蒜头形等多种类型，有的还有刺或棱。因此，锤也被称为"瓜""骨朵"。锤柄多为木质，也有铁质，铁质的柄和锤头一体铸成，这类金属制成的锤又称为"金瓜"。

锤有长柄锤、短柄锤、链子锤等。长锤多为单用，长 1.4~1.8 米，双手持用。

图 1-114

铁锤头 ①
Iron head of Hammer

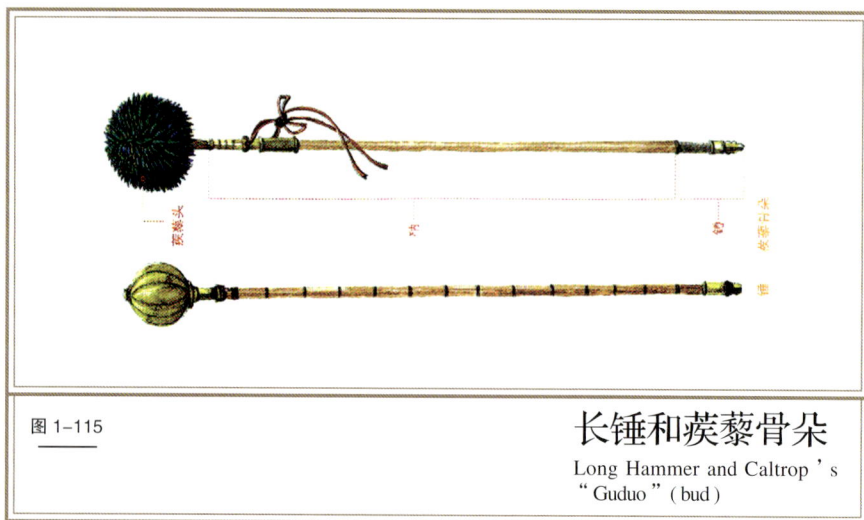

图 1-115

长锤和蒺藜骨朵
Long Hammer and Caltrop's
"Guduo"（bud）

① 铁锤头：河北省易县燕下都遗址出土。

Iron head of Hammer：It was excavated among the remains of the Secondary Capital of Yan in Yi County.

图 1-116

铜锤[1]（清）
Copper Hammer
(Qing Dynasty)

图 1-117

铁锤
Iron Hammer

----

[1] 铜锤：锤首为铜质长圆瓜形，锤柄为铁质圆柱状，外裹竹篾丝麻，柄底端为铜质多面体。
Copper Hammer：The head was made of copper in the shape of oval melon. The handle was an iron column wrapped with bamboo skin and silk–ramie. The very end top of the handle took a shape of rhombus.

第 13 节

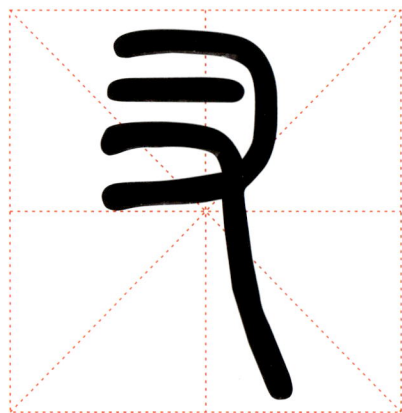

叉

叉由劳动工具演化而来，最早是古人捕鱼、狩猎和收拢谷物的工具。

兵书《六韬·虎韬·军用》中记载："鹰爪方胸铁杷，柄长七尺以上，三百枚。方胸铁叉，柄长七尺以上，三百枚。方胸两枝铁叉，柄长七尺以上，三百枚。"这可能是最早的叉用于军事的记载了。与刀、剑、枪、矛等常规兵器相比，叉处于次要地位。

顶端有两股叉的为"牛角叉"；顶端有三股叉的为"三头叉"，又名"三角叉"。汉代用两股叉。明代《三才图会·器用》中介绍，三股全部向上的叫作"钢叉""文叉"，有一股向下的叫作"武叉"，形如莲花的称为"莲花叉",还有五股叉甚至九股叉。叉柄多在七八尺,重四五斤。《武备志·军资乘·器械三》云:"镋钯、傷杷、扒、镋、大斧、铲、马叉等兵器,皆短兵中之长兵者也。"其中的马叉多为三股,刃锋面宽,"上可叉人,下可叉马"。马叉一直沿用到清代,为绿营所用。

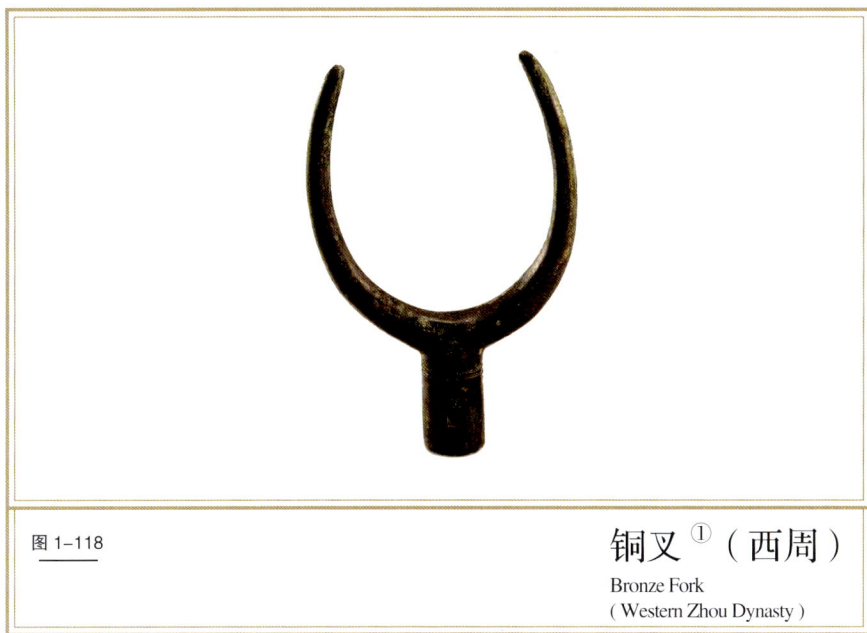

图 1-118

铜叉 [1] (西周)
Bronze Fork
(Western Zhou Dynasty)

---

① 铜叉:叉长 22.8 厘米,骹口径 3.6 厘米,镦长 12.8 厘米,口径 3.6 厘米。叉头内弯呈牛角形,双尖圆钝,短骹上部饰两道凹弦纹,下部近骹口处有对穿的方形钉孔。

Bronze fork: The tine was 22.8cm long, and the diameter of its shaft was 3.6cm. The set on the base was 12.8cm in length with the diameter of 3.6cm. The two tines were curved like an ox-horn, and the both tops were round and dull. There were two bow string patterns at the top of the tang and there was a penetrating square hole near the bottom end of the tang.

图 1-119

铜蛇头纹叉 ① **（西汉）**
Bronze Fork with snake-head design
(Western Han Dynasty)

图 1-120

三头叉
Fork with three tines

---

① 铜蛇头纹叉：云南晋宁县石寨山滇墓出土，通高 30 厘米。叉头下部与矛叶相似，上部外展分为两歧，似鱼的尾鳍。叉头后援铸銎筒，銎口呈圆形，銎筒铸成蛇的头颈形象，蛇圆眼张口，衔住叉头。叉头中部突起的脊棱像是蛇吐出的舌头，直伸叉口。

Bronze Fork with snake-head design：It was unearthed from the Dian Tomb of Shizhai Mountain in Jinning County,Yunnan Province. It was 30cm high. The lower part of the tines was similar to the spear-leaf, and the upper part was extending two branches which were like a tail fin. At the end of the tine was cast a tube with a round mouth. The tube was forged in the shape of snake-head with round eyes and opened-mouth to bite the fork head. There was a protruding ridge in the middle which was like the snake's tongue stretching upward.

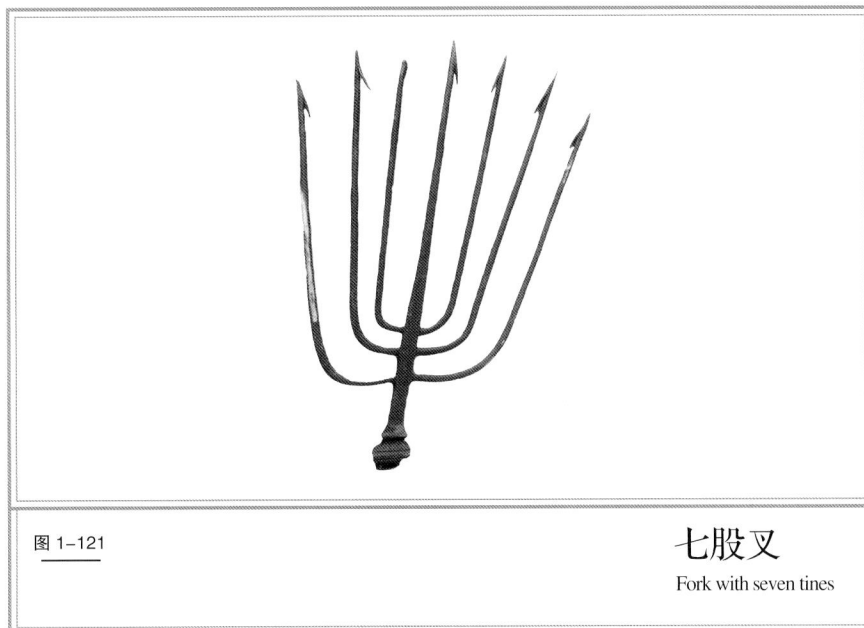

图 1-121

七股叉
Fork with seven tines

第 **14** 节

铫

铫是汉代兴起的一种长柄格斗兵器，由铍演变而来，属于矛类兵器。《说文系传》："铫，铍有镡也。"上端尖锋，形似短剑，与铍的区别是茎与骹之间加有两端上翘呈锐尖状的镡，使其具有一定的防护功能。铫有长柄也有短柄，铫长一般为 25~30 厘米，镡宽约 10 厘米。东汉以后绝迹。

图 1-122

铜铩（东汉）
Bronze Long Spear
(Eastern Han Dynasty)

图 1-123

铩
Long Spear

第 15 节

铲

　　铲也是从农具或工具演变而来的。早在新石器时代已有石铲，商代铸有青铜铲，战国晚期开始使用铁铲，明代出现月牙铲。

　　月牙铲铲头一般为铁质，刃部呈凸弧形，以銎装柄，柄为木制或铁制，有内月牙和外月牙两种。《三才图会·器用》卷八图示的"天蓬铲"为一内月牙，"形如月牙，内外皆锋刃，横长二尺，柄长八九尺或一丈，兵马步战第一利器。直推可以削手，往上推则铲首，向下推则铲足，或钩败卒之足，或于上风扬尘，妙不胜述"。《武备志·军资乘·器械三》图示的铲是一外月牙，"铲，长小尺一丈，尾有刃，以便后刺"。

古代僧侣也将铲用作随身兵器，常在铲头底部两头各凿一孔，挂上大铁环，舞动时当当作响，增加威势，也可用作行走时的开路工具或挑货扁担。

图 1-124

石铲（新石器时代）
Stone Spade（The Neolithic Age）

图 1-125

青铜铲（商后期）
Bronze Spade
（The Later Stage of Shang Dynasty）

图 1-126　铁铲（战国时期）
Iron Spade (The Warring States Period)

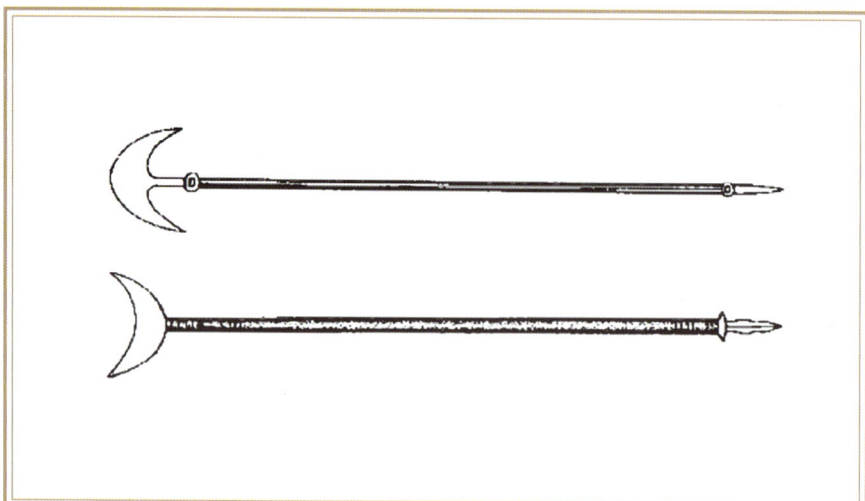

图 1-127　外月牙铲和天蓬铲
Spades with a concave and a convex blade

第 16 节

镋

　　镋，属于罕见兵器，始于明代，由枪发展而来。形似马叉，中间的利刃如长枪枪头，称为"正锋"或"中叉锋"，长一尺半；两侧分出两股，弯曲向上成月牙形，可攻可防。下接镋柄，柄长六至七尺，用法有劈、扫、刺、挑等。

　　由于镋的正锋较两侧锋刃长得多，所以刺杀效果更好。这种兵器过于长和大，分量又重，适合身高力大者使用。主要有凤翅镋、雁翅镋、牛头镋、齿翼月牙镋、锯齿镋和流星镋等几种。

图 1-128

凤翅锐 ①
Trident Halberd in the shape of
phoenix wings

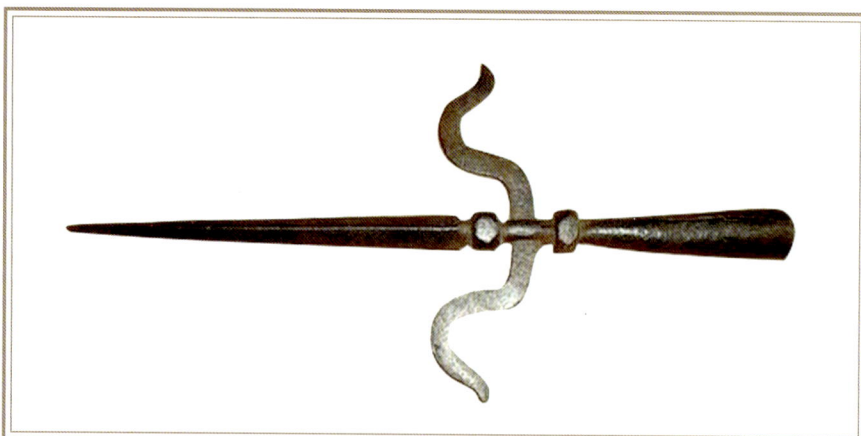

图 1-129

凤翅锐
Trident Halberd in the shape
of phoenix wings

① 凤翅锐：两边外展像凤凰翅膀而得名。

　　Trident Halberd in the shape of phoenix wings: It gained the name because the two blades on both sides looked like stretching wings of a phoenix.

图 1-130

齿翼月牙镋 [1]
Chiyi Yueya Trident Halberd

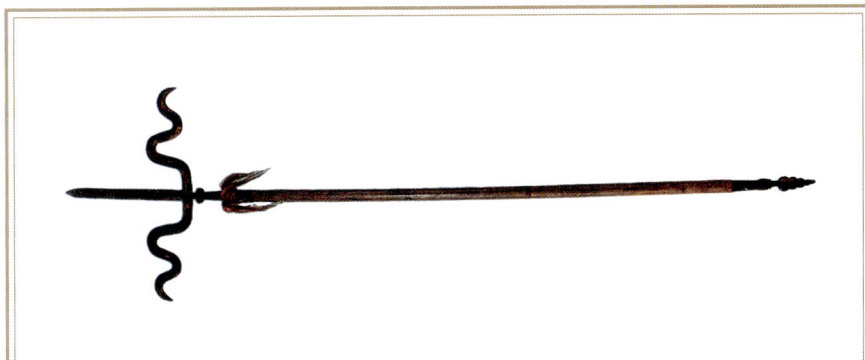

图 1-131

铁镋 [2]（清）
Iron Trident Halberd
(Qing Dynasty)

[1] 齿翼月牙镋：铁制，镋头有尖，长一尺，左右分出两股，各长八寸，状如月牙，上面植入十六个小刺，每个小刺长五分。

Chiyi Yueya Trident Halberd：It was made of iron. The head of Tang was in a length of 300 centimeters with a sharp top. There were two branches on its both sides with an overall length of 2.4 meters. They looked like a crescent and 16 barbs with a length of 150 millimeters were attached to the edges of both branches.

[2] 铁镋：长 236 厘米，镋头铁质、木柄、头系红缨，底镶镀金铜镈。

Iron Trident Halberd: It was 236cm long and the head of Trident Halberd was made of iron. It had a wooden handle and red horse tassel attached to the top. The bottom end of the handle was covered with a copper sheath of gilded gold.

第 **17** 节

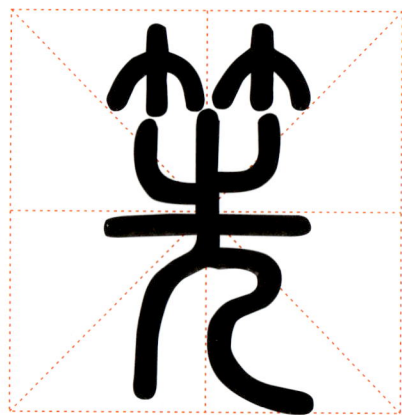

狼筅

　　狼筅是一种多枝形长兵器。明代戚继光《练兵实纪杂集·军器解上·狼筅解》："狼筅乃用大毛竹，上截连四旁附枝，节节枒杈，视之粗可二尺，长一丈五六尺。人用手势遮蔽全身，刀枪丛刺必不能入，故人胆自大，用为前列，乃南方杀倭利器。"

　　明代中晚期，为抗击倭寇，戚继光专门组织并训练了狼筅兵。在长而多节的毛竹顶端装上铁枪头，两旁枝刺用火熨烫得有直有钩，再灌入桐油，敷上毒药。战斗时，倭寇长刀虽锋利，却砍不断软枝，竹节层层深，能阻挡长枪刺入，狼筅兵在前冲阵，长枪兵紧随左右，大刀接应于后，杀得倭寇死伤无数。狼筅的独特结构增加了武器的覆盖面积，用来阻挡敌人的进攻非常有效，成为戚继光"鸳鸯阵"的武器装备之一，被称为"破阵第一利器"。

图 1-132

狼筅
Wolf Brush

图 1-133

狼筅

圆牌

长枪

长枪

队长

锐钯

长枪

长枪

圆牌

锐钯

长枪

狼筅

粪

戚继光 "鸳鸯阵" ①
Qi Jiguang's "Array of Mandarin Ducks"

---

① 戚继光 "鸳鸯阵"：明代冯梦龙《智囊补·兵智·鸳鸯阵》记载："戚继光每以鸳鸯阵取胜。其法二牌平列，狼筅各跟随牌，每牌用长枪二枝夹之，短兵居后。"

Qi Jiguang's "Array of Mandarin Ducks"：According to a text Array of Mandarin Ducks in the Eight Volume of Feng Menglong's *The Complete Brain Truster* in Ming Dynasty, it said that: "Qi Jiguang would win every time when he demonstrated the Array of Mandarin Ducks. There were two soldiers who held a shield standing in the front separately. The two holding the Wolf Brush directly followed them. Then four lancers would stand in a row to follow them. The soldiers with short weapons would stand behind."

短兵器

短兵器是古代较短的手持格斗兵器的统称，是相较于较长的手持格斗兵器而言的。一般将不及身长、多以单手操持的冷兵器列为短兵器。在中国古代，常见的短兵器如刀、剑、斧、鞭等，可以刺杀、砍杀，近战杀伤力很强。在冷兵器时代，短兵器是步兵的必备武器，很多骑兵也会配备短兵器。短兵器主要为单手握持使用，亦有为提高杀伤力而采用双手握持器械的。

和其他古代兵器一样，短兵器同样源于原始的生产工具，特别是狩猎工具。石器时代中，兵器主要为木、石、骨、角等材质。到了商代中期，短兵器跨入了金属兵器阶段。金属兵器先后经历了青铜兵器和钢铁兵器两个阶段。无论是越王勾践剑代表的青铜兵器，还是百炼钢刀代表的钢铁兵器，中国古代短兵器的发展均有着领先于世界的先进水平。

在汉代以前，在以车战为主要方式的战争中，短兵器并不是最重要的兵器。《五经正义》中记载的"车之五兵"分别是矛、戟、剑、盾、弓，而剑多为辅助兵器。进入骑兵与步兵的时代后，短兵器才有了更为重要的地位，特别是钢铁短兵器在战争中的使用，极大地提高了兵器的强度和杀伤力。宋代以后，随着热兵器的出现，中国进入冷兵器与热兵器共存的时代。

第 **1** 节

短剑

　　剑是我国古代的一种刺杀短兵器，素有"百兵之君"的美称，一般由身和茎两部分构成。剑身中间凸起称"脊"，脊两侧成坡状称"从"，从外的刃称"锷"，剑身前段称"锋"。"剑茎"一般指剑把，有圆柱和扁圆柱两种。茎端称"首"，茎和身之间有的有护手称"格"。剑既可以佩带，又可以手持。

　　作为兵器而存在的剑始于商代，最早出现于北方草原游牧民族中。我国现存最早的剑类兵器发现于内蒙古鄂尔多斯，被称为"鄂尔多斯式青铜短剑"。西周时期，青铜兵器有了进一步的发展，制作出很多富有特色、形制精美的古剑。商代常见的曲柄式短剑基本消失，直柄直刃式短剑成为主要形式。其特点是圆首、有格、圆茎或扁圆茎，有的茎上还带有箍。除了青铜材质的剑以外，也出现了少量玉、铁等材质的剑。东周时期，北方草原地区游牧民族的青铜短剑有了很大发展，传统直柄直刃式铜短剑有了新的发展，同时也出现了新型的曲刃式铜短剑。

春秋晚期至战国初期，中国古代的青铜兵器进入鼎盛时期。青铜剑的形制有了变化，且长度增大，一般多为 28~40 厘米，有的已经达到 50~60 厘米。这一时期的兵器发展有数量庞大、质量精良、形制成熟等特点。因利于近战击刺的特点，剑在实战中发展成主要的格斗兵器。特别是在我国东南吴越地区，因地处江南水乡，盛行于中原的车战在这里无法进行，而剑轻便锋利，便于近战，所以成为步兵的主要短兵器。正因为如此，春秋时期吴越地区的铸剑水平远远超过中原各国。因此，吴、越、楚被称为"宝剑之乡"，其地所铸宝剑最为有名的是 1965 年湖北江陵望山楚墓出土的越王勾践剑。汉代生产力水平提高，冶炼钢铁技术不断发展。至汉武帝时，钢铁兵器取得了飞速发展，铁剑开始取代青铜剑。东汉末年，由于环柄铁刀的普遍使用，铁刀完全取代了铁剑。从此，在战争舞台上鏖战七八百年的剑结束了作为军队的标准武器装备的历史使命，退出了军事舞台。

剑一直以礼器、武器、法器的性质发展。东周时，古人在剑上安装玉质剑首、剑格和其他一些玉质的装饰物品，称为"玉具剑"，作为礼器使用。汉以后，战争中剑已经基本不存在，其主要功能有：第一，佩带，仅仅在舆服制度中作为配饰使用；第二，成为民间体育锻炼的器械；第三，作为具有神秘色彩的宗教法器，镇恶祛邪。在明清时，剑更多地成为帝王将相的玩物，尽管其外表越来越华丽，但几乎丧失了军事意义。

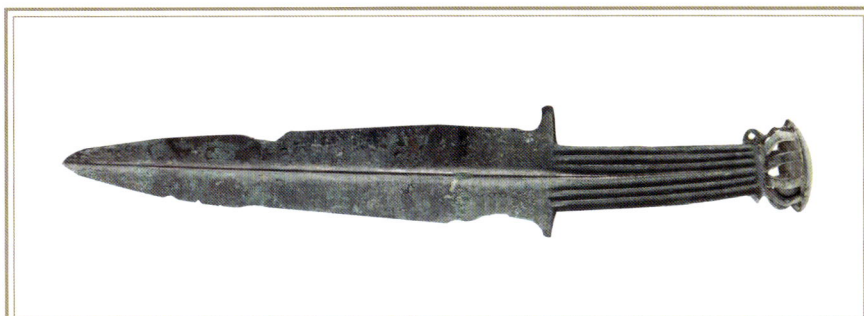

图 2-1

铃首剑 [1]（商）
Sword with bell pommel
（Shang Dynasty）

图 2-2

马首短剑 [2]（西周早期）
Half-sword with horse pommel
（The Early Stage of Western Zhou Dynasty）

---

[1] 铃首剑：山西省保德县林遮峪出土。商代后期，北方草原游牧民族形成独特的青铜文化，使用的青铜短剑一般具有铃首、兽首等装饰，工艺水平也达到相当的高度。

Sword with bell pommel：It was unearthed from the relics of Linzheyu in Baode County Shanxi Province. In the later stage of Shang Dynasty, the unique bronze culture was formed in the Northern Nomadic tribes. The bronze swords they used usually had the decorations like bell-shaped pommel or animal-shaped pommel. Their technological level had been considerably advanced.

[2] 马首短剑：北京昌平白浮出土，青铜时代早期短剑，具有明显的草原文化特征。

Half-sword with horse pommel：It was found at the site of Baifu in Changping District of Beijing. The early stage of half-sword in Bronze Age took the feature of apparent prairie culture.

图 2-3

"丰伯"铜剑 ①（西周）
Bronze Sword with inscription of "Fengbo"
（Western Zhou Dynasty）

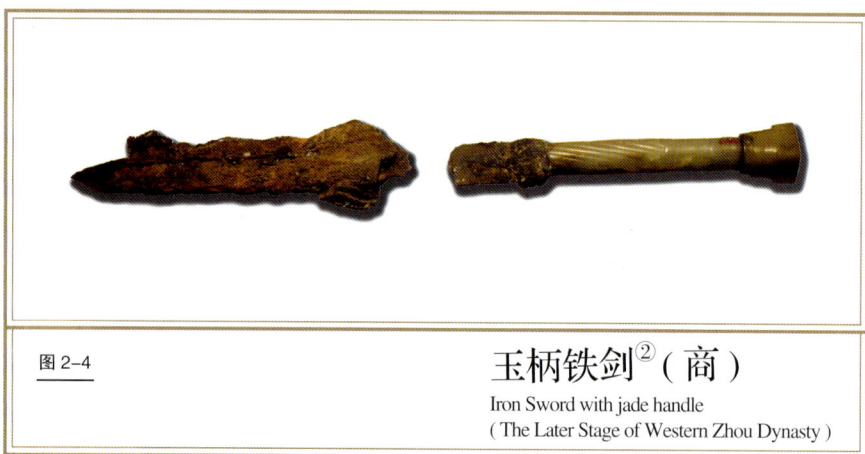

图 2-4

玉柄铁剑 ②（商）
Iron Sword with jade handle
（The Later Stage of Western Zhou Dynasty）

① "丰伯"铜剑：1964 年河南省洛阳市北窑西周墓出土。扁茎柳叶形铜短剑，剑身有"丰伯"二字铭文。

Bronze Sword with inscription of "Fengbo"：It was unearthed from the Tomb of Western Zhou Dynasty in Beiyao in 1964. The bronze sword with a flat stem was in the shape of willow leaf. There was the inscription of two characters "Fengbo" on the body of the sword.

② 玉柄铁剑：河南省三门峡市虢国墓出土。剑长 20 厘米，茎长 13 厘米；剑身铁质；剑柄由和田青玉制成，中空，里面插有铜制的芯，用于连接剑身。该剑集铁、铜、玉三种材质于一体，是中国出土的时代最早的一件人工冶铁制品。

Iron Sword with jade handle：It was excavated from the Tomb of Kingdom Guo in Sanmenxia City Henan Province. Its body was 20cm long and its stem was 13cm long. Its body was made of iron. Its handle was made of Hetian Jade, which was hollow to insert a bronze core so as to link the body and the handle. The sword was a complex of iron, bronze and jade, and was a man-made iron-smelting ware first unearthed in China.

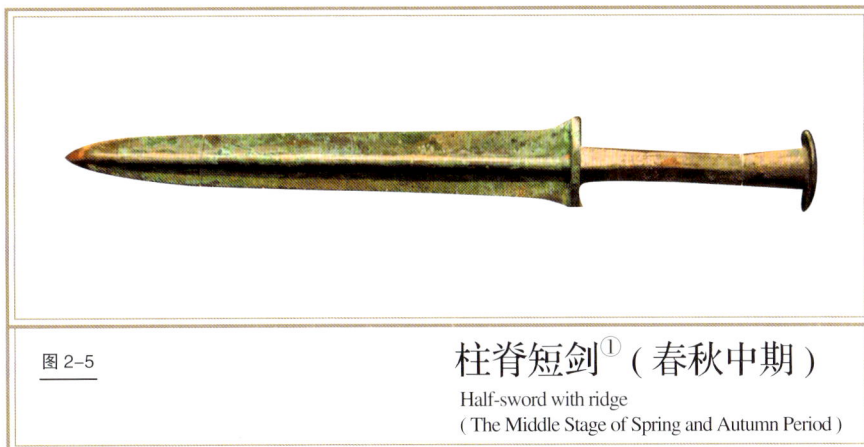

图 2-5　　柱脊短剑① （春秋中期）
Half-sword with ridge
（The Middle Stage of Spring and Autumn Period）

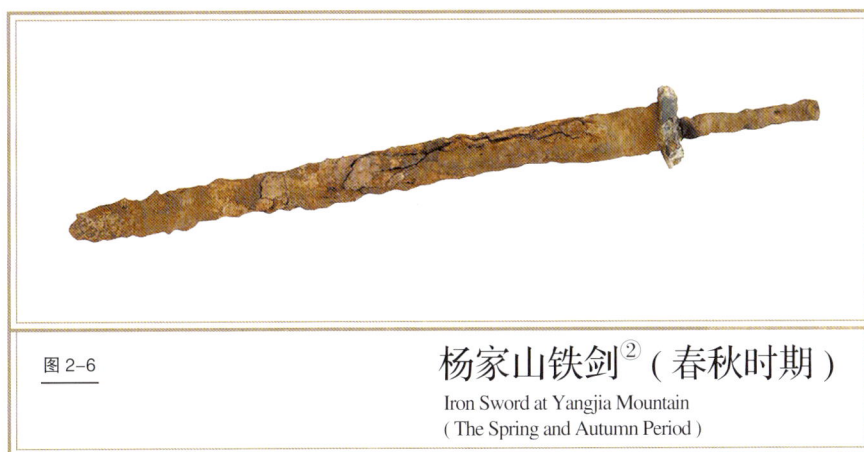

图 2-6　　杨家山铁剑② （春秋时期）
Iron Sword at Yangjia Mountain
（The Spring and Autumn Period）

① 柱脊短剑：北京延庆玉皇庙出土，代表了北方草原民族短剑的一种简约造型。

Half-sword with ridge：It was found at the Temple of Jade Emperor in Yanqing county Beijing. It stood for the simple structure of the half-sword used by the ethnics living in the northern China.

② 杨家山铁剑：湖南长沙杨家山春秋65号墓出土，是中国发现的最早的钢制品。剑通体长 38.4 厘米，茎长 7.8 厘米，剑宽 2~2.6 厘米，剑脊厚 0.7 厘米。采用块炼钢技术，剑含 0.5% 的中碳钢。

Iron Sword at Yangjia Mountain：It was excavated from No. 65 Tomb of the Spring and Autumn Period at Yangjia Mountain in Changsha city Hunan Province. It was the earliest steelware detected in China. It was 38.4cm in whole length and its stem was 7.8cm long. It was 2cm to 2.6cm in width and its ridge was 0.7cm in thickness. It adopted the chunk-steel smelting technique, and contained 0.5% medium carbon steel.

图 2-7　　　　　　　　**吴王夫差剑**[①]（春秋时期）
Sword of Fuchai
(The Spring and Autumn Period)

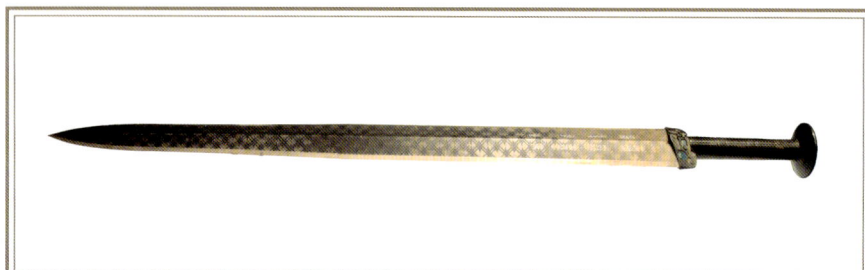

图 2-8　　　　　　　　**越王勾践剑**[②]（春秋晚期）
Sword of Goujian
(The Spring and Autumn Period)

---

① 吴王夫差剑：春秋时期吴国君主夫差所用，河南辉县出土。剑通体长 59.1 厘米，剑身宽 5 厘米。剑身上有阴刻篆字铭文："攻吾王夫差自作其之用。"

Sword of Fuchai: It was used by King Fuchai of Kingdom Wu in the Spring and Autumn Period. It was unearthed in Hui County Henan Province. It was 59.1cm in whole length and its body was 5cm in width. There were the inscription of seal script incised on its body, which read "(Belonging to) King Fuchai of Wu made for his personal use."

② 越王勾践剑：春秋晚期越国青铜器，出土于湖北江陵望山 5 号楚墓。因剑身镀了一层含铬的金属而千年不锈。经无损科学检测，其主要合金成分为铜、锡、铅、铁、硫等。花纹处含硫高，因硫化铜可防锈。剑通体长 55.7 厘米，宽 4.6 厘米，柄长 8.4 厘米，重 875 克，极其锋利。刻有 "钺王鸠浅，自乍用鐱" 八字。

Sword of Goujian: It was the bronze ware in Yue Kingdom of the Spring and Autumn Period and was unearthed from No. 5 Tomb of Chu at Wangshan in Jiangling County Hubei Province. It was stainless since its body was plated with the metal containing chrome. Based on the nondestructive scientific detection, the main alloying constituents were copper, tin, lead, iron and sulfur, etc. Its design or pattern had more sulfur content since the copper sulphide was rust-proof. It was 55.7cm in height including 8.4cm hilt. The blade was 4.6cm wide at its base. It weighed 875 grams. It was very sharp and incised with "(Belonging to) King Goujian of Yue, made for his personal use."

图 2-9

长剑 ①（战国时期）
Long Sword
（The Warring States Period）

图 2-10

宽 "燕王职" 剑 ②（战国时期）
Sword with inscription of "King Zhi of Yan"
（The Warring States Period）

---

① 长剑：中原式铜剑，剑体长而宽，剑柄装饰简洁，风格与草原文化短剑明显不同。

Long Sword：It was bronze sword used in Central Plains. Its blade was long and wide, and its hilt was simple in decoration. It had a distinction in style from the one with prairie culture.

② 宽 "燕王职" 剑：通长 62 厘米，剑身长 52.8 厘米、宽 4 厘米，茎长 9.2 厘米、宽 1.8 厘米，重 650 克。出土时剑身已断成两截，剑身后部有铭文："郾王职作武业著（鐯）剑。"燕王职即燕昭王，其名为职。此剑由燕国传入秦国并随葬入墓。

Sword with inscription of "King Zhi of Yan"：It was 62cm in length including 52.8cm blade and was 4cm in width. Its hilt was 9.2 cm long and 1.8cm wide. It weighed 650 grams. When unearthed, it had already been broken into two parts. There were inscription on the backside of the blade, which read "The sword was cast under the supervision of King Zhi of Yan State and was given to his followers." King Zhi of Yan State referred to King Zhao of Yan, whose name was Zhi. This sword was introduced into Qin State and was buried with the dead in the tomb.

图 2-11　　　　　　　　　　"繁阳之金"铜剑 ① (战国时期)

Bronze Sword with inscription of " Fanyang Zhijin "
(The Warring States Period)

图 2-12　　　　　　　　　　　　　铜剑 (战国时期)

Bronze Sword
(The Warring States Period)

---

　　① "繁阳之金"铜剑：该剑铸工精巧，十分锋利，剑身铭刻错铜纹"繁阳之金"四字，为春秋时期吴国君主夫差所用，河南辉县出土。剑身全长 59.1 厘米，宽 5 厘米，满布花纹，锋锷仍很锐利。剑身铸有篆书阴文十字："攻瘉王夫差自乍其元用。"

Bronze Sword with inscription of "Fanyang Zhijin"：The sword was exquisite and sharp. Here four characters of "Fanyang Zhijin (meaning the weapon was cast in the place of Fanyang)" were incised in elegant pattern. It was used by the King Fuchai of Wu in the Spring and Autumn Period and was unearthed in Hui County Henan Province. It was 59.1cm in whole length and 5cm in width. And it was covered with decorative patterns and its edge of the blade was very sharp. There were inscription of seal script incised on its body, which read "(Belonging to) King Fuchai of Wu made for his personal use."

图 2-13

铜剑①（秦）
Bronze Sword（Qin Dynasty）

图 2-14

玉具铁剑②（西汉）
Iron Sword with jade ornaments
（Western Han Dynasty）

① 铜剑：制造精致，长度达到 90 厘米左右，十分锋利，具有长、窄、薄、利的形制特点，说明此时工艺水平达到前所未有的高度。

Bronze Sword：It was manufactured with exquisite techniques, and was about 90cm long. Its structure was characterized by length, thinness, narrowness and sharpness. Its technology had reached an unprecedented level.

② 玉具铁剑：河北满城汉墓出土，长 71.8 厘米。玉具剑即装有玉质附件的剑，如有玉质剑首和剑格，或剑鞘上玉质的璏和摽，典雅华贵，主要用作配饰。

Iron Sword with jade ornaments：It referred to the swords decorated with jade wares, like the jade pommel and jade guard, the jade hook and protrusive part on the scabbard, which made the sword elegant and luxury. It mainly functioned as accessory. The sword in the picture was unearthed in Mancheng County Hebei Province. It was 71.8 cm long.

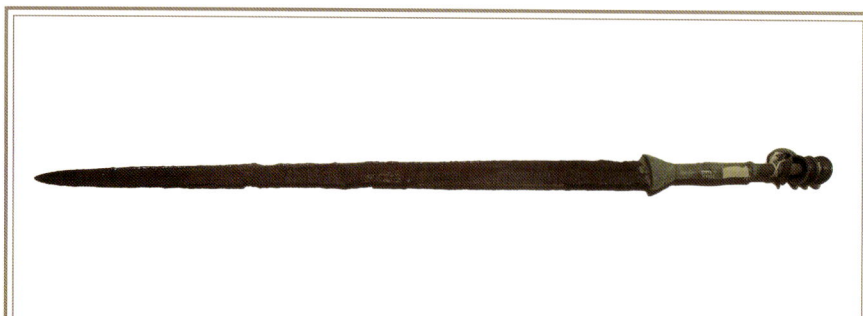

图 2-15

青铜柄铁剑①（西汉）
Iron Sword with bronze hilt
(Western Han Dynasty)

图 2-16

七星铁剑②（金）
Long Iron Sword inlaid with the
Big Dipper(Jin Dynasty)

① 青铜柄铁剑：辽宁西丰西岔沟出土。制造时往往多次加热、渗碳，反复锻打，刃部往往局部淬火，硬度极高。

Iron Sword with bronze hilt：It was excavated from Xichagou of Xifeng County, Liaoning Province. It was forged by repeated heating and carburization. Its blade was harder because of selective quenching.

② 七星铁剑：北京房山金陵遗址出土，通长 1.25 米。铜质云头大环首，剑身铁质，中脊饰银线，前段镶嵌北斗七星。

Long Iron Sword inlaid with the Big Dipper：It was unearthed from the Relics of Jinling in Fangshan District of Beijing. It was 1.25m in length. Its bronze pommel was in the shape of a big ring, and its blade was made of iron. Its ridge was decorated with silver wire. The design of the Big Dipper was inlaid in the front part.

图 2-17

钢剑（明）
Copper Sword（Ming Dynasty）

图 2-18

红鱼皮鞘出云剑①（清）
Sword with clouds design and a Scabbard covered
with red-fish skin（Qing Dynasty）

---

①红鱼皮鞘出云剑：乾隆御用剑之一，长 100 厘米。
　　Sword with clouds design and a Scabbard covered with red-fish skin：It was used by Emperor
Qianlong (1736–1795) in Qing Dynasty, and was 100cm long.

第2节

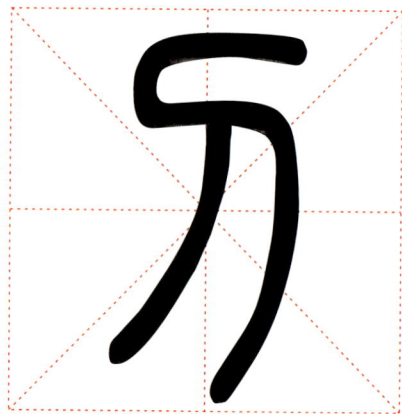

短刀

短刀是我国古代的一种砍杀短兵器。《释名》云："刀，到也，以斩伐到其所乃击之。"短刀为单面长刃的短兵器。

早期的刀并不以兵器的性质出现。铜刀脱胎于石刀，体形很小，泛指可用于切、削、割、剁、刺的工具，与匕合用亦为膳食器。商代，中原地区的铜刀体形仍较小，刀柄与刀身分离，形制有了凸刃和凹刃、环状柄与兽状柄等区别。当时的刀主要用来砍削器物、宰牛羊或防身自卫，还未正式用于战争。直到西周，刀在以车战为主的战争中发挥的作用并不大，商代大量使用的青铜短刀基本消失。与同时代的铜剑相比，刀的做工粗糙，形体笨拙，远不如铜剑精巧锋利。同时，商代、西周出现了制作精美的玉质刀，但缺乏实战效应，主要是作为礼器而存在。

和剑一样，使刀以兵器性质出现并用于实战的是北方草原游牧民族。商代后期少数民族的刀颇具民族特色，其形制基本特征是凸背曲刃，柄与身接触处的刃部一侧有突齿，并装饰有各种纹路。柄首主要有兽首、环首、铃首三种。

到了汉代，随着车战的没落以及骑兵作用的凸显，在中原地区刀受到了军事家的重视。考古发现的环首长刀、环首短刀、秃头短刀等，证明刀已经登上了战争舞台。汉代开始，刀的材质发生巨大变化。随着百炼钢技术的发展，铁刀日益精良，不仅取代了青铜刀，更在战争中取代了剑，成为军队中最主要的短柄格斗兵器。魏晋南北朝时期，环首铁刀是使用最广泛的兵器。唐代，环首刀有了新的形制，为直体单刃，刀身狭长，刀柄一般是铁茎外包裹木把后缠绕丝绳。唐代钢铁刀的制造技术有了进一步的发展，加上通过丝绸之路的贸易往来，中亚出产的优质铁矿石、成品钢铁传入中国，因此制造出一批精品钢刀。

在宋代，刀已经明确分长柄、短柄，长柄刀实质已经属于长兵器，短柄刀则突破汉唐以来环首刀的形制。与此同时，在制作工艺上，宋代已经开始使用"夹钢"工艺。到了元代，由于蒙古贵族更喜欢剑，因此在军中剑的使用较刀更为普遍。刀、剑一般刃锋利，做工精致，镶嵌宝石，十分精美，其性质和佩带方式沿袭了唐宋时期汉人的风格。明代同样分短柄刀与长柄刀，短柄刀的形制受到了日本长刀的影响，和宋刀有了极大的不同，一般刃狭长而弯，极锋利。清代，刀是清军主要格斗兵器，同时皇室、官佐也十分喜欢佩刀。短柄军刀在军中一般分为三大类：一是兵卒用刀，双手持握，可大力劈砍；二是官佐佩刀，与明代有所区别，钢刃窄薄，刀上有血槽；三是皇室用刀，制作精美。

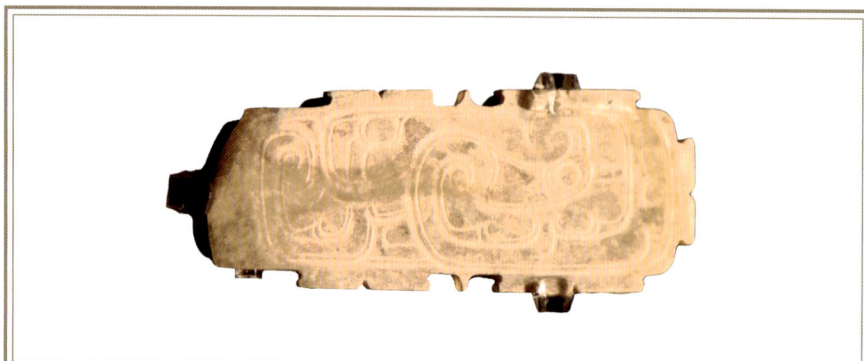

图 2-19   **玉凤纹刀**[①]（ 西周 ）
Jade Sabre with phoenix design
（ Western Zhou Dynasty ）

图 2-20   **三凸纽环首刀**[②]（ 商 ）
Sabre with ring-shaped pommel scattered with
three buttons（ Shang Dynasty ）

---

   ① 玉凤纹刀：北京房山琉璃河出土。玉刀两面纹饰均以双勾阴刻线作凤纹，凤昂首直立，高冠长尾。

Jade Sabre with phoenix design：It was found at the Relics of Liuli River in Fangshan District of Beijing. Both sides of the blade were incised with phoenix design in grooved lines. The phoenix was standing upright with high coronet and long tail.

   ② 三凸纽环首刀：山西省石楼县二郎坡出土。

Sabre with ring-shaped pommel scattered with three buttons：It was unearthed from the site of Erliangpo in Shilou County Shanxi Province.

图 2-21

镂空环首刀 [①]（商）
Sabre with hollow-out pommel in the shape of ring
（Shang Dynasty）

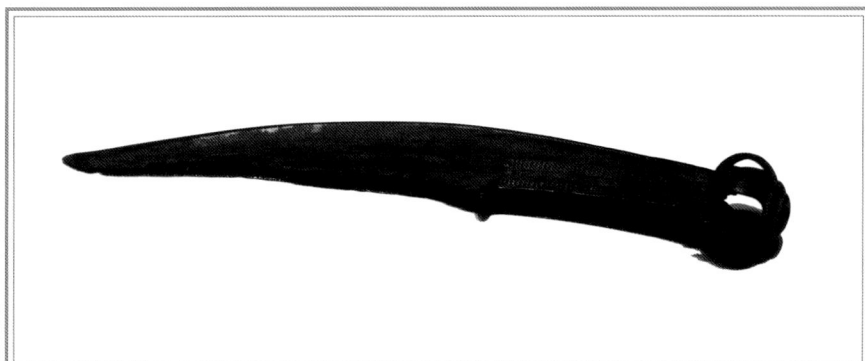

图 2-22

铃首青铜刀（商）
Bronze Sabre with Bell-shaped Pommel
（Shang Dynasty）

---

① 镂空环首刀：山西省石楼县义牒村出土。

Sabre with hollow-out pommel in the shape of ring：It was found in Yidie Villege of Shilou County Shanxi Province.

图 2-23

铜刀[1]（商）
Bronze Sabre（Shang Dynasty）

图 2-24

斜刃铜割刀（战国时期）
Bronze cutting-knife with oblique blade
（The Warring States Period）

[1] 铜刀：河北藁城台西出土。
Bronze Sabre：It was excavated from the site of Taixi in Gaocheng County.

图 2-25

铁刀（西汉）
Iron Sabre（Western Han Dynasty）

图 2-26

"永初六年"钢刀 ① （东汉）
Steel Sabre with inscription of "The Sixth Year in
Yongchu Period"（Eastern Han Dynasty）

---

① "永初六年"钢刀：山东兰陵出土。刀背有错金隶书铭文："永初六年五月丙午造卅湅大刀吉羊宜子孙。"

Steel Sabre with inscription of "The Sixth Year in Yongchu Period"：It was unearthed in Lanling County Shandong Province and was inscribed with clerical script inlaid gold on the back of the blade, which read "The sabre was made in May of the sixth year in Yongchu period after boiled for many times, Year of the Sheep".

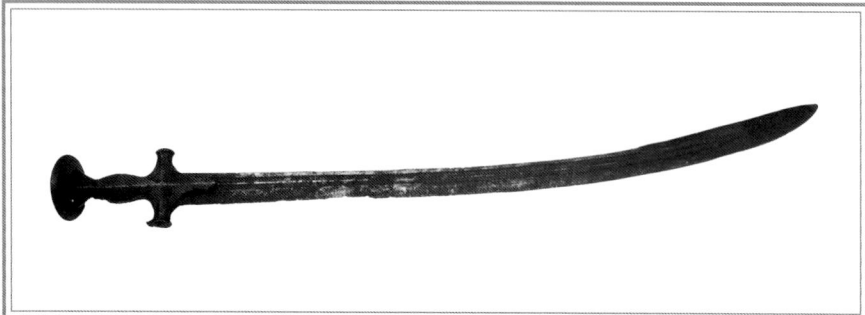

| 图 2-27 | 战刀①（西藏古格王朝时期）
Sabre（The Period of Guge Dynasty in Tibet） |

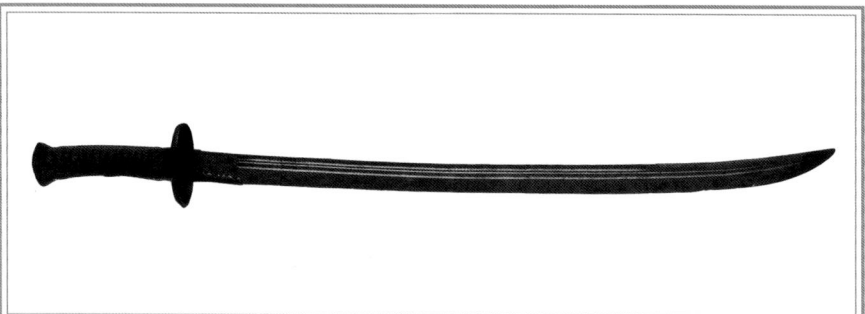

| 图 2-28 | "万历十年登州戚氏"军刀②（明）
Sabre with inscription of "Forged under the supervison of Qi in
Dengzhou in the Tenth Year of Wanli Period（Ming Dynasty） |

---

① 战刀：古格王朝的前身可以上溯到象雄国，王朝大概是在9世纪统一西藏高原的吐蕃王朝瓦解后建立的，到17世纪消亡，前后世袭了16个国王。古格王国时期金属制造业已经达到相当高的水平。

Sabre：The predecessor of Guge Dynasty could date back to the kingdom Xiangxiong. It was established in the 9th century to unify the states on the Tibet Plateau after the collapse of the Tubo Dynasty. Until the end of 17th century, there were 16 kings successively inherited to be the emperor of Guge Dynasty. The metal manufacturing industry had been quite advanced at the Period of Guge Kingdom.

② "万历十年登州戚氏"军刀：明万历十年（1582）戚继光任总兵时铸造。

Sabre with inscription of "Forged under the supervison of Qi in Dengzhou in the Tenth Year of Wanli Period"：It was forged in the tenth year of the Period of Emperor Wanli in Ming Dynasty when Qi Jiguang was appointed as General in Chief.

图 2-29

渥巴锡腰刀 [1]（清）
Broadsword of Ubashi Khan（Qing Dynasty）

图 2-30

蒙古刀具 [2]（清）
Mongol Sabre（Qing Dynasty）

---

① 渥巴锡腰刀：渥巴锡（1742—1775），清代卫拉特蒙古土尔扈特部首领。1771年1月，渥巴锡率领本部17万人东迁，回到其祖先的家园。7月到达西部蒙古，9月乾隆皇帝册封他为乌讷恩素诛克图旧土尔扈特部卓里克图汗，以其所部为旧土尔扈特部。

Broadsword of Ubashi Khan：Ubashi Khan（1742—1775）was a Torghut-Kalmyk prince and the last Khan of the Kalmyk Khanate in Qing Dynasty. In January 1771，he led the return migration of approximately 170,000 Kalmyks from their pastures on the left bank of Volga River to Dzungaria, their ancestral hometown. In July they arrived in Mongolia in the West, and Emperor Qianlong of Qing Dynasty conferred the title of Khan of Old Torghuts. The First Phase of their movement became the Old Torghuts.

② 蒙古刀具：蒙古军所使用的刀一般刃锋利，做工精致，镶嵌宝石，十分精美，其性质和佩带方式沿袭了唐宋时期汉人的风格。

Mongol Sabre：The Mongol Sabre was very sharp. It looked elegant since it was inlaid with precious stones and forged with delicate skills. Its nature and the approach to wearing followed the style of Han People in Tang and Song Dynasties.

第 3 节

鞭

　　随着青铜兵器退出战争舞台以及钢铁冶炼、锻造技术的不断发展，在唐宋以后出现了一些与刀、剑有着极大差别的短兵器，其中非常具有代表性的是鞭和锏。因为二者形制相似，所以历代都把鞭、锏相提并论，并因在短兵器中不及刀、剑用途广泛，被视为杂兵。在材质与性质方面，鞭与锏也有很多的相似之处。

　　从材质上看，鞭有单、双和软、硬之分，使用的材质多为铜、铁、钢、铁木、纯木、皮革等。具体来看，硬鞭多为铜制或铁制，软鞭多为皮革编制。硬鞭有竹节鞭、虎尾鞭等数种，使用技法主要以挡、摔、点、截、扫、盘、板、戳、拦、撩、拨以及绞压等为主，身法上转折圆活、刚柔合度，步伐轻捷奋迅，与手法紧密配合。

  鞭一般适用于马战与步战。硬鞭一般用于马战，持鞭之将多持双鞭。唐宋以前，鞭并未在军队中广泛使用。而在宋代，鞭、锏已经在军队中有了一定的普及。之后随着冷兵器的发展，鞭慢慢退出了历史舞台，更多地成为一种民间武器。

  民间有很多流传已久的关于鞭的"流派"，其中最有名的有：秦家鞭，此鞭长四尺，通体为长铁杆，其上下二端各有一突出的圆球，无明显的鞭把和鞭尖的区别；雷神鞭，其鞭长四尺，鞭把与剑把相同，鞭身前细后粗，共为十三节，形如宝塔，把手处有圆形铜护盘，鞭重三十斤，通体为铁制；水磨钢鞭，鞭长三尺五寸，鞭把为五寸，鞭身长三尺，鞭身后粗前锐，呈方形，鞭头鞭把三处均可手握，能两头使用；竹节鞭，其鞭长四尺半，把手为圆形，上有若干突出圆结，把手前有圆形护盘，鞭身前细后粗，呈竹节状，共有九节或十一节不等。

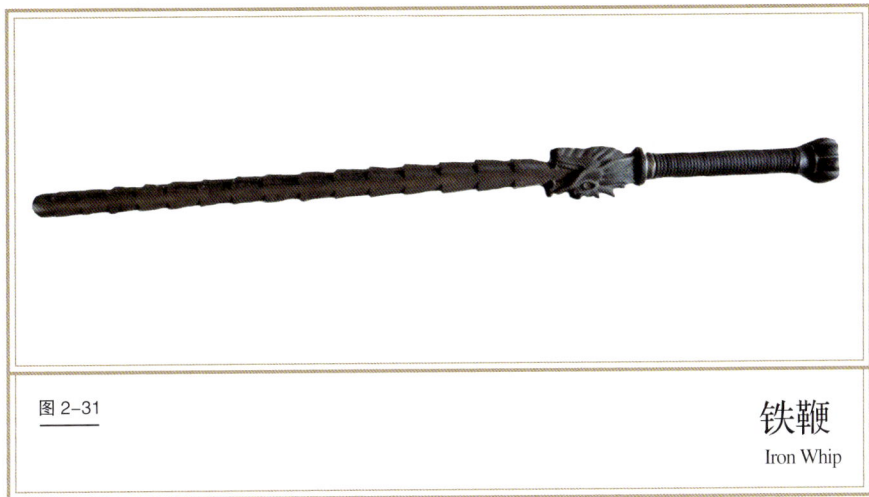

图 2-31

铁鞭
Iron Whip

图 2-32

木柄龙头铁鞭

Iron Whip with a dragon design on the wood handle

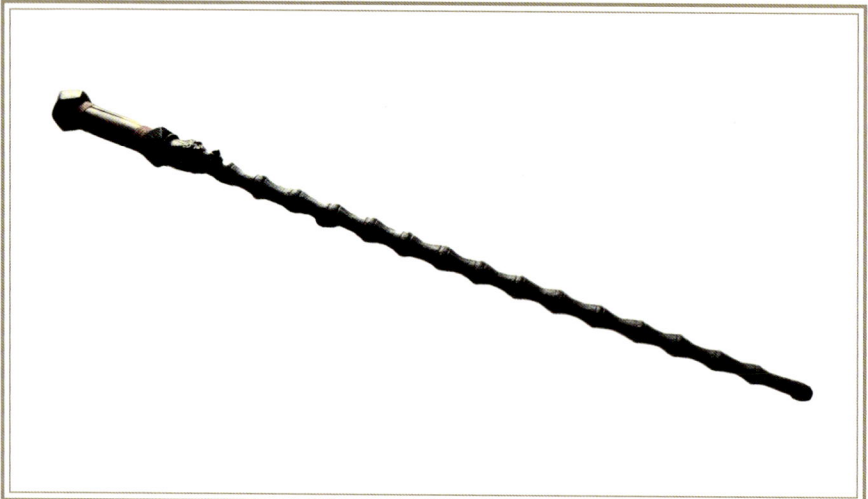

图 2-33

龙吞束腰竹节铁鞭（明）

Iron Whip with bamboo-like joints held in the mouth of dragon design (Ming Dynasty)

图 2-34

杵式双铁鞭 [1]（清）
Double-handed Whips in the shape of pestle
(Qing Dynasty)

图 2-35

剑式铁鞭 [2]（清）
Iron Whip in the shape of sword
(Qing Dynasty)

① 杵式双铁鞭：鞭身呈竹节状，柄部作金刚杵状，内为铁柱，外包圆木，柄两端以铁铸须弥座，通长 104 厘米，清宫旧藏。

Double-handed Whips in the shape of pestle：The lash was like bamboo joints. Its handle was made in the shape of vajry pestle. An iron column was in the middle of the handle to be wrapped with timber. On the both ends of the handle were forged vajrasana. It was 104cm in overall length and was kept in Qing Palace.

② 剑式铁鞭：鞭身呈竹节状，前端尖细，护手呈圆盘状，鋄（wàn）金夔龙纹，黑漆木柄，缠黑丝绦带，黑漆鞘，通长 104 厘米。

Iron Whip in the shape of sword：The lash was bamboo like joints with a sharp top. Above the handle was a disc-shaped plate. It was covered with the gilded pattern of Kui Dragon. The handle was in black lacquer wound with black silk braid. Its scabbard was painted in black. It was 104cm long.

第 **4** 节

锏

铜经常和鞭一起出现，是一种与鞭相似的短柄打击兵器，一般无刃，有柄。锏和鞭的主要区别在于，锏一般有棱无节，顶端也无尖，整体风格简洁，持锏者需要有强大的上臂力量。

从材质上看，锏一般以铜或铁制成，在冶炼锻造技术较为发达的年代，钢制锏也被广泛使用。锏的形制变化不大，一般长而无刃，多棱，长度为一米左右，由锏把和锏身组成。锏身呈方锥形，棱角突出，锏把与锏身连接处有护手。锏体断面呈方形，有槽，所以也称"四面金装锏"或"凹面锏"。锏的用法与刀、剑、鞭接近，主要有击、枭、刺、点、拦、格、劈、架、截、吹、扫、撩、盖、滚、压等。在实战中，多双锏并用，利于步战，一般是身强力壮的兵士使用，杀伤手段简单粗暴，也常用于骑兵，杀伤力十分可观。

一些学者认为，锏与剑同时出现，锏的使用技法在秦汉之后也已经出现。但根据考古证据来看，锏在两晋之前很少出现。隋唐之后，和鞭一样，锏在战争中作为破甲利器受到一定的重视，在宋代战争中使用较为广泛。

出土文物中，常见的锏主要有：八棱锏、平棱锏、凹面锏、四棱锏、浑圆锏、狼牙锏等。除了在战争中作为兵器使用，也常被民间当作武器使用。

图 2-36

铁锏 [①] （元）
Iron Mace（Yuan Dynasty）

① 铁锏：此锏长而无刃，四棱，通长 73.5 厘米。

Iron Mace: It was long and blunt, and was molded with four ridges below the head with a length of 73.5 cm.

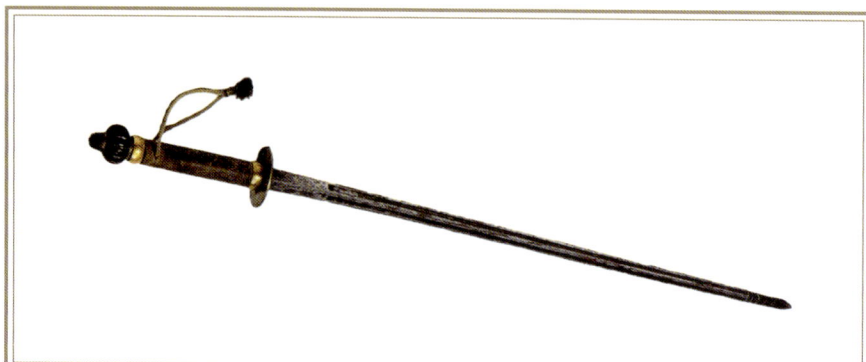

图 2-37

钢锏^①（清）
Steel Mace (Qing Dynasty)

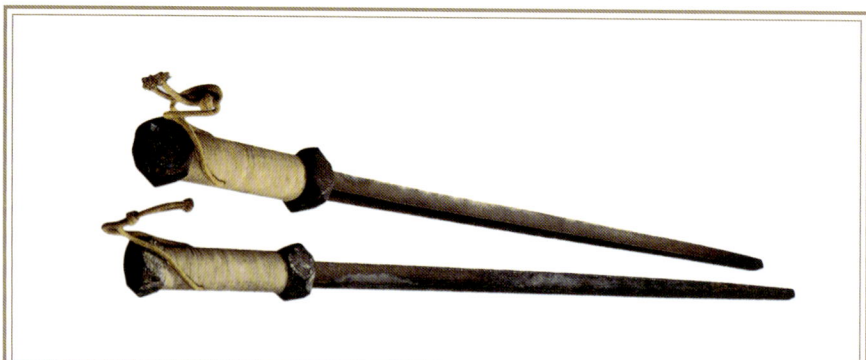

图 2-38

铜双锏^②（清）
Double-handed Copper Mace
(Qing Dynasty)

① 钢锏：此锏锏身呈四棱柱状，护手圆盘状，柄首作铜爪棱形，通长 103 厘米，为清宫旧藏。

Steel Mace: It was in the shape of four ridges. It had a disc-shaped hand-guard and a pommel in the prismatic shape of copper claw. It was 103 cm long and is stored in the Qing Palace.

② 铜双锏：此双锏锏身呈四棱柱状，护手以及柄首作多面体，通长 74 厘米，为清宫旧藏。

Double-handed Copper Mace: It was in the shape of four ridges, and its hand-guard and pommel was made in the prismatic shape. It was 74 cm long and is stored in Qing Palace.

第 **5** 节

短斧

在中国古代兵器中，短斧和短锤有着很多的相似之处。早在石器时代，人类充分利用力学原理，将木棍或直骨与石器或骨器结合，发明出最早的简单机械，其中有利刃的可视为石斧，以球状为主的可视为石锤，这是人类最早的劈砍锤击兵器。

尽管在材质上经历了石骨、青铜、钢铁的变化，用途和名称也有所不同，又有长短之分，但斧身的式样基本相同，均为一侧是扇形刃，一侧是长方体，下部装有木柄。在形制上，短斧与长兵器中的斧相似，有单、双斧之分，为古时步兵所用。短柄因形状扁宽，也称为"板斧"。斧的主要用法有：劈、砍、剁、抹、砸、搂、截等。斧的使用，主要是利用杠杆原理和冲量等于动量的改变量原理来运作的，由此也可以看出古代中国军事家与工匠的智慧。

石器时代以石斧为主；商代时青铜斧开始在军队中使用；到了周代，斧已经慢慢从战争中退出，作为装饰物成为权力的象征，或作为斩杀的刑具。

春秋战国时期，短斧在少数游牧民族地区开始流行。隋唐时期，短斧开始登上战争舞台。在这一时期，斧的刃部加厚，手柄缩短，重量有所减轻。兵士在使用短斧时，能够单手持握，其砍杀效果有了极大的提高。这一时期斧的代表式样有凤头斧、长柯斧等，其形制已经开始有短兵器的特点。宋朝以后，短斧在战争中广泛使用，受到了各朝各代军事家的重视。除《武经总要》记载的开山、静燕、日华、无敌、长柯斧之外，还有专门攻城用的凤头斧、峨眉斧，以及用于守城的挫王斧等，斧柄一般长二尺五到三尺五。在清代，斧更是被编进十大类军器中，装备于八旗前锋营。柄长大约一尺六寸的短斧，携带方便，使用灵活，杀伤力强。

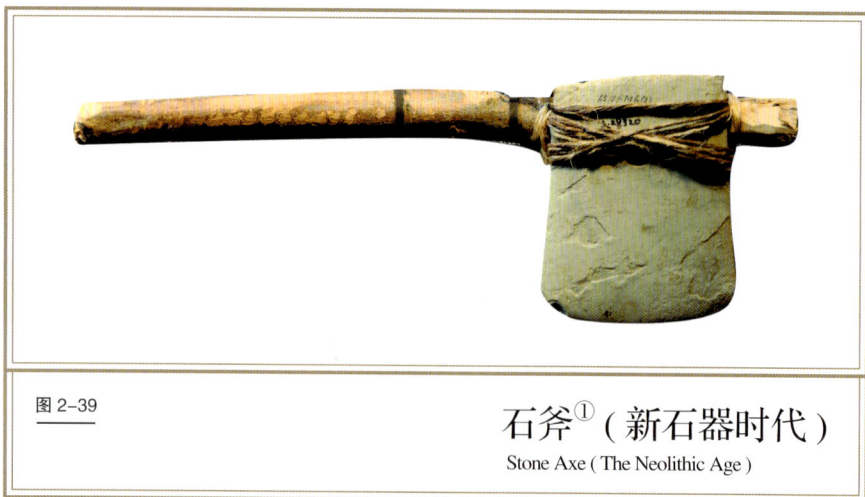

图 2-39

石斧①（新石器时代）
Stone Axe (The Neolithic Age)

① 石斧：出土于湖北荆门屈家岭文化遗址。
Stone Axe: The stone axe was unearthed from the Cutural Relics of Qujialing in the upper-middle reaches of the Yangtze River.

图 2-40

石斧（商后期）
Stone Axe (The Later Stage of Shang Dynasty)

图 2-41

管銎斧 [1]（西周早期）
Axe with a circular-shaped hole for a handle
(The Early Stage of Western Zhou Dynasty)

[1] 管銎斧：北京丰台出土。銎指器物上套插木柄的中空部位。此斧的大圆孔与銎都具有西北地区草原兵器的特点。

Axe with a circular-shaped hole for handle：It was found in Fengtai District of Beijing. The circular hole was used to fasten the wooden handle. This axe illustrated features of weapons related to the culture of Northern Grasslands.

图 2-42

铜斧①（西周早期）
Bronze Axe
（The Early Stage of Western Zhou Dynasty）

图 2-43

銎斧②（春秋时期）
Axe with handle receptacle
（The Spring and Autumn Period）

---

① 铜斧：北京昌平白浮出土，属于北方草原民族的短柄兵器，斧背两侧还残留有木柄的朽木。

Bronze Axe: It was excavated from the Relics of Baifu in Changping District of Beijing. It belonged to the weapons with short handles used by the ethnic groups on the Northern grasslands. On the both sides of the shaft receptacle there were residues of the wooden handle.

② 銎斧：山西省长治市分水岭 269 号墓出土，形似戈，其内为鸟首衔援，两侧蟠螭缠绕，螭间为一小龟，形象生动。

Axe with handle receptacle: It was unearthed from the No. 269 Tomb of Fenshuiling in Changzhi city Shanxi Province. It looked like a dagger. Its blade was designed in the shape of bird–head with the wedge in its mouth. On the opposite side of the bird mouth was covered with a vivid design of snake–like dragon and a turtle.

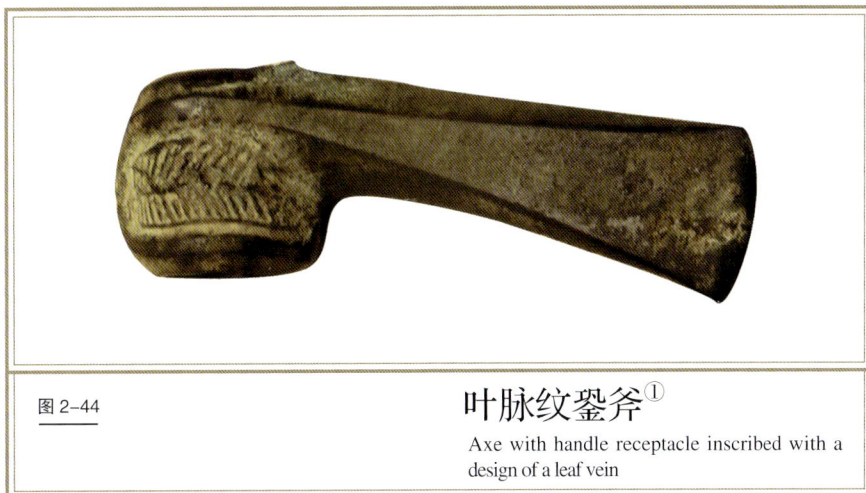

图 2-44

叶脉纹錾斧①
Axe with handle receptacle inscribed with a design of a leaf vein

①叶脉纹錾斧：新疆巩留县阿尕尔生墓葬出土，距今约3000年。
Axe with handle receptacle inscribed with a design of a leaf vein：It was excavated from the Tombs of Aga Ersheng in Gongliu County. It is at least 3000 years old.

第6节

短锤

和大多数古代兵器一样，锤同样从生产工具中产生。在原始社会，人类在狩猎活动中经常使用浑圆的石球进行投掷，用以杀伤猎物。而这一方式也被应用于战争中，在战斗中用锤硬砸、硬架，很有威力。

早期的锤柄都是用木料制成，作为打击部分的锤头则是铜、铁所制，这些用金属制成的锤又称为"金瓜"。商代以后，青铜长锤取得了一定的发展，但并未广泛使用。直到隋唐之后，特别是到了宋代，锤才在战争中广泛使用。在宋代，受少数民族影响，战争中短锤被广泛使用。短锤一般以双锤形式出现。短柄双锤非常沉重，舞练者需要有较大的力量。

　　古时锤也被称为"椎"，有长柄单锤、短柄双锤及链子锤等。从形制上看，锤形似瓜，故亦称"立瓜""卧瓜"，也有四方八棱等形。古代持锤者称为"金瓜武士"。此外，锤也分为硬锤、软锤。由于锤的特点各异，使用方法也大不一样。长柄锤多单用，短柄锤多双使。短柄锤多沉重，使用时硬砸实架，其用法有涮、拽、挂、砸、架、云、盖等。软锤一般讲究巧劲，也与铁链、绳索连接使用。

图 2-45

石锤 [1]（旧石器时代）
Stone Hammer（The Paleolithic Age）

---

　　[1] 石锤：旧石器时代常见，先后在侯家窑－许家窑遗址、南庄头遗址、板井子遗址等出土。
　　Stone Hammer: It was commonly used in the Paleolithic Age. This kind of hammer was successively excavated from the relics of Houjiayao and Xujiayao, the site of Tunan Zhuangtou and the site of Banjingzi.

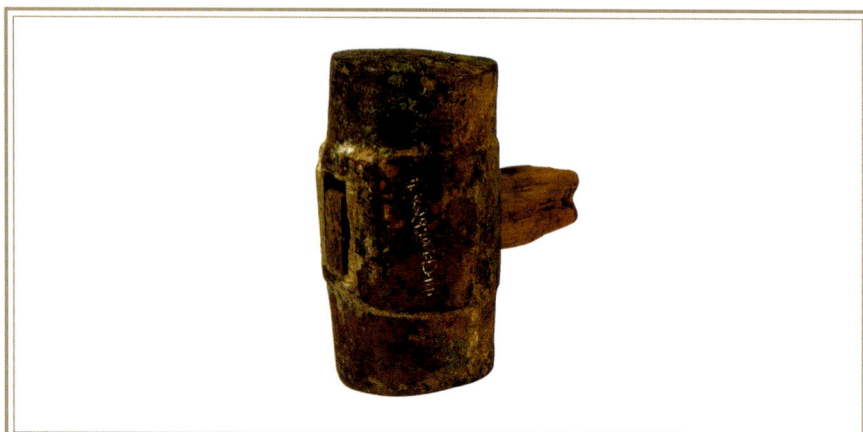

图 2-46

铜锤 [1]（汉）

Bronze Hammer（Han Dynasty）

图 2-47

短锤

Short Hammer

① 铜锤：此铜锤高 8.6 厘米，直径 4.5 厘米，重 1.12 千克。

Bronze Hammer: It was 8.6cm in height and 1.12 kilogram in weight. The diameter of the hammer head was 4.5cm.

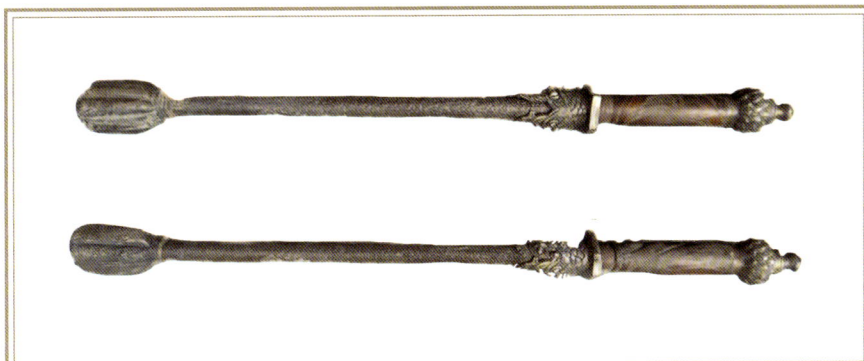

图 2-48　　　　　　铁双锤①
Double-handed Hammers

图 2-49　　　　　　铜锤②（清）
Bronze Hammer (Qing Dynasty)

① 铁双锤：历史上很多武将在后人的小说、演义中被描绘成善用双锤，如《隋唐演义》中的李元霸、裴元庆、秦用、梁师泰，《薛刚反唐》中的薛葵，《岳家将》中大闹朱仙镇的岳家军八大锤：严成方、岳云、狄雷、何元庆等。

Double-handed Hammers：Many generals in history were described as being skillful at swinging double-handed hammers in the fictions or historical novels written by the later generation, such as Li Yuanba, Pei Yuanqing, Qinyong, Liang Shitai (*Romance of Sui and Tang Dynasty*) and Xue Kui (*Xuegang Destined to Rebel in Tang Dynasty*) in Sui and Tang Dynasties，Eight Hammers in Yuejia Army like Yan Chengfang, Yue Yun, Di Lei and He Yuanqing(*Generals of the Yue Family*).

② 铜锤：嵩山少林古兵器展览馆藏。

Bronze Hammer：It was stored in Shaolin Museum of Ancient Weapons on Songshan Mountain.

图 2-50

铜锤^①（清）
Bronze Hammer (Qing Dynasty)

---

① 铜锤：长 58 厘米，锤首为铜质长圆瓜形，锤柄为铁质圆柱状，外裹竹篾丝麻，柄端为铜质多面体。

Bronze Hammer: It was 58cm long. The head of the hammer was made of copper in the shape of a round melon. Its handle was made of iron in the shape of column, which was wrapped with bamboo strips, silk and linen. On the bottom end of the handle was there a copper prism shaped pommel.

第 **7** 节

钩

钩是一种短柄格斗兵器，最早出现于春秋末期的吴国。《吴越春秋·阖闾内传》记："阖闾既宝莫耶，复命于国中作金钩，令曰：'能为善钩者，赏之百金。'吴作钩者甚众。"有学者认为，钩是由戈演变而成。春秋时期，钩与戈、戟并用。钩有单钩、双钩、鹿角钩以及挠钩等，是一种多刃的兵器，技法有钩、缕、掏、带、托、压、挑、刨、挂、架等，演练时起伏吞吐如浪。

春秋时期并未发现有出土文物，直到秦朝时期，才有了钩的实物的出现，秦俑坑中出土两柄钩。秦钩形似弯刀，齐头无锋，两边有刃，可推可钩。汉代时发明出一种防御性兵器，称为"钩镶"，其中镶起着盾的作用，钩则可钩束敌兵并以利刃杀之。

　　钩也常被民间视作武术器械。武术中所用的钩有单、双之分；也因钩的形式不同而有不同名称。如：鹰嘴钩，其钩尖如扁担头；鹿角钩，其钩身有叉，形如鹿角；挠钩，长杆杆端有两钩向下弯曲。常见的钩是双钩，比较难练，相传清代中期河北献县人窦尔敦曾以双钩闻名。

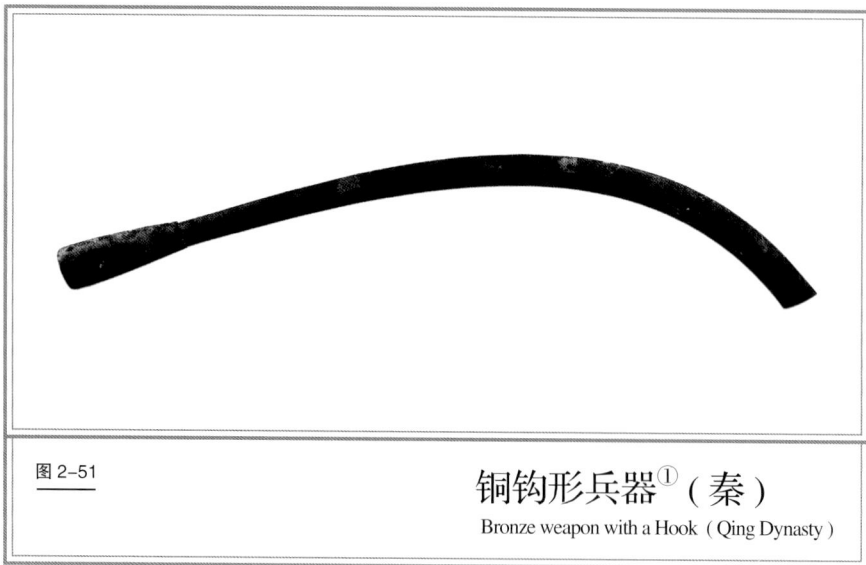

图 2-51

铜钩形兵器①（秦）
Bronze weapon with a Hook（Qing Dynasty）

　　① 铜钩形兵器：整体形似弯刀，通长 66 厘米，刃宽 3.2 厘米，光素无纹，质朴无华，可钩可砍，在当时是极具杀伤力的武器。

　　Bronze weapon with a Hook：It looked like a curved sabre. It was 66cm long and its blade was 3.2cm wide. The appearance was plain without designs. It was simple but could be used for chopping or hooking, so it was a lethal weapon at that time.

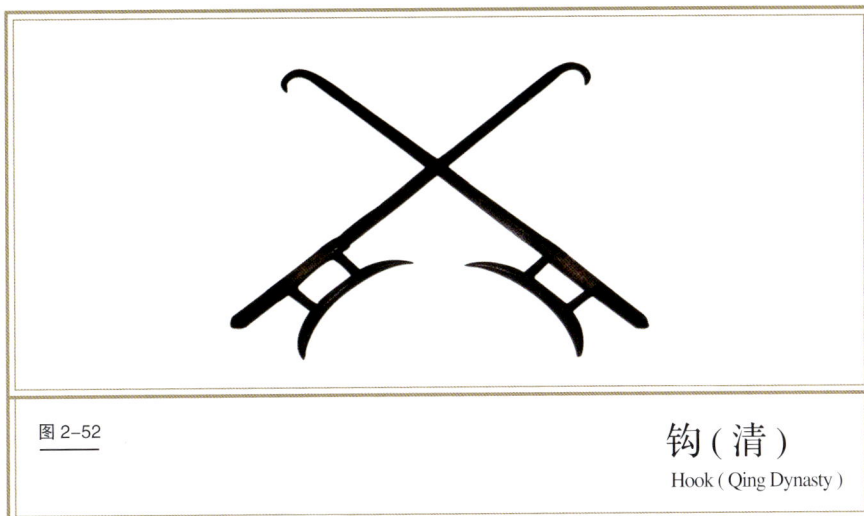

图 2-52

钩（清）
Hook (Qing Dynasty)

图 2-53

月牙双钩[①]（清）
Double-handed Hooks with crescent blade
(Qing Dynasty)

①月牙双钩：铁质，长 100 厘米，前端作弯钩状，末端起尖，手握处缠素丝带，其前以双横档连接月牙形利刃。

Double-handed Hooks with crescent blade: It was made of iron and 100cm long. There was a hook on the top with a tip. The grasping part was wound with a silk ribbon, in front of which two bars were used to link the crescent blade.

第**8**节

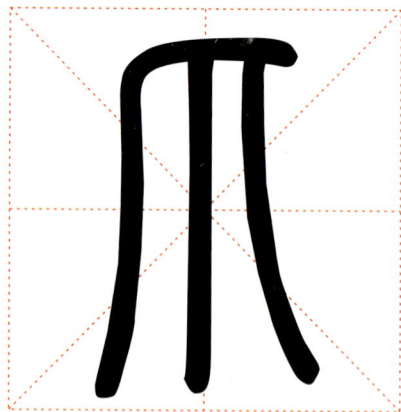

爪

爪是一种使用率比刀剑等常规武器要低得多的奇门兵器，使用起来比较困难，但若能用好，则会具有巨大的威力。爪一般分为在末端系绳子的飞爪和套在手上的爪两种。飞爪可以用来攀爬墙和树木，也可以用作攻击武器；而套在手上的爪则是一种近身格斗武器，一般不会太长，一尺左右，是模仿野兽的爪子而打造的一种武器，其特点是凶狠奇诡。

在一些历史记载及话本小说中，最有名的爪是"飞虎爪"，是一种很厉害的暗器。爪为精钢打造，略似手掌，有五个钢爪，每个爪又分三节，可张可缩，其最前一节末端尖锐，犹如鸡爪。钢爪掌内装有机关，可控制各爪。钢爪尾部系有长索，与机关相连。

　　以飞爪击人，只要将长索一抽，钢爪即猛然内缩，爪尖可深陷入肉，敌人万难摆脱。据传，清代时，山西大盗荣康以此闻名，号称"飞爪天王"，后将此技传给天津镖局毛某。毛某艺成后，走镖时竟不插镖旗，只在镖车上悬一飞爪。群盗一见此物，即自行退避。民国以来，武林中所用飞爪已无机关，只是固定的三爪或五爪，多用于爬越高墙。

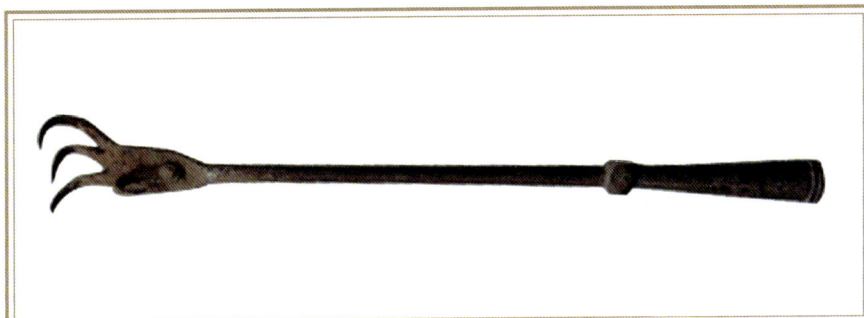

图 2-54

爪
Claw

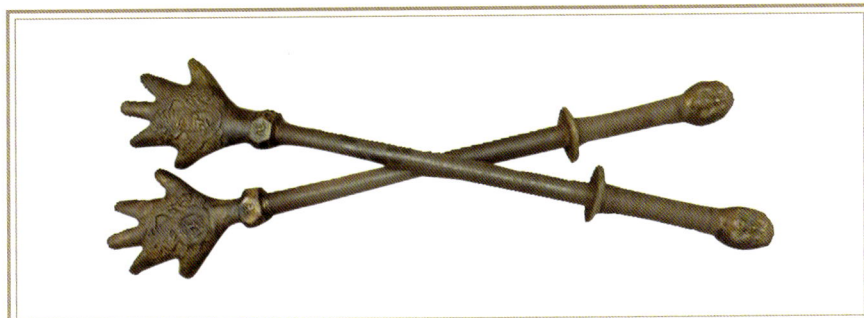

图 2-55

双爪
Double-handed Claws

第 **9** 节

拐

　　拐可看作一种带有把手的棒，主要流行于民间和武术界，可双拐同用，也可配合其他兵器使用。拐的手握部分多变，拐身、拐把均可持握，可打可戳，可攻可守。

　　据说拐是由农具或老人的拐杖演变而来，根据长度分长拐和短拐，根据外形分为二字拐、十字拐、卜字拐、上下拐、钩镰拐、原样拐等。在明清时期，拐在我国南部拳法中曾盛行，民国时期依然有大量国术家习练此种武器。

　　传统拐术所用的拐主要用硬木制成，木料一般是红橡木等，需要经过一定的处理进行硬化和防腐。传统上木料需要数年的土埋和化学反应后才能被采用。

拐由较长的拐身和较短的手柄组成，使用时可以握手柄，也可以握拐身。防守时，如果握住手柄，拐身可以保护整条前臂。手柄的末端往往有一段直径较大的类似门把的设计，除了防止脱手外，还可以在握住手柄时保护手指。

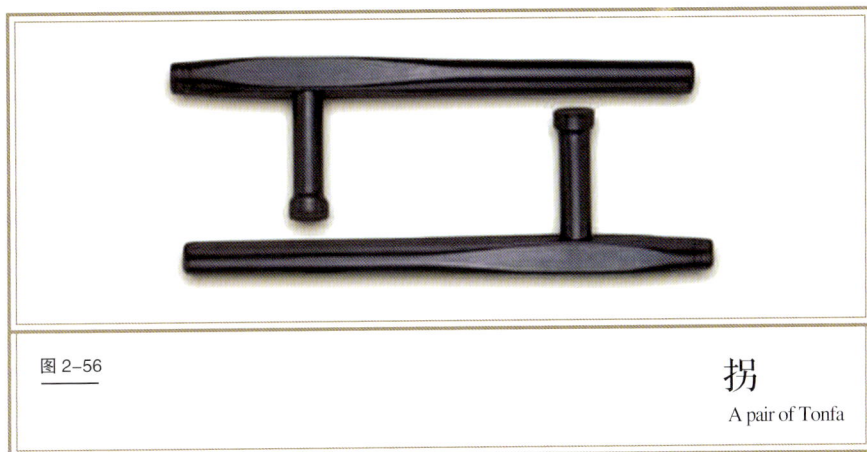

图 2–56

拐
A pair of Tonfa

图 2–57

拐
A pair of Tonfa

第 **10** 节

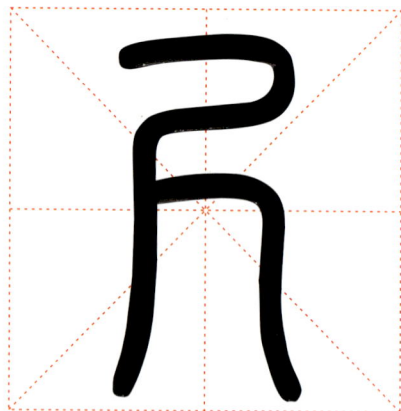

铁尺

　　铁尺为我国传统器械，也叫"点穴尺"，16世纪传至琉球，日本吞并中国附属国琉球后，铁尺也随之传至日本，多为练空手道者使用，所以又名"笔架叉""浪人叉""空手道短叉"。其形如圆柱、圆棱，四面不内陷，上粗下细，易于携带，可暗藏腰间，可正持也可反手持。通常双手各持一支，所以也称为"双铁尺"。有的铁尺两侧有向上旁枝，旁枝多用于格挡时卡住对方的兵器，因此对付刀剑或更长的兵器有较大的优势。铁尺大约起源于唐宋时期，为我国衙役捕快的常用武器，主要特点是套路短小精悍、攻防紧凑、使用灵活。

　　据传，铁尺在湖南各地流传甚广，其套路不一，打法也不尽相同。

以流传株洲地区的铁尺为例，它系清朝少林寺僧人雷明光所创。雷明光祖籍河南，年轻时因反清复明失败，入少林寺削发为僧，后潜心研究南北诸家武功，取武术名家器械之精华而创编"铁尺功"，自此苦练日久，造诣颇深，铁尺功被列入少林看家功法，不得轻使。少林遭劫后，传人钟金彪逃到醴陵日月寺定居授徒，铁尺便在株洲地区特别是客家人中流传。

图 2-58

铁尺
Iron Ruler

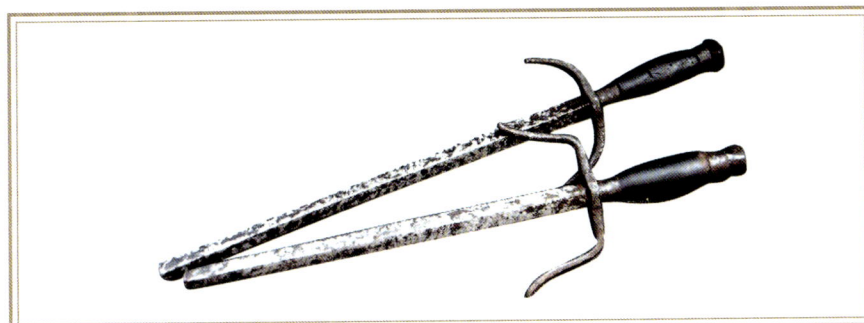

图 2-59

铁尺
Iron Ruler

第 **11** 节

啄锤

　　啄锤是北方少数民族独有的兵器，具有管銎斧与管銎戈两种功能，特点是中间有銎，銎的一侧呈斧形或锤形，另一侧呈戈状。

　　北方草原游牧民族在西周、东周时期将啄锤广泛应用于战争中。东周时期，云南古滇国少数民族的青铜器有了很大的发展，创造了独具特色的青铜文明，其遗址出土了很多具有浓郁民族特色的兵器。到了汉代，铜啄仍被使用于战争中，并有了更多的装饰。

　　唐宋以来，受北方游牧民族的影响，中原军队也装备了少量啄锤。李筌《太白阴经》记载有唐代骑兵配备的"啄锤斧钺"，但地位远不及长枪和佩刀等主要兵器。

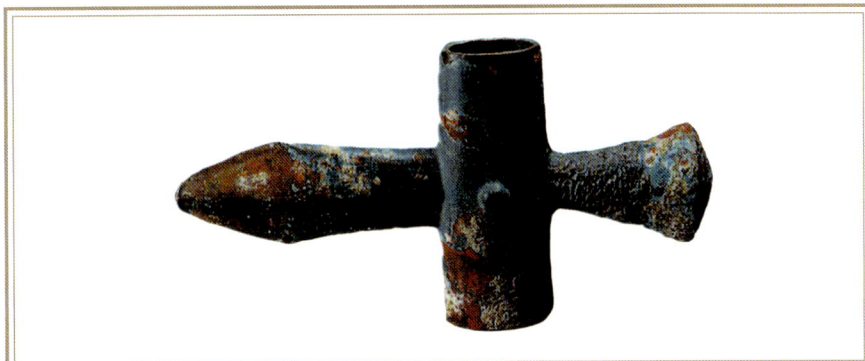

图 2-60 　啄锤^①（西周晚期至春秋早期）
Pecking Hammer（The Later Stage of Western Zhou Dynasty
to the Early Stage of Spring and Autumn Period）

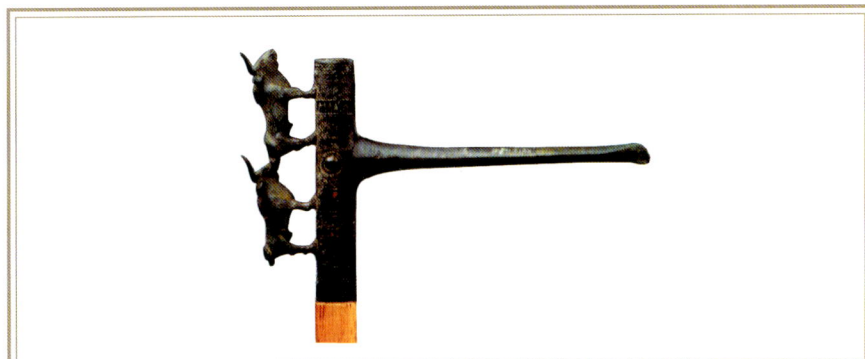

图 2-61 　铜啄^②（战国晚期至西汉初期）
Bronze Pecking Hammer（The Later Stage of the Warring
States Period to the Initial Stage of Western Han Dynasty）

① 啄锤：西周晚期至春秋早期东胡人所用，出土于内蒙古宁城，长 14.7 厘米，銎长 7.2
厘米。

Pecking Hammer: It was used by the Donghu people (a Northern nomadic nationality) from the later
stage of Western Zhou Dynasty to the initial stage of the Spring and Autumn Period. It was excavated from
Ningcheng in Inner Mongolia. It was 14.7cm long and had a 7.2 cm long eye for the shaft.

② 铜啄：汉代滇族常见兵器，此件铜啄出土于云南省江川县李家山，长 26.1 厘米，高 14.8
厘米。

Bronze Pecking Hammer：It was a weapon frequently seen in the Kingdom of Dian. It was found at
the site of Lijia Mountain in Jiangchuan county Yunnan Province. It was 26.1cm long and 14.8cm high.

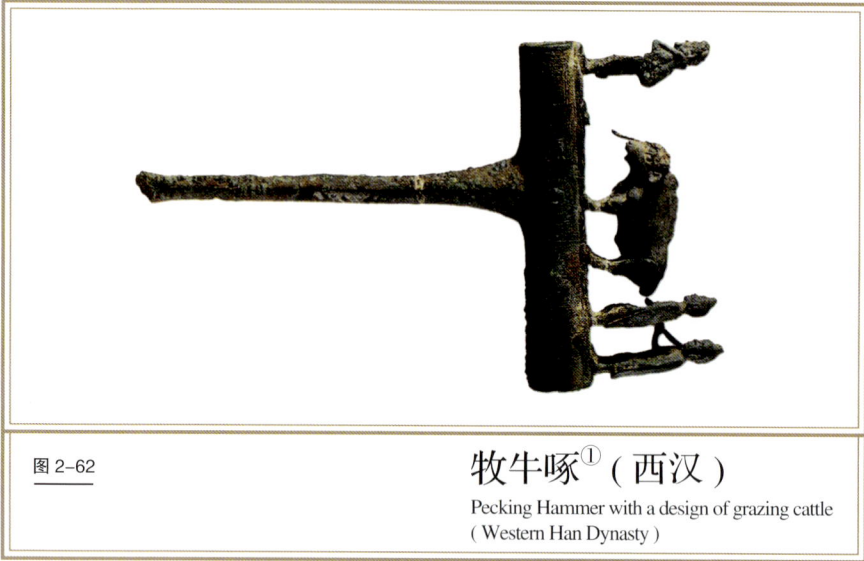

图 2-62

牧牛啄①（西汉）
Pecking Hammer with a design of grazing cattle
(Western Han Dynasty)

---

① 牧牛啄：云南晋宁石寨山出土，长 20.4 厘米，高 15.1 厘米，为西汉西南夷滇国所造。

　　Pecking Hammer with a design of grazing cattle：It was unearthed from the site of Shizhai Mountain in Jinning County Yunnan Province. It was 20.4cm in height and 15.1cm in length. It was made in the Kingdom of Dian where the Southwestern ethnic groups were living in the Western Han Dynasty.

远射兵器

远射兵器是我国古代兵器的重要组成部分，其发展历程见证了朝代的变迁，反映出历代人们的生产、生活、战争、礼制等各个方面的发展变化。远射兵器主要包括投枪、飞镖、飞石索、抛石机、弓、箭、弩等，在古代战争中能够相对远距离地对敌人进行杀伤。远射兵器在冷兵器时代曾发挥过重要的作用。由于火枪、火炮等热兵器的出现，冷兵器逐渐退出战争舞台或处于次要地位，唯有弓箭一直长盛不衰。

弓箭是中国乃至世界历史上最古老、最重要的兵器之一，也是古代战场上最有杀伤力、最危险的兵器之一。在中国古代流传着"羿射九日""纪昌学射"等故事，反映了远古时代的人们依靠弓矢与自然作斗争的图景。1963 年，在中国山西朔县峙峪村的旧石器时代晚期遗址（距今约 2.8 万年）中发现了一枚用燧石打制的箭镞，确凿地证明了中国先民在距今约 2.8 万年前已经在使用弓箭。中国古人认为"弓生于弹"（《吴越春秋·勾践阴谋外传》），弹弓极有可能就是弓的前身。

弓箭是原始人最重要的狩猎工具，在新石器时代晚期成为最重要的原始兵器。弓箭是古人的一项重要发明，对于以农耕、狩猎和畜牧为生的原始民族具有极大的作用，可以有效地抵御猛兽和获取更多的猎物。恩格斯说："弓箭对于蒙昧时代，正如铁器对于野蛮时代和火器对于文明时代一样，乃是决定性的武器。"

弓箭在冷兵器时代兵器家族中的地位举足轻重，被认为是兵器之首，很多著名战争都留下了使用弓箭的历史记录。中国古代出现了很多名弓，相传有后羿的落日弓、项羽的霸王弓、吕布所用的"龙舌"等，以射术成名的有李广、徐晃、黄忠、秦琼、薛仁贵等，但射术最精湛的非养由基莫属，很多练射箭的人都奉养由基为祖师爷。养由基最初为楚庄王近卫军成员，后成为楚国名将，百步外射柳叶百发百中，成语"百步穿杨"即源于此，京剧《清河桥比箭》讲的就是养由基善射的故事。

我们从弓箭的起源、种类、功能、演变和发展以及在军队中的地位和作用等方面解读远射兵器，以增强对这一古老冷兵器的认识。

第 **1** 节

箭

　　箭分为箭头、箭杆和箭羽。随着朝代的发展，箭的制作工艺、材料不断进步。箭开始精工细作后，样式更为精细，仅箭头就可分为前锋、刃、翼、脊、后锋、本、关、铤等部分。

　　古代的箭头称为"镞"。石器时代，箭镞的材料通常选用石头、兽骨、蚌壳、角等，加工、打磨为石镞、骨镞等，形状多为棒形、叶形、三角形。在增强镞和箭杆的牢度上，古人下了一定的功夫。从原始的打制石镞到精致的骨镞，再到石镞和骨镞共用。

　　青铜器时期，箭镞开始采用铜制作，更加尖硬锐利。青铜镞在商周时期为有脊双翼式，春秋战国时期为三棱式。中国最早的青铜镞发现于青海乐都柳湾聚落遗址，是锻造而成的三棱镞。其形似弹头，两翼稍长，具有超强杀伤力。此时的人们对箭的两刃进行打磨，对称的双翼在飞行中可以起到平衡作用，使镞可以更准确地击中目标，且更具穿透性。

东周时期，箭矢发展成熟。春秋中前期仍以承袭于西周的双翼带铤式铜镞为主，但有所改进，形体渐趋窄瘦，同时出现了新式的菱形铜镞和三棱铜镞。战国时期，三棱铜镞逐渐取代了双翼式铜镞而成为主要的形式。从双翼式铜镞到三棱铜镞，镞头日渐短小，但一些铜镞的镞铤却不断加长，因此战国时期出现了长铤镞，有的铤甚至长达30~40厘米。箭杆仍多以竹制，也有木制的，尾装鸟羽。从出土的实物来看，弓用箭大概70厘米，弩用箭大概50厘米。

秦代开始尝试用铁制箭头铤部。西汉冶铁业发达，全铁制箭头问世，最早铁箭头多采用锻制，比铜箭头更加坚韧。从魏晋到隋唐，铁箭分类简单，发展路线就是使箭头更硬更长，以便穿透铁甲，增强杀伤力。

唐代箭分为竹箭、木箭、兵箭、弩箭。前两种用于狩猎，后两种用于战斗。箭镞用钢制成，刃部坚硬，能穿透坚甲。

宋代对兵器精雕细刻，箭的样式更加精细，出现了铁脊箭、锥箭等。据考古学家证实，在出土的宋代文物中共有371件钢铁箭头，大概分为四棱镞、三棱镞、三翼镞、菱形铁镞等。

元朝的军事制度是蒙古旧制和中原王朝军制的结合体，军事力量比较强盛。弓箭是元代战争的主要利器，以复合弓为主，也有单体弓。

明代经济繁荣，军事力量强盛。弓箭由于比较方便携带，用途较广。明代箭的种类较多，主要是根据镞的样式而定，常常见于射人、射马、演习，常见箭有鞭箭、袖箭、筒子箭、流星箭等。

图 3-1

石镞
Stone Arrowhead

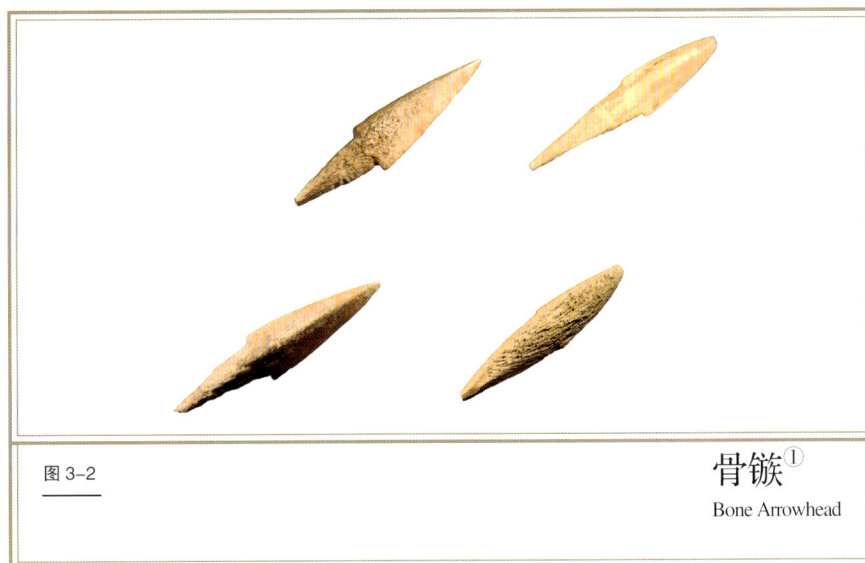

图 3-2

骨镞[1]
Bone Arrowhead

① 骨镞：1977 年浙江余姚河姆渡遗址 T234、T243、T232、T211 第四文化层（距今 7000—6500 年）出土，分斜铤式、柳叶式和圆铤式三种。

Bone Arrowhead: The four pieces (numbered by T234, T243, T232, T211 respectively) of the bone arrowheads were excavated at the Relics of Hemudu in 1977, which represented the fourth cultural layers about 7000 years ago. They could have the inclined plug, willow leaf shaped plug and round plug.

图 3-3

青铜箭镞（西周）
Bronze Arrow
（Western Zhou Dynasty）

图 3-4

铜镞
Brass Arrow

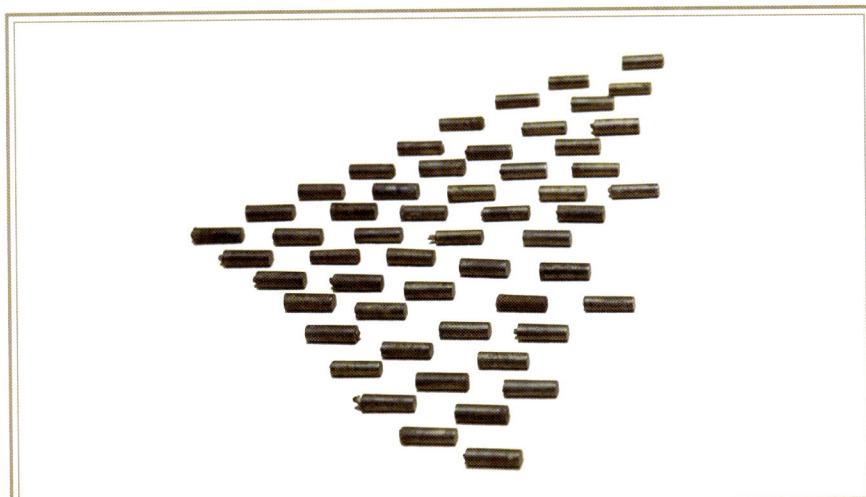

图 3-5

铁镞
Iron Arrow

图 3-6

银镞
Silver Arrow

图 3-7

墩镞①
Dun Arrow

图 3-8

平头箭镞②
Flat Head Arrow

---

① 墩镞: 箭头是木制的墩子, 没有杀伤力, 射人会造成疼痛感, 主要起警告作用, 功能类似于现在的橡皮子弹。

Dun Arrow: Wooden arrowheads, with the goal to stun the target without penetration, not to kill, but cause pain when the target was hit. They are similar to the present rubber bullets.

② 平头箭镞: 一般是圆锥形, 主要用于射马, 又称马箭。

Flat Head Arrow: It was forged into a cone, with the main aim of shooting horses, hence named as horse arrow.

图 3-9

双翼镞①
Two-winged Arrow

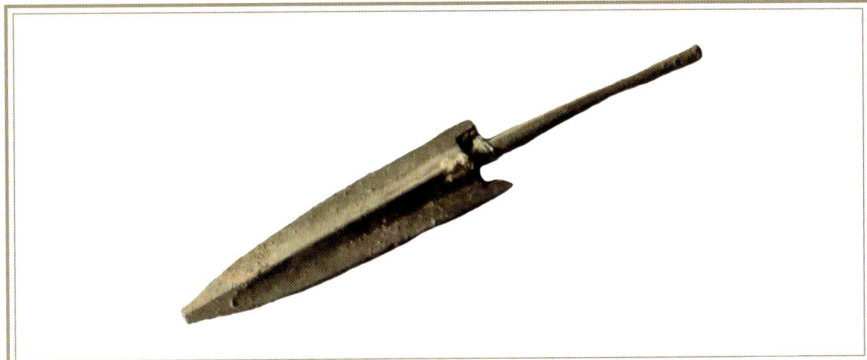

图 3-10

三翼镞②
Three-winged Arrow

① 双翼镞：多见于夏商至春秋时期，此类箭镞双范铸造，生产效率高，但相较后来出现的三翼、三棱镞轻，杀伤力和穿透力弱。

Two-winged Arrow: It was very common in the Xia Dynasty and the Spring and Autumn Period. They were cast in two moulds, but compared with three-winged or three-bladed arrows of the later times, two-winged arrows were relatively lighter with weaker lethality and penetrating power.

② 三翼镞：三翼镞在飞行中所受的空气阻力比较均匀，使箭的稳定性更好；而三翼之间形成的夹角具有与双翼镞叶面上的血槽同样的功能，使三翼镞杀伤力与穿透力兼顾的特征更加明显。

Three-winged Arrow: It evenly encountered the air resistance in the flight, which better stabilized the arrow. The angles formed by the three wings had the same function as blood grooves on the two-winged arrow, which accented the characteristics of three-winged arrow—combining lethality and penetrating power.

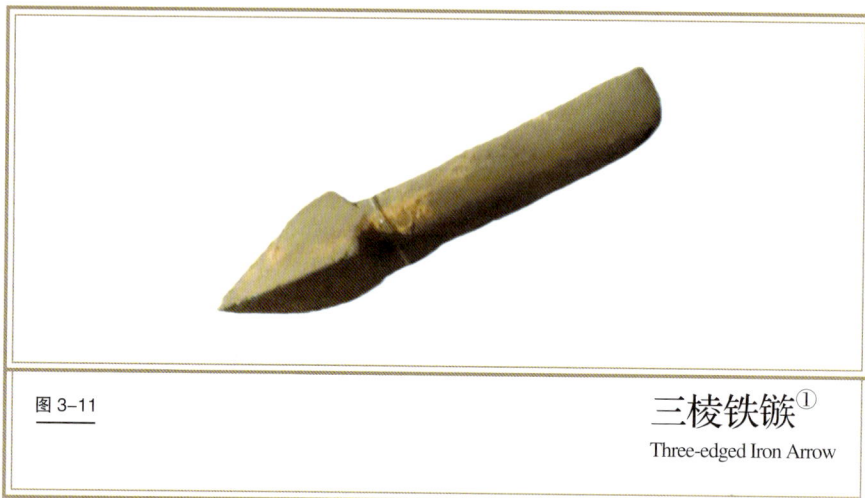

图 3-11

三棱铁镞①
Three-edged Iron Arrow

图 3-12

翎箭
Arrows with feather fletching

① 三棱铁镞：镞身呈三角形，但无外伸之翼。脊三条棱成刃，镞体近似流线型，边棱的曲线类似现代的弹头，使箭在飞行时阻力更小、方向性更好、更为精准，具有更强的杀伤力。

Three-edged Iron Arrow: It took the shape of pyramid, but without extended wings. Streamlined, looking like bullets, three-edged arrow not only reduced the air resistance during the flight, enhancing its orientation and preciseness, but also strengthened its lethality.

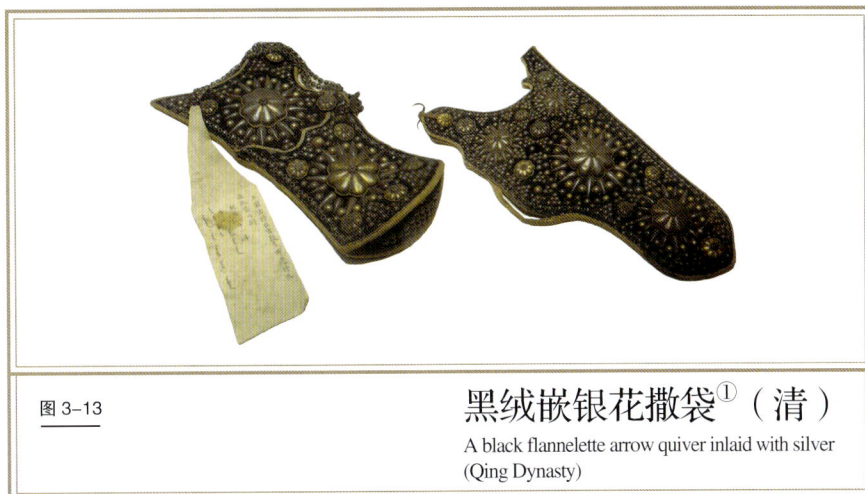

图 3-13

黑绒嵌银花撒袋^①（清）

A black flannelette arrow quiver inlaid with silver
(Qing Dynasty)

---

① 黑绒嵌银花撒袋：清代乾隆皇帝御用箭袋。

A black flannelette arrow quiver inlaid with silver: Dedicated for Qianlong Emperor (1711 −1799 A.
D.), the sixth emperor of the Manchu−led Qing Dynasty (1636 −1912 A. D.)

第 **2** 节

弓

弓是抛射兵器中最古老的一种弹射武器。它由富有弹性的弓臂和柔韧的弓弦构成，当把拉弦张弓过程中积聚的力量在瞬间释放时，便可将扣在弓弦上的箭或弹丸射向远处的目标。

中国最早的弓大概出现于 3 万年以前。《释名·释兵》这样解释"弓"这一名称的来源："弓，穹也。张之穹隆然也。"弓上面张开像穹隆的地方称"弓干"；弓的末端称"箫"，常以角质加固；左侧箫固定弦的缺口称为"弭"；右侧箫固定弦的圆孔称为"驱"；两箫中间有一皮质的弦；弓的中央人所握的地方称"弣"；弣和箫中间的部分称为"渊"。

早期的弓箭制造粗陋，"弦木为弧，剡木为矢"，一根木条或竹竿拴上弓弦，再把削尖的木棍当作箭，就可以使用了。到了东周时期，弓的制作水平有所提高，能使用多种材料制造复合弓，弓的形制构造基本定型。复合弓的制作方法是：先在竹和木制造的弓身上傅角被筋，再缠丝涂漆。弓身中部形成反曲，可以加大弓的弹力，使其射击性能和杀伤力显著提高，成为战争中的重要远射兵器。春秋时期的贵族从小就要学射箭，"射"成为贵族士大夫必须学会的"六艺"之一。

古代的制弓技艺十分讲究，取料制作都要注意气候条件。加工制弓干的木料必须是在冬天，因为冬天的木料材质坚硬，加工后纹理细致；而制角则在春天，因为春天阳气润泽，角不会发脆；加工兽筋要在暖和的夏天，兽筋不易挛结；秋季再用胶、漆、丝三种材料将干、角、筋组合在一起；冬季固定弓体，弓体不易变形，隆冬冰冻时检验漆纹是否开裂；到下一年春季再加上弓弦，这才算完成了整张弓的制作。之后还要经过火焙、测力、试射，方能交付使用。一张普通的弓，要一年才能造成，至于制造一张良弓，就更费时费力了。据《考工记》记载，西周军队中所用的弓根据使用者的身长和体力，分为上、中、下三个型号：上弓长六尺六寸，约等于152厘米；中弓六尺三寸，约等于145厘米；下弓六尺，约等于138厘米。

到了汉代时，实战的弓箭种类增多，制作工艺得到大幅度提升，造出用于步战、水战、骑战的各种弓箭，有虎贲弓、雕弓、角端弓、路弓、强弓等，不仅弓力强劲，而且装饰有铜箍、玉角，十分精致美观。

到了唐代，弓箭分为长弓、角弓、梢弓、格弓四种。长弓用作步战，角弓用于骑战，梢弓和格弓分别是狩猎用弓和皇朝禁卫军用弓。

从北宋到清初，弓箭一直是军队的主要作战兵器之一，特别是少数民族朝代如元和清，士兵专精骑射。但是唐宋以后直到明清，弓的形制日趋单一化，大致只分为常用弓和练习弓，前者注重射击的准确度，后者练习张弓的臂力。

元代作为一个少数民族在马上打下的朝代，蒙古兵所用的弓主要是"马克打"大弓、"卡蛮"大弓、顽羊角弓等，箭矢则有响箭、批针箭等。

明代特别重视弓的选材与制作，一张弓所用的材料往往分别来自许多地方。明代除沿用宋代4种弓——黄桦弓、黑漆弓、白桦弓和麻背弓以外，还有开元弓、小梢弓、西番木弓3种，箭则增加了透甲锥箭等20多种。

清代时，弓箭装饰得更加漂亮。当时，弓按照官阶品级制定不同的尺度纹饰，箭也按照战斗、狩猎、校阅、发信号等不同用途划分出40多种不同形态。

在中国古代历史上，各代朝臣都十分重视弓箭的制作和使用。因为在古代战争中，"两军相遇，弓弩在先"。无论是攻守城镇还是伏击战、阵地战，都可以弓箭为利器，先下手为强。火器问世以后，弓箭仍以其轻巧灵便、精准率高的优点继续效力于军中，一直沿用到清朝末年。

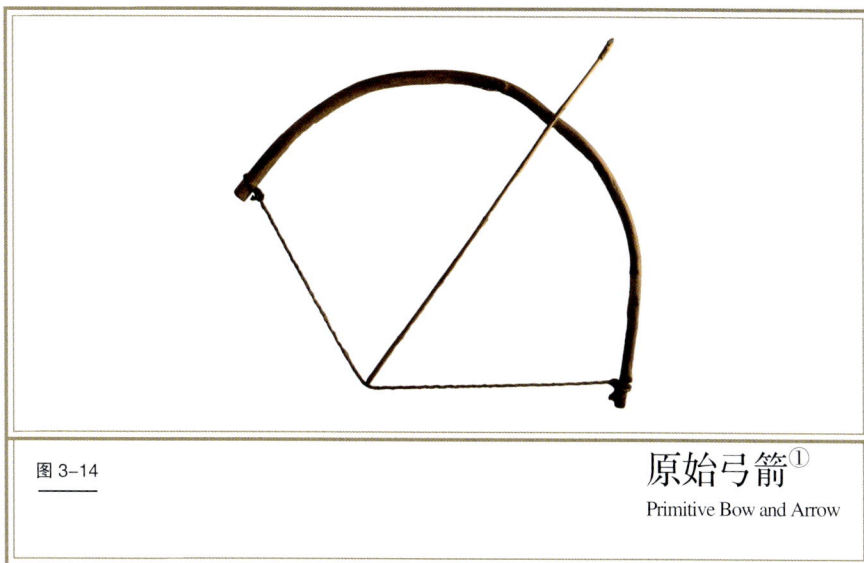

图 3-14

原始弓箭①
Primitive Bow and Arrow

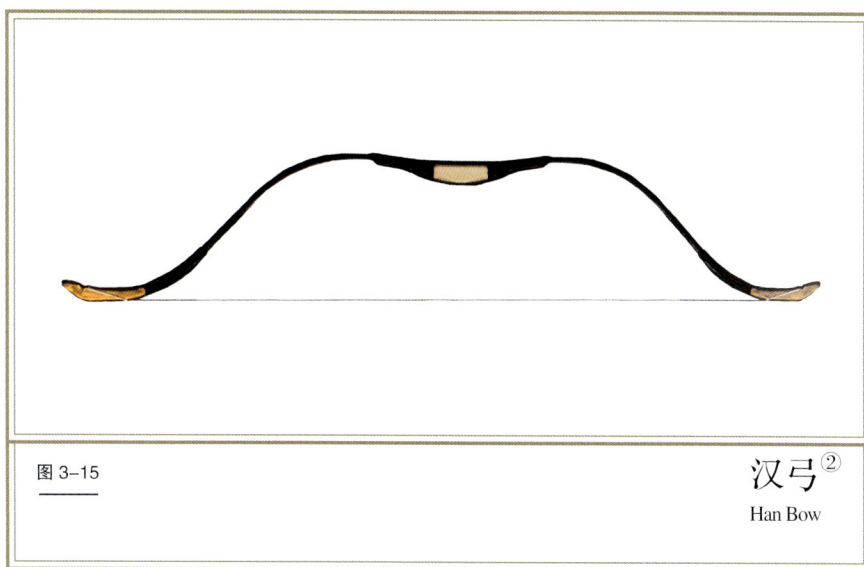

图 3-15

汉弓②
Han Bow

① 原始弓箭：将树枝弯曲用绳索绷紧即成，制弓材料单一，由竹或木制成。

Primitive Bow and Arrow: The primitive bow and arrow was composed of a string joining the two ends of a curved bamboo or a branch. The material was monotonous.

② 汉弓：使用复合材料，一般由兽角、筋、竹木材、丝、漆、胶等复合而成，射击距离、穿透力和杀伤力巨大。

Han Bow: A composite bow, usually made from horn, sinew, wood, bamboo, string and glue laminated together, with long range shooting, strong penetrating power and massive lethality.

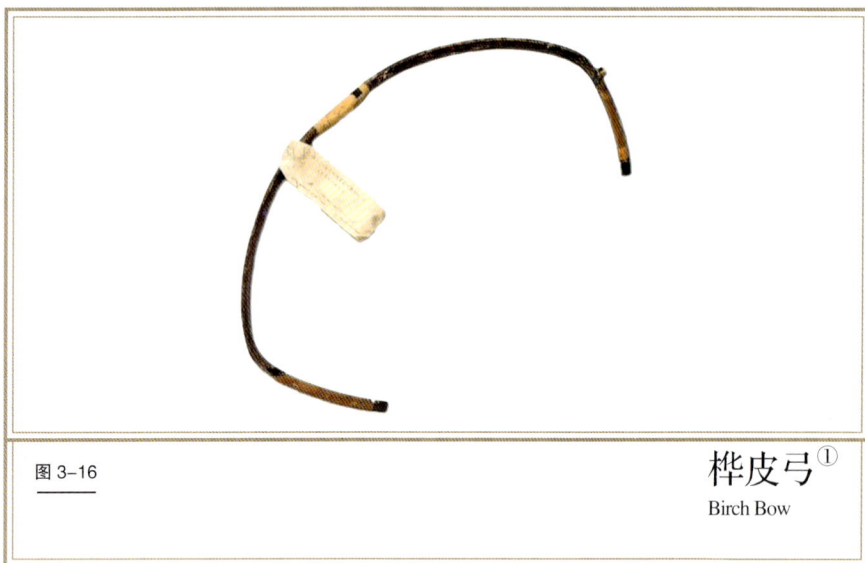

图 3-16

桦皮弓①
Birch Bow

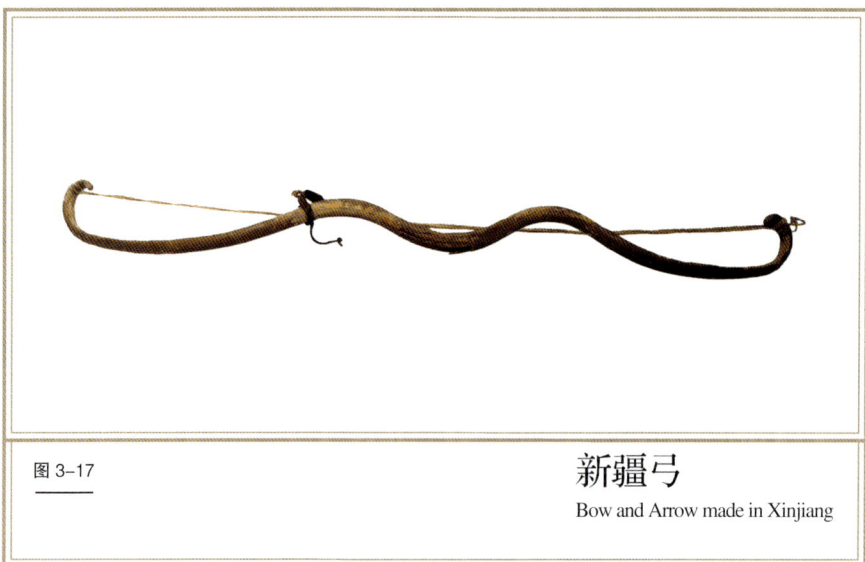

图 3-17

新疆弓
Bow and Arrow made in Xinjiang

① 桦皮弓：清代乾隆皇帝御用弓。

Birch Bow: It was dedicated to Qianlong Emperor , the sixth emperor of the Manchu-led Qing Dynasty.

第 3 节

弩

弩是中国古代最强劲的武器，是由弓发展而来的借用机械力进行射击的武器。用弓作战，射出的箭常常难以取准，而且射程有限，于是就出现了用机械发射的弩。汉代刘熙在《释名·释兵》中解释道：弩，怒也，有执怒也。弩的出现应不晚于商周时期，春秋时期弩已经成为常见的武器。

战国时期，弩已经普遍用于实战，且种类繁多。三国时，诸葛亮发明了"元戎连弩"，可连续射出 10 支箭。北宋时出现了巨大的床弩，射出的箭很长很大，箭头犹如巨斧，射程可达 1400 米。当时，在小型弩方面也有不少发展，出现了各种暗发弩，如装在背上的背弩（又名"紧背低头花装弩"），箭长仅 2 寸；装在马镫下面的硝弩；装在袖中的袖炮；预先设下，待敌触发的伏弩（窝弩），等等。

西汉时因为跟北方匈奴长时间交战，作为汉军步兵对抗匈奴骑兵的利器，弩得到了进一步发展。西汉对强弩做了进一步的改良，不但在秦代增大望山的基础上又添刻度，使弩拥有了稳定的弹道参照，而且随着铜弩廓取代木弩廓，弩身对拉力的承受力也大大增强了，极大地提高了弩作战时的可靠性。

到了十六国、南北朝时期，骑兵称雄于战场，弩不便于骑兵在马上使用，且为了克制骑兵的冲击力，所以进一步向威力强、射程远、使用机械力量的床弩发展。

弩在宋代得到极大发展，偏重步兵的宋廷将其视作对抗北方骑兵民族的利器。"神臂弓"的发明使宋军的有效射程可至 370 米。床弩则从两弩至四弩，从小型至巨型，种类繁多，两床和三床弓还能在弦上绑一个装有数十支普通箭的铁兜子，使床弩拥有了杀伤人马的功能。

弩的衰落是在元朝。元朝的骑兵极其强悍，弩的作用空前降低，于是弩从宋代的极盛一跌而至元代的极衰。随着火器的继续发展，弩逐渐退出了战争的舞台。

在清朝年间，军队已经不再使用弩作为战斗武器了。弩不再受到重视，逐渐被淘汰了。

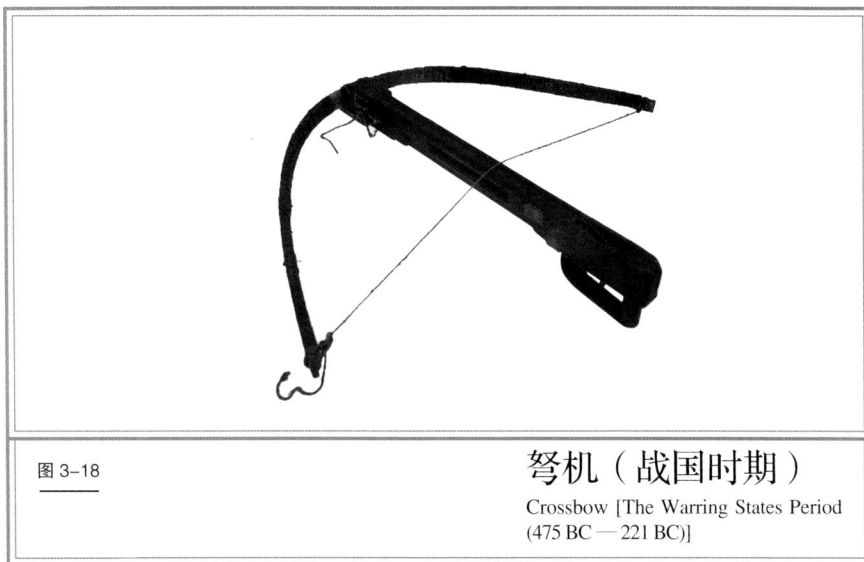

图 3-18

弩机（战国时期）
Crossbow [The Warring States Period
(475 BC — 221 BC)]

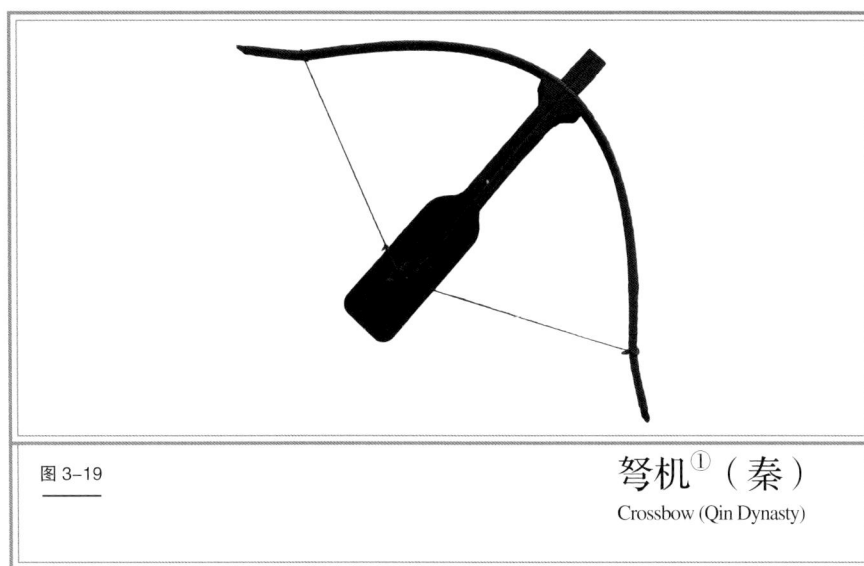

图 3-19

弩机①（秦）
Crossbow (Qin Dynasty)

① 弩机：设计非常巧妙，灵活运用了杠杆原理，实际使用的时候，可以承担很大的来自弓弦的拉力，但扣动扳机时所需要的力道却非常小，有利于维持射击的稳定性，有效提高了射击精度。弩的构造一般分为：弩弓、弩臂、弩机、弭、弦五部分。

Crossbow: It was designed ingeniously, applying the level principle. In practical use, it could endure the drawing power of the string, but needed little strength when triggered, which wais useful to maintain the stability of shooting with higher accuracy. Usually, a crossbow was composed of a bow, a tiller, a trigger, a string and a frame.

图 3-20

铜弩机^①（战国时期）
Bronze Crossbow Trigger Mechanism
[The Warring States Period (475 BC —221 BC)]

图 3-21

镏金铜弩机^②（汉）
Gilded Bronze Crossbow
[Han Dynasty (206 BC—220 AD)]

---

① 铜弩机：由牙、钩和悬刀组成，无廓，用铜枢安在木壁框槽中，属于"臂张弩"，是秦军攻灭六国时使用的武器。

Bronze Crossbow Trigger Mechanism: Bronze crossbow in the Warring States Period was installed in a wooden tiller, a main weapon used by Qin army to defeat and annex the other six ducal states.

② 镏金铜弩机：此弩机有铜廓（机匣），其中的机件有望山（照门，类似现代瞄准器上的标尺）、悬刀（扳机）、钩心（又名牛，即棘爪）、两个贯穿各部件的轴孔及使之组合为整体的键，反映了汉代弩机的基本结构和制作工艺。

Gilded Bronze Crossbow: It was composed of aiming device, a trigger and a butt plate, reflecting the basic structure and craftsmanship of this period.

图 3-22

彩漆弩^①（战国晚期）
Colorful Lacquer Crossbow
(The Late Warring States Period)

图 3-23

漆木双矢并射连发弩^②（战国时期）
Lacquered wooden repeating Crossbow (The Warring States Period)

---

① 彩漆弩：长 32.7 厘米，是为数不多的通体彩绘的战国弩。

Colorful Lacquer Crossbow: It was 32.7 cm in length, one of few wholly-painted crossbows.

② 漆木双矢并射连发弩：高 17.2 厘米，长 27.8 厘米，宽 5.4 厘米，木质，外刷黑漆，结构分为矢匣、弩体和小木弓三部分；手持发射，一次可同时发射 2 支弩箭；矢匣内可储矢 20 支，可连续发射 10 次。

Lacquered wooden repeating Crossbow: It was 17.2cm in height, 27.8cm in length, 5.4cm in width, painted with black lacquer, which was composed of a casket for arrows, a bow and a small wooden tiller, hand held. With 20 arrows in the casket, it could shoot two arrows simultaneously, ten times in succession.

图 3-24

诸葛连弩①（三国）
Zhuge repeating Crossbow
[Three Kingdoms Period (220 AD—280 AD)]

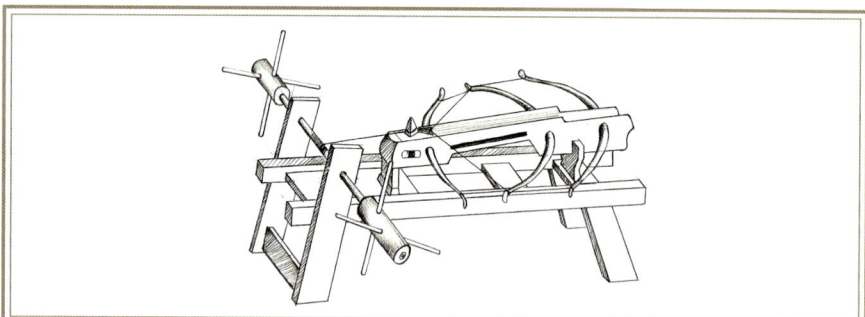

图 3-25

弓床弩②（宋）
Bench Crossbow
[Song Dynasty (960 AD—1279 AD)]

---

① 诸葛连弩：三国时期蜀国的诸葛亮发明的一种连弩，又被称作元戎弩，一次能发射 10 支箭，火力很强，但是体积、重量偏大，单兵无法使用，主要用来防守城池和营寨。

Zhuge Repeating Crossbow: It was invented by Zhuge Liang in State Shu of Three Kingdoms Period, which could shoot ten arrows at a time. This allowed a higher rate of fire than a normal crossbow, but because it was bulky and heavy, a soldier could not operate it by himself. The main purpose was to attack or defend cities or camps.

② 弓床弩：此为宋代三弓床弩，装于中部的弓应为主弓，主弓自弓弭处用短绳与前弓相连；还应装有滑轮或小环，使后弓之弦并在一处。当转动绞轴通过牵引绳拉紧主弓的弓弦时，前后弓随之张开，发射时三弓同时回弹，箭乃以强力射出。

Bench Crossbow: This was a stationary windlass device with triple-bow. The bow in the middle was the leading bow, which was connected with the bow in the front and the bow in the rear by ropes. When rotating the windlass, the three bows were extended. The three bows bounced back after the trigger was pulled with arrows being shot away.

软兵器

软兵器是中国古代兵器中较为特殊的一种，主要包括两类：一类是由圆环将器身各部分相连，材质多为木质或金属，形态较硬；一类则由木质或铁质的握把与橡胶或皮麻制成的器身组成，形态柔软。软兵器虽然"软"，但打击力度较强，在个人格斗中发挥着一定的作用，后来主要演化为武术器械。

第 **1** 节

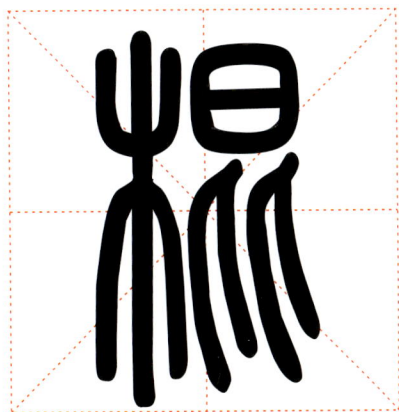

节棍

　　节棍属于经过强化的棍类兵器，其基本样式为几节坚硬、沉重的木棒或金属短棒，以铁链或坚绳相连，最具代表性的有两节棍、三节棍、梢子棍等。此类兵器弯折较为自由，难以防御，是有效的攻击器械。在中国，把多节棍作为一种兵器使用可追溯到春秋战国时代，《墨子》中的"连梃"，即为此种兵器的最早记述。

　　两节棍，又名双节棍、二节棍、双截棍、二龙棍，短小精悍，是防身御敌的重要武器。关于两节棍的起源有两种说法：一说来自西北游牧民族。《武经总要》记载："铁链夹棒，本出西戎，马上用之，以敌汉之步兵，其状如农家打麦之连枷，以铁饰之，利于自上击下，故汉兵善用者，巧于戎人。"这里所说的铁链夹棒就是两节棍的前身。一说起源于中原本地，是从中原地区农业民族的农具——连枷演化而来。

三节棍由三条等长的棍中间以铁环连接而成，有长三节棍和短三节棍之分。常规三节棍全长等于使用者直立时直臂上举至手指尖的高度，而民间武师的三节棍也有"伸开一丈"之说。因而放开使用如同长器械一般，可做远距离击打；折叠则是一短棍，约同臂长，携带十分方便，常做自卫防身之物。

梢子棍由长短不同的两根木棍以金属环相连接而成，其中短棍又称"梢子"，所以称为梢子棍；形状与农家打麦脱粒用的连枷相似，故俗称"连枷棍"；古时还称连梃、铁链夹棒、铁连枷、盘龙棍等。梢子棍分为大梢子棍和小梢子棍两种。大梢子棍两节木棍长度悬殊，长棍长140~155厘米，称为"棍身"；短棍长40~50厘米，称为"梢子"。小梢子棍由大梢子棍缩短而成，其棍身长45~60厘米，梢子长15~20厘米。据《墨子》记载，连枷棍在春秋战国时代已经是守城御敌的重要兵器。北宋《武经总要》中亦记载："若登者渐多，则御以狼牙铁拍；手渐攀城，则以连枷棒击之。"

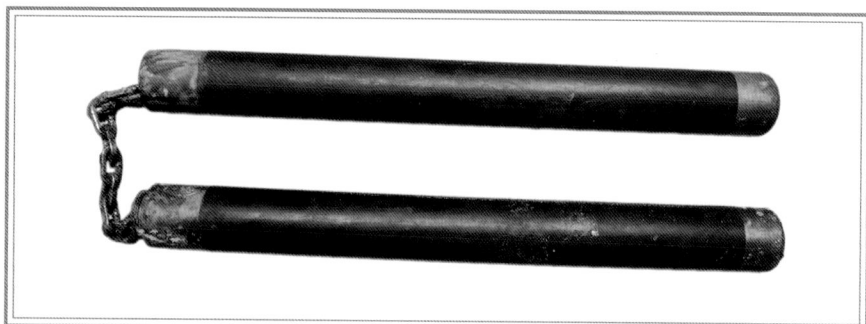

图4-1　　　　　　　　　　　　　　两节棍
The two section Chain Stick

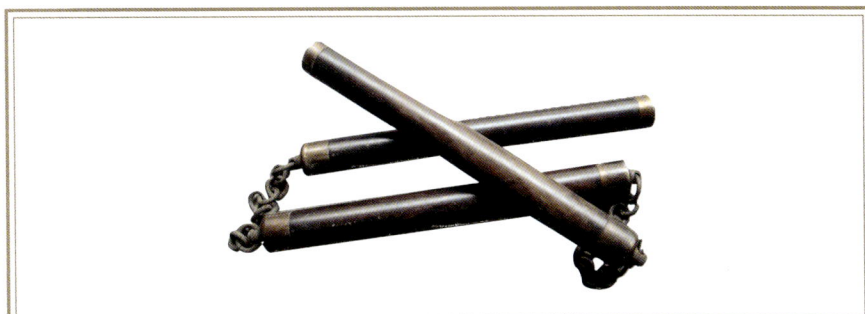

图 4-2

三节棍
Three section Chain Stick

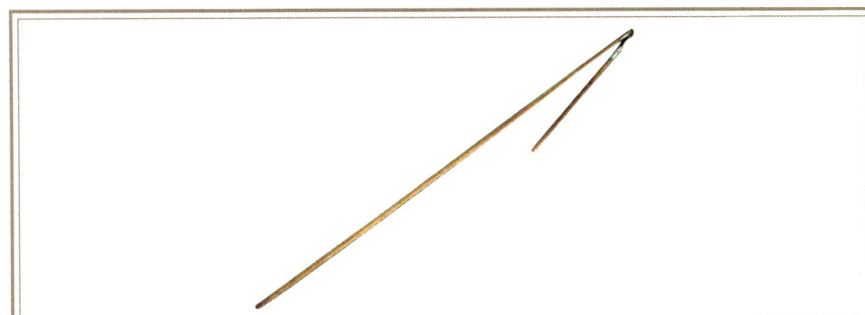

图 4-3

大梢子棍
Long Shaozi stick

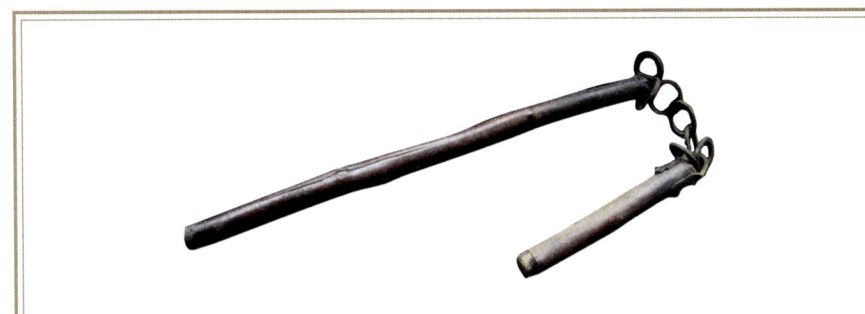

图 4-4

小梢子棍
Short Shaozi stick

第 **2** 节

软鞭

————————————

　　软鞭是鞭的一种，由鞭头、握把、用金属环相连而成的若干条金属短棒组成，具有较强的打击力。软鞭的顶端为鞭头，形状多是枪头形或圆锥形，用金属环与鞭节相连，具有刺戳功能；最尾端是握把，多为圆柱形；鞭身由数量不等的金属棒组成，以金属环相连；可缠在腰际、肩上或折叠藏起，便于携带。

　　软鞭有三节鞭、七节鞭、九节鞭、十一节鞭、十三节鞭等，七节及以上的节鞭通常统称为"九节鞭"。其使用时以圆周运动为主，借助于手臂摇动和身体各部位的转带，增加惯性动力以改变圆心及方向，上下翻飞、灵活多变、可收可放。《武经总要》记载有"连珠双铁鞭"，鞭首上连缀一条短铁链，上系两节铁棍，被认为是多节鞭的最早形态。另外，还有橡胶带或者皮、麻类编织而成的，如蛇形软鞭、筲鞭、杆子鞭、皮鞭等，以抽打为主。杆子鞭，又称虎尾鞭，最早流传于西北地区，为草原牧民所用，后经改造成为一种专用兵器，一节木棒的一端为一铁吊，上套3~4个圆环，环上缚一条牛皮拧制的绳索，绳头系一铁锤。

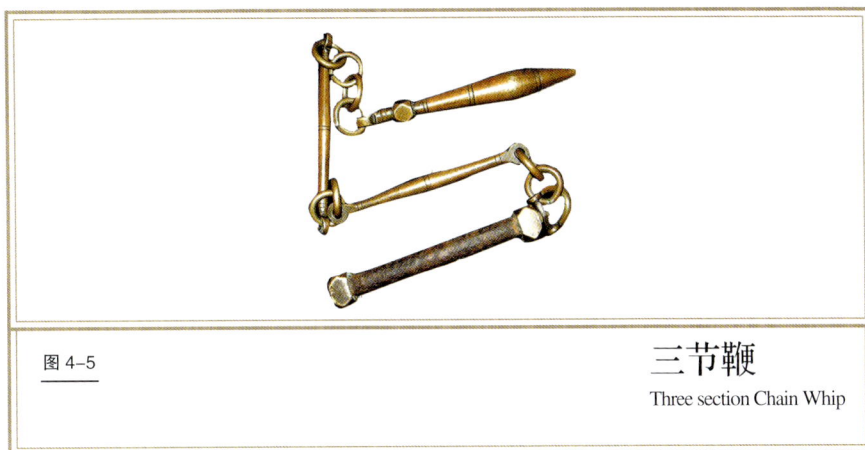

图 4-5

三节鞭
Three section Chain Whip

图 4-6

九节鞭
Nine section Chain Whip

图 4-7

蛇形软鞭
Snake-shaped Chain Whip

第**3**节

流星锤

　　流星锤是将金属锤头系于软索或铁链一端或两端制成的软兵器，由远古狩猎工具"飞石索"发展而来。流星锤由锤身、铁链或软索、把手三部分组成，分为单流星锤和双流星锤。其锤有瓜形、棱形、刺球形、浑圆形、梭形等，锤的重量大小根据使锤者的力量而定，一般4~6斤。锤身多用铜、铁铸造，末端有孔，贯穿铁环；软索以蚕丝、人发、鹿脊筋丝之类编制，粗如手指，长3~10米；把手以竹木制成，缚于软索或金属链末端。使用流星锤者平时将索链折成几折，藏于袖中，用时可一抽而出。

图 4-8　　　　　流星石球^①（战国时期）
Meteor stone ball（The Warring States Period）

图 4-9　　　　　流星锤^②
Meteor Hammer

①流星石球：石头制成的圆球，使用时将绳子系在球中间的穿孔上，掷出以攻击目标。

Meteor stone ball: It was made of stone, with a rope fastened to the hole through the center when used, thrown out to attack the target.

②流星锤：锤头为实心铁球，外镀银，直径 5 厘米，其上铸环，系黄丝绳，绳长 6.2 米。

Meteor hammer: It had a solid iron head, gilded with silver, 5 cm in diameter. It was casted with a ring, tied with a yellow rope, which was 6.2 meter in length.

图 4–10　南瓜状流星锤
Pumpkin-shaped Meteor Hammer

图 4–11　棱形流星锤
Diamond-shaped Meteor Hammer

图 4–12　浑圆形流星锤
Ball-shaped Meteor Hammer

图 4-13

狼牙流星锤①
Fang Meteor Hammer

图 4-14

链子锤②
Single-head Meteor Hammer

① 狼牙流星锤：锤头以铁或铜铸成，上面有狼牙钉若干，钉头向外，极为锋利。

Fang Meteor Hammer: It had heads with some sharp fang-shape spikes, made of iron or copper.

② 链子锤：单流星锤的一种，分锤身、索链两大部分。锤形如小瓜，多为铜铁所制，链长不等，链尾有环，可套于手上。

Single-head Meteor Hammer: It was composed of chain and head. Mainly made from copper, the head shapes similar to a melon. The length of meteor hammer was different, with a ring on one end, which was held.

暗

器

所谓暗器，是指那种便于在暗中实施突袭的兵器，是中国传统兵器中较为特殊的一类。暗器体积小，重量轻，便于携带，大多有尖有刃，近距离攻击、防卫或者投掷均可，速度快，隐蔽性强。暗器历史悠久，早在新石器时代就已出现，宋元以后广泛发展，及至明清，随着中国武术的快速发展，暗器逐渐由军队作战进入民间，至今仍有一部分活跃在民间武术流派中。

第1节

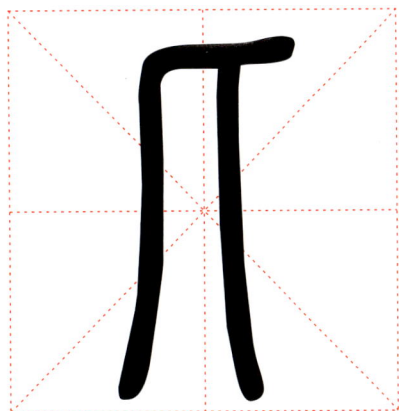

匕首

匕首是一种以刺为主兼砍击的兵器，形制似剑，长度大多在 20~30 厘米之间，有单刃和双刃之分。因其短小锋利，易于藏匿，是近距离搏斗和暗杀的有效武器。有时为了增加匕首的刺杀效能，用毒药淬之。《史记·刺客列传》就有记载："燕太子丹使轲刺秦王，豫求天下之利匕首，得赵人徐夫人匕首，取之百金。使工以药淬之。以试人，血濡缕，人无不立死者，乃装为遣荆卿。"

早在新石器时代就出现了制作精致的匕首，有石质、骨质和角质的，也用作切削器。商周以后逐渐出现青铜匕首、钢铁匕首。到了汉代，军中骑士多配匕首，一般官吏除了佩剑还带有匕首，用以防身自卫。唐以后，匕首多敛藏防身，或为侠客所用，不再是常备兵器。

图 5-1

带铃匕首^①（西周早期）
Dagger with bell
（Western Zhou Dynasty）

图 5-2

铜匕首（战国）
Bronze Dagger
（The Warring States Period）

图 5-3

铜匕首（汉）
Copper Dagger
（Han Dynasty）

① 带铃匕首：西周早期北狄所用，通长 26.5 厘米，青铜质。
Dagger with bell: It was made of bronze, 26.5cm long, used by northern nomadic tribes

图 5-4　　　　　　　　　　　匕首①（汉）
Dagger
(Han Dynasty)

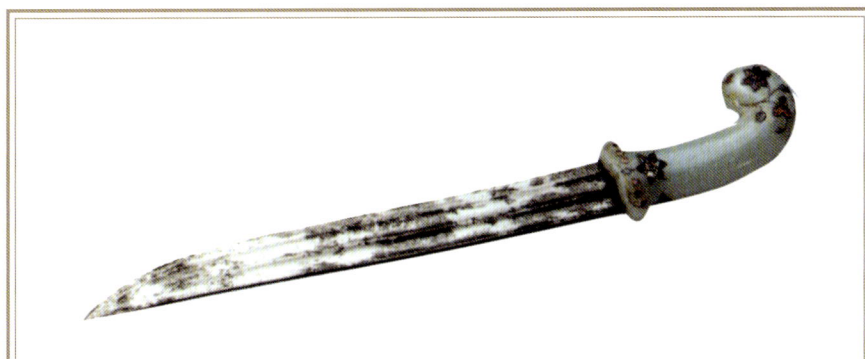

图 5-5　　　　　　　　玉嵌宝石花柄匕首②（清）
Dagger with a jade-inlaid handle
(Qing Dynasty)

① 匕首：长23.4厘米，宽4.2厘米。锋尖锐，脊棱突出，两刃有棱，格细小呈菱形，茎扁，圆首，胎体轻薄。

Dagger：23.4 cm in length, 4.2 cm in width, shaped diamond, sharp and light, pointed, with double edges of blade and round handle.

② 玉嵌宝石花柄匕首：单刃，长48厘米。

Dagger with a jade-inlaid handle：This dagger is 48 cm in length, with single edge of blade.

图 5-6

牛角柄匕首① （清）

Dagger with a horn handle
(Qing Dynasty)

---

① 牛角柄匕首：单刃，长 50 厘米。
Dagger with a horn handle：This dagger is 50 cm in length, with single edge of blade.

第 2 节

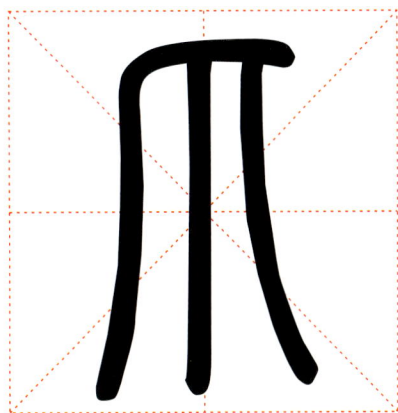

飞爪

　　飞爪是在系绳上拴有铁质钩爪的一种暗器。飞爪多带有两个钩爪，钩爪形如手掌，铁质，共四趾，连接着一半圆形或圆形的掌，趾尖非常锐利。爪趾上有许多伸缩自如的关节，爪后系有一条2~3丈长的绳索。为便于使用，绳索末端结成一圆圈套于腕上。

　　飞爪不但能杀伤敌人，还能擒拿敌人。一旦击中目标，锋利的爪尖足以使人受伤；若抽动绳索，制动爪趾各小节机关，爪尖便会向内猛扣，深隐入内，使目标无法摆脱。此外，飞爪也可用来攀登高墙等障碍物。

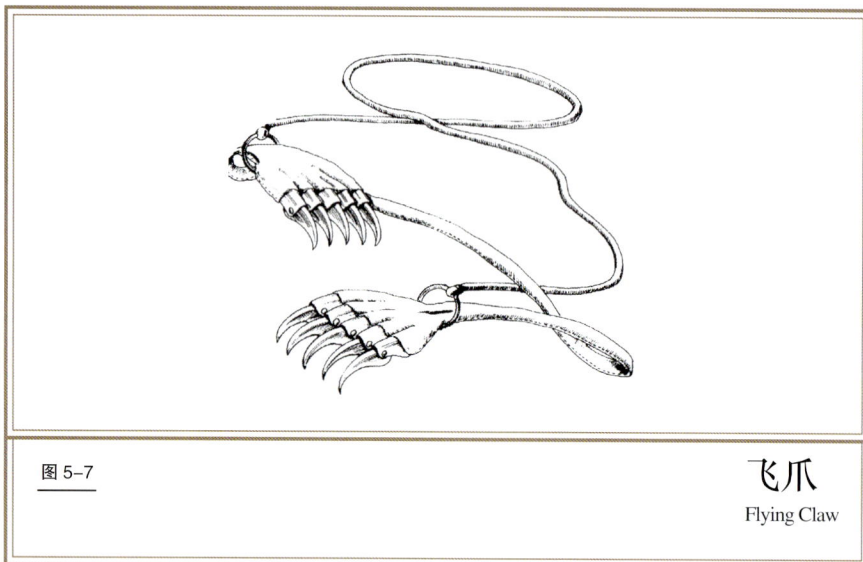

图 5-7

飞爪
Flying Claw

图 5-8

铁飞爪①（金）
Iron Flying Claw
[Jin Dynasty (1115 AD—1234 AD)]

---

① 铁飞爪：此器三爪翻翘锚形，铁质，高 15 厘米，前端爪弯尖锐，爪尾扁柱末端卷系索孔。

Iron Flying Claw: This weapon was shaped like an anchor, with three sharp reversed toes, made of iron, 15 cm in height. Its top could be attached to a rope.

第 **3** 节

镖

　　镖是一种常见的手掷类暗器。镖头呈尖状，一般由铁、铜等金属制造。镖的大小、长短和轻重不一，适合较近距离使用。常见的有脱手镖、金钱镖、绳镖等。

　　脱手镖，也称飞镖，有三棱、五棱、圆筒等形状，尖部均锋利无比，长度在 8~14 厘米，重四两半至半斤。脱手镖可分为带衣镖和光杆镖。带衣镖的末端系有红绿绸布，称作镖衣，掷出时绸布如箭羽，可以稳定飞行方向；光杆镖则不带镖衣，更加隐蔽，但飞行稳定性较差。镖一般系在腰间，9 支或 12 支为一套，每套中有一支镖比其他的长而重，为绝手镖，用于紧要关头，最大射程可达 60 米。

　　金钱镖又名"罗汉钱"，把古代常见的圆形方孔钱币的圆边磨成刃而成。此镖易于制造，便于大量携带，可攻击眼睛、咽喉等部位，但攻击距离有限。

绳镖是在镖的尾部系一长绳，属于索击类暗器。镖为纯钢所铸，呈三棱形。相对于脱手镖而言，绳镖有可回收利用的优势。

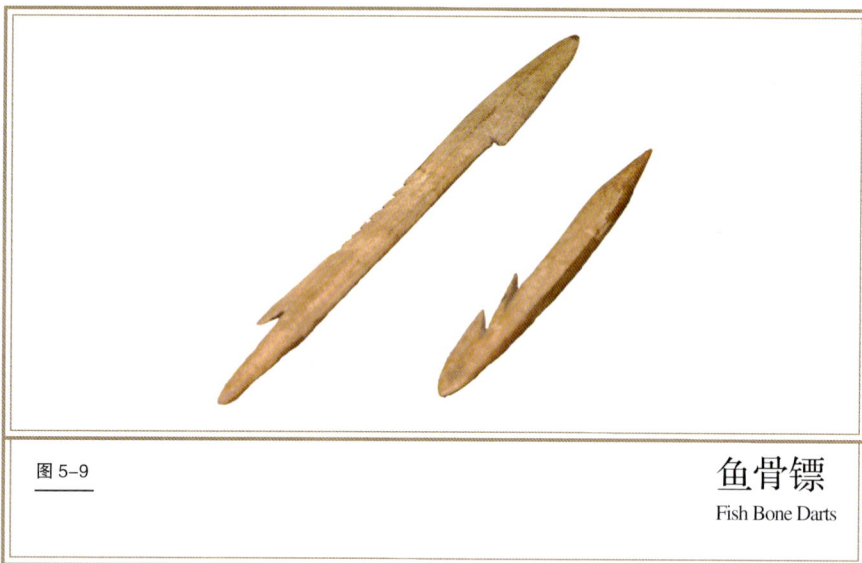

图 5-9

鱼骨镖
Fish Bone Darts

图 5-10

脱手镖
Hand thrown Dart

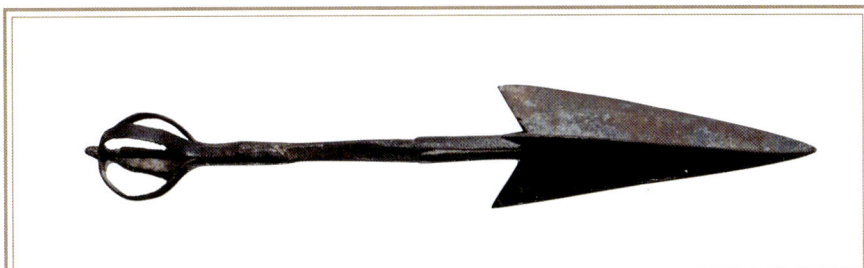

图 5-11

脱手镖
Hand thrown Dart

图 5-12

金钱镖
Coin Dart

图 5-13

金钱镖
Coin Dart

图 5-14

绳镖
Rope Dart

第 **4** 节

袖箭

　　袖箭是藏于袖中的暗箭，是利用弹簧的弹力发射短箭的筒状发射器。箭装于筒中，内设由钢丝盘成的弹簧，一按机括箭即发出。袖箭的最早记载见于《元史·顺帝纪二》："辛未，禁弹弓、弩箭、袖箭。"茅元仪《武备志》卷 120 称："袖箭者，箭短而簇重，可御人三十步之远。"常见的有单筒袖箭和梅花袖箭。

　　单筒袖箭每次只能发一箭，相传为北宋云阳（今属四川省）白鹤宫霞鹤道人所创。箭筒的外廓为铜铁所铸，长约 24 厘米，直径约 2.4 厘米。筒顶有盖，连接于筒身，不能启闭，盖子中间有一个小孔，为装箭处。筒盖旁边一寸的地方，有一片钢制的活络蝴蝶翅，是启闭的开关。筒内的弹簧下端连于尾盖，上连一圆铁片。箭为竹杆铁头，长约 15 厘米。另

配一个箭插,存箭 12 支。使用前,将箭杆压入筒内,弹簧被压紧,蝴蝶
翅将杆凹陷卡住;发射时,拨动蝴蝶翅,箭被弹射而出。

梅花袖箭筒内装六个小管,每管装箭一支,正中一箭,周围五箭,
排列成梅花状,可连续发射,故此得名。梅花袖箭的箭筒稍粗,直径
约 3.5 厘米。每个小管各有一蝴蝶片控制开关,匣盖之后有铁圈,发射
一箭之后,须将筒壁旋转一定角度,使之连续射出。小管内装配方法与
单筒袖箭相同。

图 5-15

单筒袖箭

Single barrel Sleeve Arrow
loaded with a dart

图 5-16

单筒袖箭

Single barrel Sleeve Arrow

第**5**节

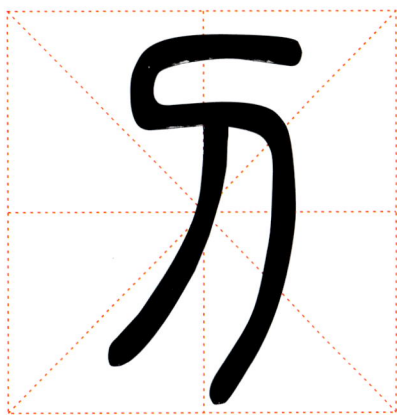

柳叶飞刀

　　柳叶飞刀是一种双刃飞刀，因形似柳叶而得名，属于手掷类暗器。刀身长约 20 厘米，柄长 4 厘米；刀中脊稍厚，双刃很锋利；通刀重约 170 克 。刀刃和刀柄均为铁质。为了甩投时飞行平稳，增加命中率，有时在刀柄末端拴上约 6 厘米长的彩绸，叫刀衣。每刀以 12 口为一鞘，刀身在内，刀柄在外，系于使用者后背，用时弯腰以手拔出掷之。

图 5-17

柳叶飞刀
Willow-leaf flying knife

图 5-18

柳叶飞刀
Willow-leaf flying knife

防护具

《韩非子》里面讲"以子之矛，攻子之盾"，自古便没有最锋利的矛，也没有最坚固的盾。在冷兵器时代，一场战争的胜利，除了先进的刀剑等武器外，坚固的盾牌、甲、胄等防护具也是很重要的决定条件。

第**1**节

盾

　　盾是一种用来抵挡攻击的防护型兵器，对刀剑的劈砍、枪箭的刺击都有防御效果。盾的使用历史久远，很早的史籍中便有记载。从材质上看，主要有皮革、木材、藤以及金属等；从外形上看，主要是方形和圆形两种；从曲面上看，战国前为平面盾，战国后多为弧形盾用以抵挡扎刺类兵器。盾的构造主要有盾背和把手两部分，一般来说，盾背面向敌人的一面会画有图，或鬼怪或神兽，用以恐吓敌人。步兵用盾形制较大，特别是在攻城时可以很好地减少伤亡；车骑兵用盾多短而窄，利于使用。盾在一定程度上可以起到抵御攻击、减少伤亡的作用，但防护范围和方向不足，而且使用时需一手持盾抵挡，一手持武器攻击，影响了机动性。

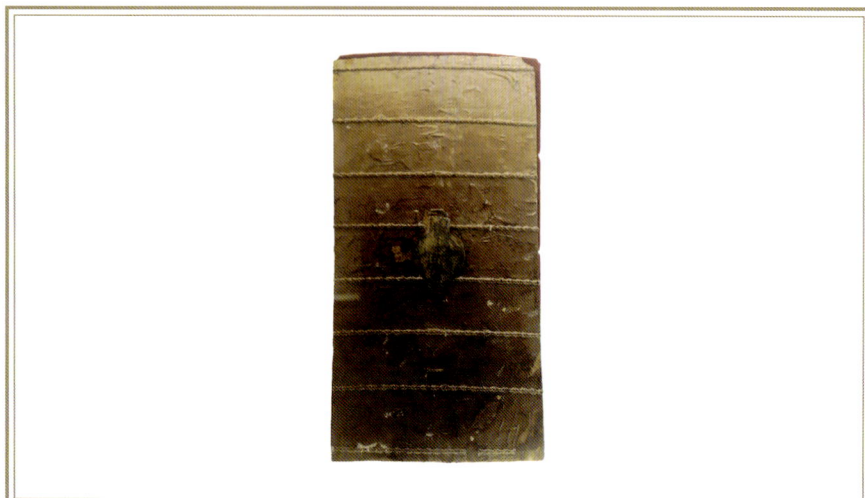

图 6-1

盾（战国时期）

Shield [The Warring States Period
(475 BC — 221 BC)]

图 6-2

龙凤纹盾（战国时期）

Shield with painted dragons and phoenixes
(The Warring States Period)

图 6–3

皮盾
Shield made of Animal Hide

图 6–4

藤盾[①]（西藏古格王朝时期）
Vine Shield (Tibetan Gurge Kingdom)

---

① 藤盾：用坚藤制成，具有很好的坚固性和伸缩性，明清火器流行时代重新被大量使用，能有效地抵御刀剑以及箭矢、弹丸等。

Vine Shield: This weapon was made of vines, which was solid and contractive. The vine shields were put in massive use again when firearms were popular in the Ming and Qing Dynasties (1368 AD – 1911 AD), which were effective against swords, arrows, knives, etc.

| 图 6-5 | 蛇面盾饰①（西周早期）
Shield Painted with a snake
[The Early Western Zhou Period (1046 BC—771 BC)] |

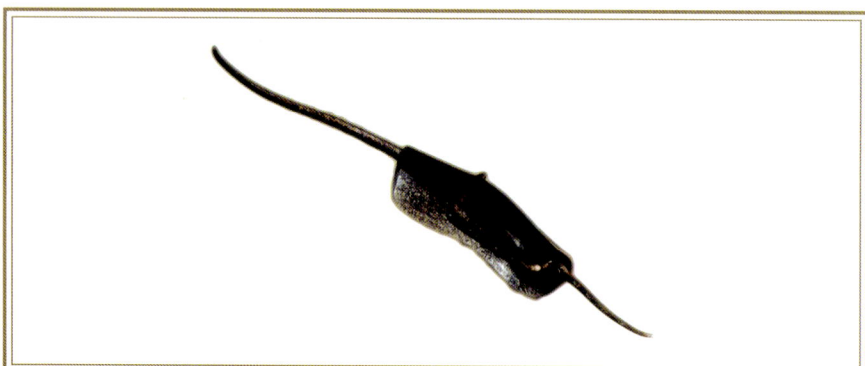

| 图 6-6 | 钩镶②（汉）
Shield with hooks
[Han Dynasty (206 BC—220 AD)] |

① 蛇面盾饰：北京昌平白浮出土。手持盾多以竹、木、藤制成，故常以盾饰镶嵌其上，具有加固、装饰盾牌和威慑敌人的作用。

Shield Painted with a snake: The weapon was excavated in Changpin county, Beijing. Hand-held shields are mainly made of bamboo, wood or vine, usually inlaid with decorations serving as reinforcing and decorating the shields, as well as frightening enemies.

② 钩镶：汉代常见的复合兵器，由钩和盾结合，上下带钩，配合环首刀攻击敌人；中后是带把手的小型铁盾，用于抵挡敌方进攻。

Shield with hooks: A commonly used composite weapon in Han Dynasty, composed of a small shield and hooks at both ends of the handle. The small iron shield is effective to protect the user's hand against the attack.

第**2**节

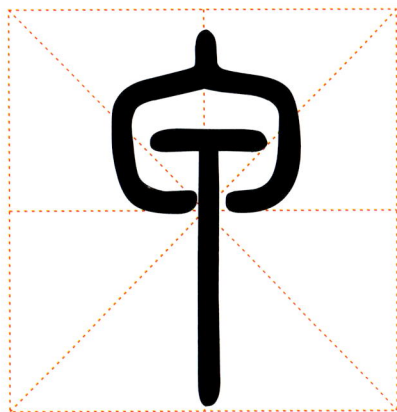

甲

铠甲是古代将士行军打仗所用的防护具，皮革制成的称为"甲"，金属制成的称为"铠"。唐宋以后，"铠""甲"通用，不分材质，均指防护具。

从材质来看，铠甲可分为皮甲、青铜甲、石甲、铁甲、藤甲、木甲、纸甲以及复合甲；从形制来看，分为单片式板甲、整片式札甲。

铠甲的种类有：商代铁甲、练甲，秦代将军铠，汉代鱼鳞甲，南北朝裲裆铠，唐朝明光甲、光要甲、细鳞甲、山文甲、乌锤甲、白布甲、皂绢甲、布背甲、步兵甲、皮甲、木甲、锁子甲、马甲等13种，宋代瘊子甲，元代柳叶甲、铁罗圈甲，明清时期的布面铁甲。

图 6-7　　　　　　　　　　　　　　石甲①（秦）
Stone Armor [Qin Dynasty
(221 BC —206 BC)]

图 6-8　　　　　　　　　　　　　　铁甲②（汉）
Iron Armor [Han Dynasty
(206 BC —220 AD)]

① 石甲：秦代将士所着防护具，甲片手工磨制，虽具一定防护能力，但制造周期长、产量低。

Stone Armor: It was one of main protection tools used by generals and soldiers of Qin Dynasty. The plates were hand–made. They played the role of protection to some extent, but having the disadvantages of long production cycle and low yielding.

② 铁甲：汉初的札甲发展成鱼鳞铁甲，甲片由大变小，甲身在只有胸甲、背甲的基础上发展出护臂、护腰，制作更加精细，防护能力更好。

Iron Armor: It developed into lamellar armor with smaller fish–scale plates, from protecting chest and back to protecting arms and waist as well. The armour had fine craftsmanship and better protection.

图 6-9

明光铠^①（唐）
Bright Light Armor (Tang Dynasty)

图 6-10

锁子甲^②（清）
Mail Armor (Qing Dynasty)

---

① 明光铠：甲身前后装有护心镜，金属材质的护心镜打磨光滑，在太阳的照耀下会反射"明光"，因此得名。明光铠样式繁多，有的会装有护肩和护膝，而且其存在的时间极长。

Bright Light Armor: It was inlaid with metal mirrors on the chest and the back respectively. After being polished elaborately, it reflected the bright light of the sun, hence the name "bright light armor". There were a variety of the bright light armors, with which added with shoulder protection and knee protection, existing for a long time.

② 锁子甲：又称环锁铠，一般由铁丝或铁环套扣缀合成衣状，每环与另四个环相套扣，形如网锁，配合皮甲，具有很好的防御能力。

Mail Armor: It was a type of armor consisting of small metal rings linked together in a pattern to form a mesh. Every ring was interlocked with the other four rings, having good defensive capability.

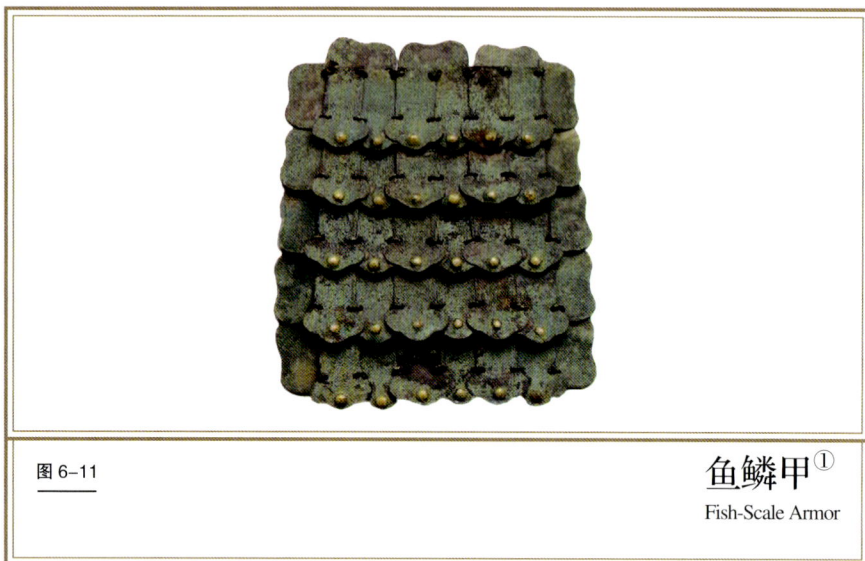

图 6-11

鱼鳞甲①
Fish-Scale Armor

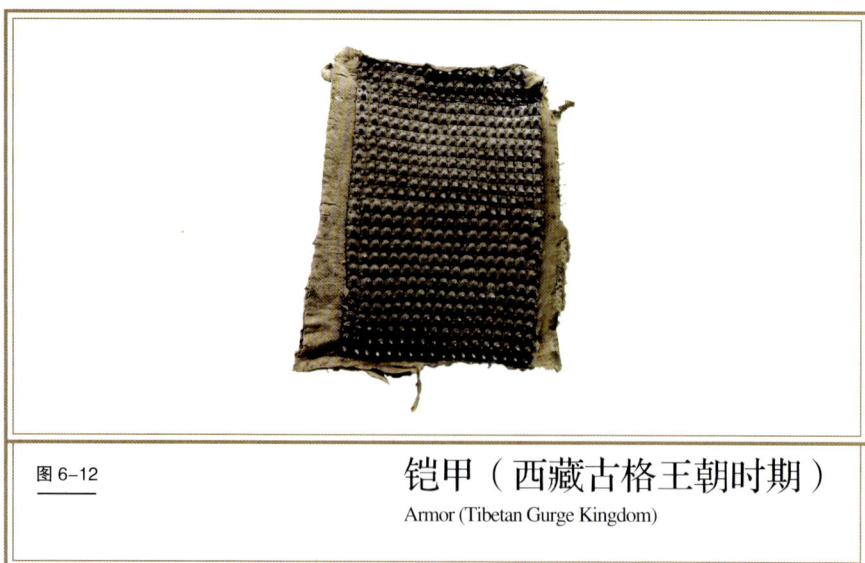

图 6-12

铠甲（西藏古格王朝时期）
Armor (Tibetan Gurge Kingdom)

① 鱼鳞甲：甲片可以收缩，间接地增加了护甲厚度，极大地提高了防护能力。另外其固定的绳索藏于甲片之内，使其不易被割断。

Fish-Scale Armor: The plates of this armor were contractive, which indirectly thicken the plates and greatly improve its ability to protect. Besides, the ropes served to fasten the plates were hidden beneath the armor were difficult to cut.

图 6-13

八旗军甲胄①（清）

Armors of the Eight Banners (Qing Dynasty)

① 八旗军甲胄：着布面铁甲，造价低，覆盖面广，依正黄、镶黄、正红、镶红、正白、镶白、正蓝、镶蓝的八旗建制所生产的甲胄是清军得以入关建朝的强力军事保证。图中所示依次（上左 1、上左 2、上左 3、上左 4、下左 1、下左 2、下左 3、下左 4）为：正黄旗甲胄、镶黄旗甲胄、正白旗甲胄、镶白旗甲胄、正蓝旗甲胄、镶蓝旗甲胄、正红旗甲胄、镶红旗甲胄。

Armors of the Eight Banners: They were administrative / military divisions under Qing dynasty into which all Manchu households were placed. These armors, made of iron, covered with cloth, cost low and could protect the whole body, which was a key success to the establishment of the Qing Dynasty. Along with the armors from the left to the right in the upper side are they belonging to Plain Yellow Banner, Bordered Yellow Banner, Plain White Banner and Bordered White Banner. Along with the armors from the left to the right at the bottom are they belonging to Plain Blue Banner, Bordered Blue Banner, Plain Red Banner and Bordered Red Banner.

第**3**节

胄

　　胄为中国古代战争中防护头颈的装备，与甲配套使用。《说文》：
"胄，兜鍪（móu）也。从月，由声。""由"意为"光滑"，"月"指
"人体"，"月"与"由"联合起来表示"光滑的青铜护具"。胄是先
秦时期的称呼，战国时称为"兜鍪"，北宋时称"头鍪"，宋以后多称
"盔"。

　　胄是中国古代兵器中存世量最少的一种，完整者屈指可数。新石器
时期已出现最早的胄，多用藤条或兽皮粗制而成。进入青铜时代，除继
续使用皮胄外，开始使用铜铸造的胄，也有皮革为主、重点部分用铜加
固的皮铜合制的胄。

从材质上看，有青铜胄、铁胄、皮胄等；从形制上看，有不包耳式、包耳式、护颈式、护鼻式、罩面式以及全包式。

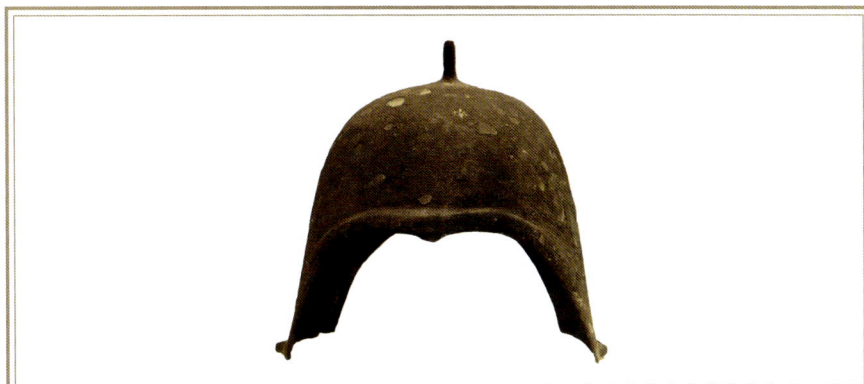

图 6-14

青铜胄（战国时期）
Bronze Helmet [The Warring States Period
（475 BC—221 BC）]

图 6-15

铁胄^①（战国时期）

Iron Helmet (The Warring States Period)

---

①铁胄：由 89 块铁片编缀而成，燕下都遗址出土，是目前仅见的先秦铁胄。

Iron Helmet: This helmet was composed of 89 iron pieces plated, excavated at Yanxiadu (now Baoding, Hebei Province). It was the only extant helmet before the Qin Dynasty (221 BC – 206 BC).

图 6-16　素面铜胄①（战国时期）
Bronze Helmet (The Warring States Period)

图 6-17　铁胄②（战国时期）
Iron Helmet (The Warring States Period)

---

① 素面铜胄：胄脚边沿四周有小孔，可穿上绳索佩戴；胄顶留有插戴领缨的洞孔。

Bronze Helmet: This helmet had small holes along the edge, which were used to tie ropes for wearing. On the top of it, there was a small hole for inserting a tassel.

② 铁胄：又称"兜鍪"，战国时开始流行。外层为铁制甲片编制而成，可很好地保护头颈；内衬多为皮革或者丝质，便于佩戴。

Iron Helmet: The helmet was popular in the Warring States Period. The outer layer was composed of iron plates, which could effectively protect the head while the inner layer was usually made of leather or silk, which was easy to wear.

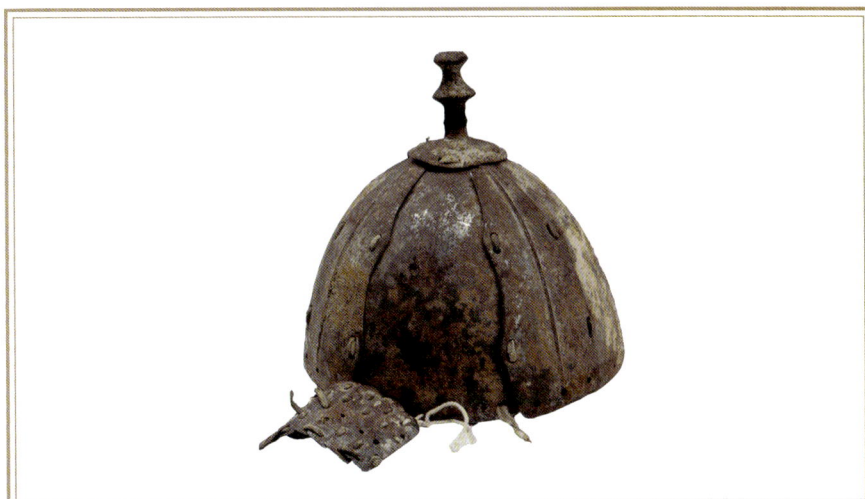

图 6-18 头盔（西藏古格王朝时期）
Helmet of a Tibetan King

图 6-19 蒙古头盔
The Mongolian Helmet

图 6-20

头盔（明）
Helmet (Ming Dynasty)

图 6-21

头盔①（清）
Helmet (Qing Dynasty)

① 头盔：铁制，帽檐和护颈宽大，内衬为皮制或织物，胄顶雁翎因军衔高低而不同，胄身嵌有铆钉以及虎头装饰。

　　Helmet: This helmet was made of iron, with a broad brim and a big neck guard. The lining was made of leather or fabric. The length of the tassel on the top varied according to the different ranks of officers. The helmet was inlaid with rivets and tiger heads as ornaments.

火器

在中国古代，火药的发明经历了漫长的历史过程。早在汉朝，火药的主要成分——硝石、硫黄已被人们当作药物使用。两晋、隋唐时期，炼丹家在实践中已经发现了硝石、硫黄和木炭等混合物的燃烧性能，并采用"伏火法"炼丹。自火药发明以后，利用火药作为杀伤源的武器逐渐被研制出来，并应用于战争。火器即利用火药等的燃烧、爆炸作用或发射的弹丸进行杀伤和破坏的兵器。火器的威力和破坏力远大于冷兵器，因而逐渐成为继冷兵器之后攻城守城的主要武器。北宋时期编著的《武经总要》一书中列举了火球、火药鞭箭、蒺藜火球、霹雳火球等八种火器。原始的火药兵器开始用于装备军队，宣告了冷兵器时代的结束，中国古代兵器的发展从此步入了新时代。

南宋后期，由于火药的性能已有很大提高，人们可在大竹筒内以火药为能源发射弹丸，并掌握了铜铁管铸造技术，从而使元朝具备了制造金属管形射击火器的技术基础，中国火器实现了革新和发展，出现了具有现代枪械意义的新式兵器——火铳。

元末明初，太祖朱元璋在重新统一中国的战争中，较多地使用了火铳作战。到洪武年间，铜火铳的制造达到了鼎盛时期，成为军队的普遍装备，不仅火铳结构更趋合理，也形成了比较规范的形制。永乐时，更创立了专习枪炮的神机营，成为中国最早专用火器的新兵种。到嘉靖年间，北方长城沿线要隘几乎全部构筑了安置盏口铳和碗口铳的防御设施。火铳的大量使用，标志着火器的威力已发展到一个较高的水平。明代中期，长期陷于发展迟缓状态的封建经济以及统治阶级的闭关锁国政策，使中国逐渐丧失了明初时所保持的世界兵器领域绝对领先的地位。到明中叶，发明了火铳的中国不得不从舶来品中汲取养分，仿制了比火铳更先进的"佛朗机"和"红夷炮"，以及单兵使用的鸟铳等。中国火器的制造又进入了一个新阶段。

地雷是一种埋入地表下或布设于地面的爆炸性火器，在我国约有500年的历史。相对于地雷而言，水雷是"埋"在水中或水底的雷，是最古老的水中兵器，最早是由中国人发明的。1558年明朝人唐顺之编纂的《武编》一书中详细记载了一种"水底雷"的构造和布设方法，它用于打击当时侵扰中国沿海的倭寇。

第 **1** 节

火箭

　　火箭是早期的燃烧性火器之一，在《三国志·魏明帝纪》中便有记载。公元 228 年，魏国第一次把火把装在箭上射出，正是运用这种火箭，魏国守将郝昭才焚烧了蜀军攻城的云梯，保住了陈仓（今陕西宝鸡东）。

　　古时候的火箭由箭头、箭杆、箭羽和火药筒四大部分组成。火药筒外壳用竹筒或硬纸筒制作而成，里面用火药填充，筒上端封闭，下端开口，筒侧边有一小孔引出导火线。点火后，火药在筒中燃烧，产生大量气体，高速向后喷射，产生向前推力，其实这就是现代火箭的雏形。火药筒相当于现代火箭的推进系统；锋利的箭头具有很强的杀伤力，相当于现代火箭的战斗部；尾端安装的箭羽在飞行中起稳定作用，相当于现代火箭的稳定系统；箭杆相当于现代火箭的箭体结构。中国古代火箭外形图首次记载于公元 1621 年茅元仪编著的《武备志》中。

明朝时期，火箭得到了进一步完善，箭头除了普通的形状，还有了刀形、枪形、剑形、燕尾形等；同时还出现了将许多支火箭结成一束发射的多发式火箭和以火药做推进动力的多级式火箭，尤以"火龙出水"及"飞空砂筒"两种最为精密。

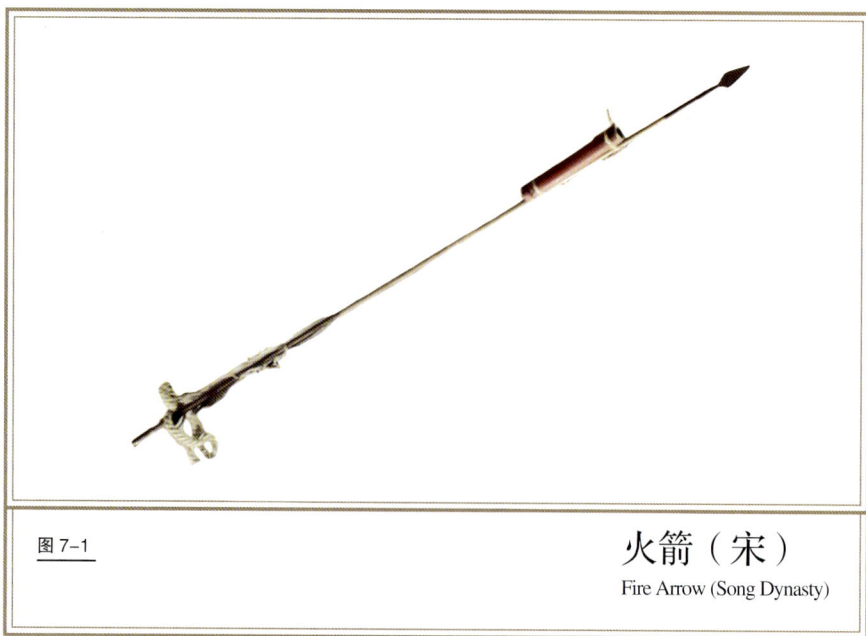

图 7-1

火箭（宋）
Fire Arrow (Song Dynasty)

图 7-2　　神火飞鸦① （明）
Shen Huo Fei Ya (Ming Dynasty)

图 7-3　　"一窝蜂" 火箭②
Fire Arrow called "Nest of Bees"

---

① 神火飞鸦：外形如乌鸦，"鸦身"用细竹或芦苇编成竹篓形，内部填充火药，腹部下方绑上 4 支火箭，与背上通出的 4 根 1 尺多长的火线相连。点燃火箭后，火药燃气反冲力将"飞鸦"射至 100 丈开外。到达目标时火箭发射药用尽，"飞鸦"落地，炸药自动点燃，可炸敌营或敌船，水陆两用。

Shen Huo Fei Ya: It literally means "Divine Fire Flying Crow". It was made of bamboo battens or reeds woven into a crow-shaped basket. The ancient Chinese would put gunpowder inside this bird-shaped basket, and then they would cover this basket with cloth. Finally, they would attach two pairs of fire arrows to each side of this bird-shaped rocket. Four fuses, about 33.33 cm long, would connect the rockets with the gunpowder inside the basket. When ignited, the Divine Fire Flying Crow would fly towards the targets. The range of this primitive rocket was about 300 metres. The "crow" was very powerful upon explosion and could initiate a raging fire strong enough to burn the enemy's camp on land or boats on water.

② "一窝蜂"火箭：将多支装有火药筒的火箭安置在一个口大底小的火箭桶中，桶内有分层箭格板，每支火箭分插一格，而后把火线挤在一起，伸出筒外。使用时将火线点着，各火药筒的火药燃气同时喷出，众箭齐发。

Fire Arrow Called "Nest of Bees": Many fire arrows tied with gunpowder tubes were in-loaded in a big-opening-small-end barrel. There were different layers of partitions, in which each of the partition was in-loaded with an arrow. Each fuse is twisted together, stretching out of the barrel. When the bunch of fuses were ignited, the arrows were shot, one after another.

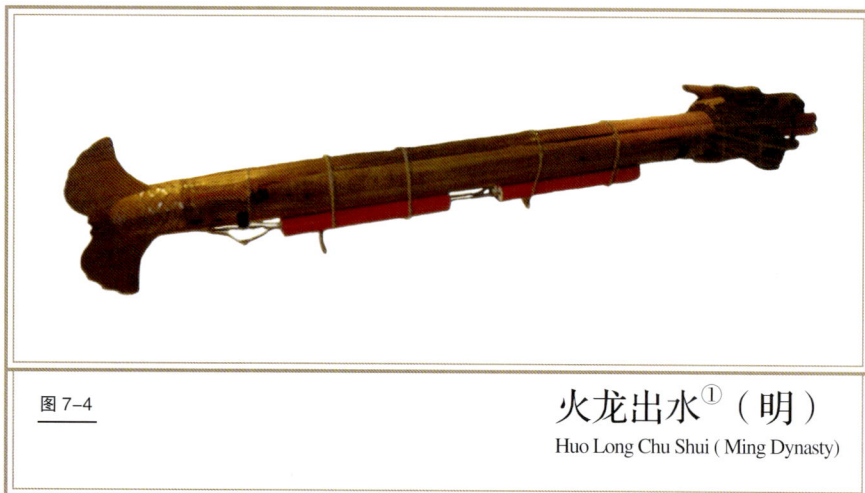

图 7-4

火龙出水① （明）
Huo Long Chu Shui (Ming Dynasty)

---

① 火龙出水：水陆两用火箭，二级火箭始祖，发明于明朝中期，是当时世界上最先进的远程火箭。首尾是龙形，龙头下面、龙尾两侧各装一个半斤重的火药筒，四个火箭引信汇总与火龙腹内火箭引信相连。

Huo Long Chu Shui: Literally, "fire dragon coming out water". It was an amphibious weapon, the rudiment of a two-stage rocket. Invented in the Ming Dynasty, it was the most advanced long-range weapon at that time. It was formed in a dragon. A pair of 250- gram gunpowder tubes were fastened beneath the head and the tail respectively. The fuses of the four tubes were connected with the fuse of gunpowder inside the barrel.

第2节

火球

　　火球，同"火毬（qiú）"，球心以硝石、硫黄、木炭及其他可燃物混合组成，用多层纸、布等裱糊为壳，壳外多用沥青、松脂、黄蜡等可燃性防潮剂涂敷。

　　火球是中国古代战争中使用的一种球状抛掷火器，出现于宋代初年（公元 1000 年前后）。靖康元年（1126）金军进攻宋都汴京（今河南省开封市）时，双方曾大量使用火球。火球的制作方法是将含硝量低、燃烧性能好的黑火药团成球状，有的还掺入有毒或发烟物质及预制杀伤元件，用纸或麻包缚数层，外敷松脂，以防潮和助燃。火球主要用于攻守城池作战。古代战争中使用较多的有霹雳火球、蒺藜火球、毒药烟球等多种球形火器。

　　火球在使用时要借助抛石机、弓、弩、弹射装置等冷兵器的机械力，把火球上的火药包抛射至敌方，达到烧杀、阻碍、毒杀、熏灼等作战目的。北宋初的兵器制造者已经能够巧妙地把轻重型射远冷兵器的射远作用同火器的燃烧作用结合在一起，创制出一种既能增强射远冷兵器的杀伤、焚毁威力，又能增加火器作战距离的新式兵器，运用在水陆各种类型的作战中，这也是冷兵器与火器并用时代的特点。

图 7-5

蒺藜火球[①]（宋）
Caltrap Fireball (Song Dynasty)

① 蒺藜火球：宋代出现的带有杀伤物的球状抛掷火器。在球中放置三枝铁刃，火药团之，中间用长麻绳穿起。燃放时待火焰起后，用炮掷入敌船纵火。突出球外的倒须可刺入目标。
　　Caltrap Fireball: It was ball-shaped shooting fire weapon with great lethality, which appeared in the Song Dynasty. The ball was loaded with gunpowder and iron spikes. After ignited, the fire ball was shot at the enemy's warships by cannon. The barbs outside could create mayhem against targets.

图 7-6

霹雳火球①
Thunderbolt Fireball

图 7-7

毒药烟球②
Poisonous smoke Fireball

---

① 霹雳火球：球心为干竹，薄瓷如铁钱者 30 片和火药 1.5~2 千克裹竹为球，放时声如霹雳，故以此命名。爆炸时碎瓷片使敌人受伤，燃烧时产生大量烟焰以达到熏灼敌人之效用。

Thunderbolt Fireball: The center of the ball was a section of hollow bamboo, inlaid with 30 pieces of porcelain, as thin as coins and 1.5 – 2 kg weight gunpowder. When exploding, the fireball sounded like thunderbolt, hence the name. After explosion, the broken porcelain could wound enemies, and the exhaust smoke could choke and disable them.

② 毒药烟球：可释放毒烟的球状抛掷火器，重量大概是 5 斤，可以使敌方士兵口鼻出血，该武器的出现也标志着中国古代以火药爆炸的杀伤力而起主要作用的火药兵器走上了战争的舞台。

Poisonous smoke Fireball: A ball-shaped throwing fire weapon which could emit poisonous smoke, weighing approximately 2.5 kg, which could cause enemies to bleed from the mouth and nose. The weapon marked the fact that Chinese people began to use the gunpowder weapons.

图 7-8	竹火鹞（左）与铁嘴火鹞（右）[1]
	Bamboo Fireball (the left) and Iron Fireball (the right)

---

① 竹火鹞：编竹为笼，腹大口狭，外表糊纸张数层，内填火药、卵石等，与铁嘴火鹞相类似，束草为尾。铁嘴火鹞：木身铁嘴，束草为尾，将火药装至鹞尾内。

Bamboo Fireball: It was made of bamboo battens and reeds weaved into a cage, shaped into a drum, pasted with layers of paper and stuffed with gunpowder and stones. Iron fireball: It was made with wooden cage and iron top. The gunpowder was stuffed into straw tail.

第**3**节

火枪

　　火枪是在传统长矛的基础上改装绑缚燃料筒制成，由南宋绍兴二年（1132）宋将陈规守德安府时创制。使用时，先点燃喷筒中的火药喷发火焰，发射之后，也可当冷兵器刺杀敌人。为增强这类武器的杀敌效果，常在火药中添加毒物，使其喷射出毒火焰或毒烟雾。

　　火枪是用一个或两个竹筒装上火药，绑缚在长枪枪头下面，与敌人交战时，可先发射火焰烧灼敌人，再用枪头刺杀。这种火器在南宋时非常盛行。火枪由中国发明，并在欧洲发扬光大，欧洲的军队对于火枪这样的装备是非常热衷的，尤其是德国和英国。德国的火枪技术和火枪普及率乃是欧洲第一，不论是在发明了火门枪的火药时代，还是普鲁士王朝战争时期，火枪的运用都处于领先地位。

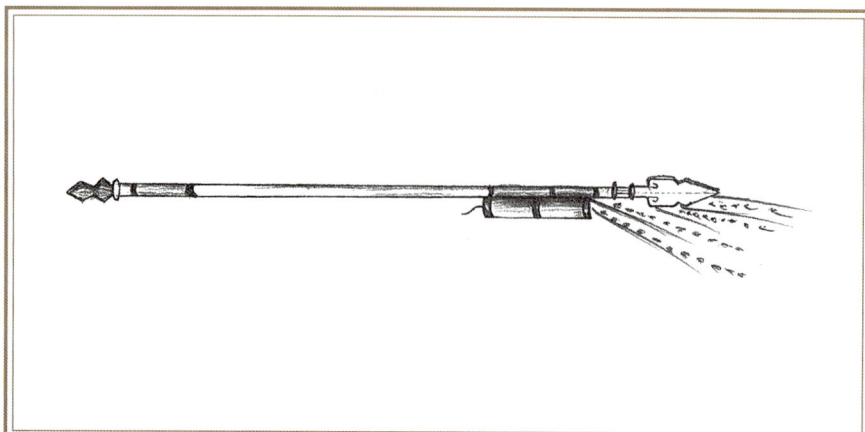

图 7-9

梨花枪[1]（明）
Lihua Spear (Ming Dynasty)

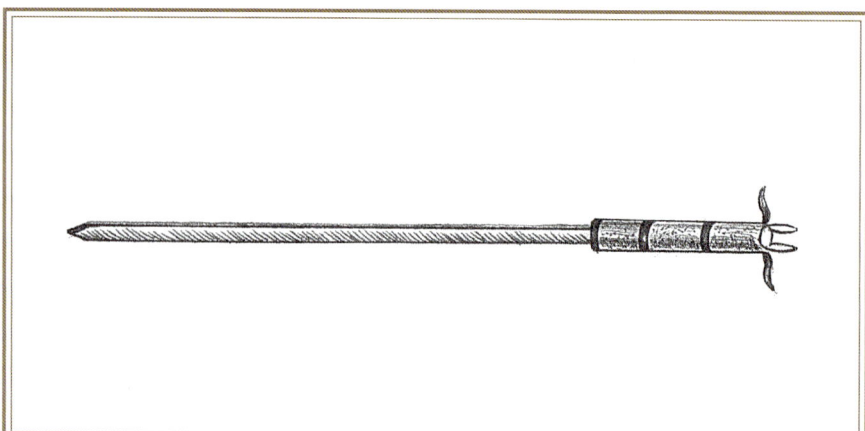

图 7-10

梨花枪（清）
Lihua Spear (Qing Dynasty)

①梨花枪：在枪的前端绑缚火药筒，临阵时可先燃放，喷火烧敌，然而再辅之以格斗。

Lihua Spear: A gunpowder tube was tied to the front end of the spear, which could be ignited to burn enemies and used as a spear to thrust at enemies.

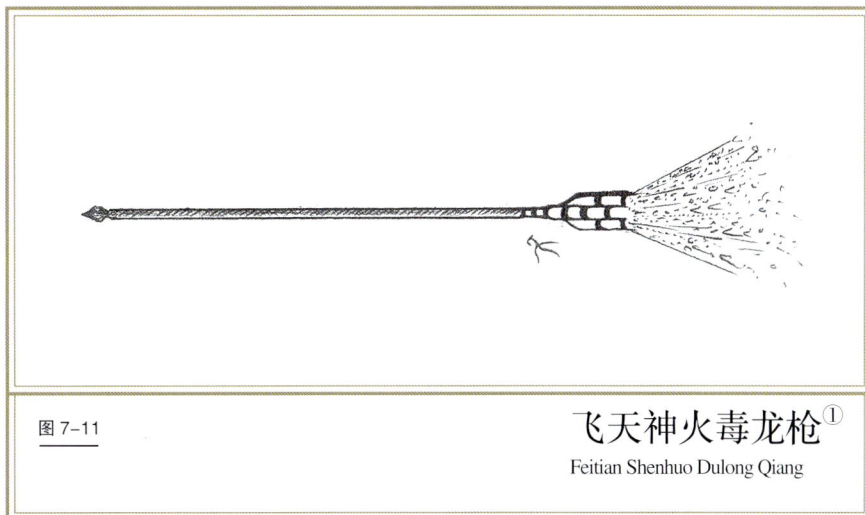

图 7-11

飞天神火毒龙枪①
Feitian Shenhuo Dulong Qiang

① 飞天神火毒龙枪：用铜或铁制造，中空，内设铅弹一枚，刀刃上蘸毒药，刀刃两旁缠火药筒。远距离可发铅弹，中距离可发毒火，近距离用刀刃刺杀敌人。

Feitian Shenhuo Dulong Qiang: Literally, "Flying Magic Fire Poisonous Dragon" Spear. It was made from a hollow copper or iron tube, and loaded with a lead pellet. The blade was poisoned, two sides of which were tied with gunpowder tubes. In long range, the lead pellet could be shot out. In the middle range, poisonous flame would gush out while in the short range, blade could be used to stab enemies.

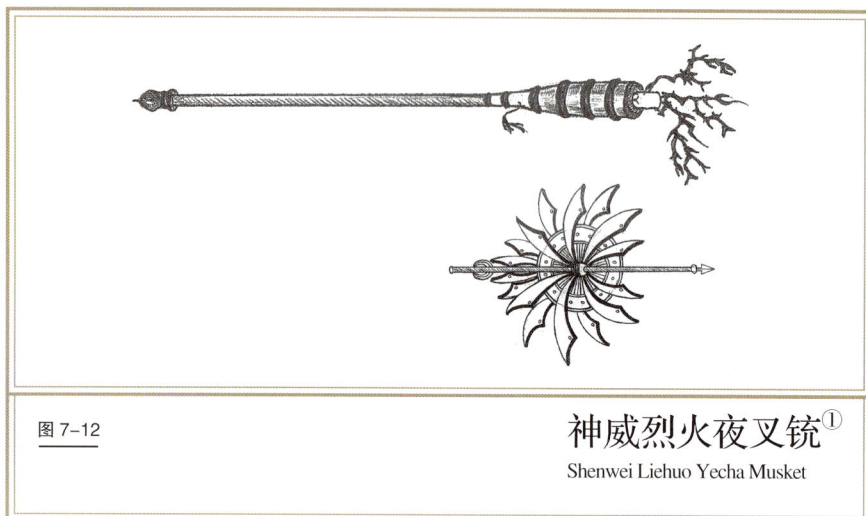

图 7-12

神威烈火夜叉铳[①]
Shenwei Liehuo Yecha Musket

---

① 神威烈火夜叉铳：《武备志》曰："铳与常铳相同，不必另造，借用坚木车为法马，马上钉利簇，上蘸虎药，布裹神火铁线，缚紧簇上。遇人马则钉入骨，遇镝重则焚粮草，遇船则烧蓬帆、簇制三棱倒钩，遇物钉入，则拔不出。器虽常制，而利害百倍。"

Shenwei Liehuo Yecha Musket: Literally "Mighty Flaming Yaksha". According to *Treatise on Armament Technology*, the musket was general and the wooden carriage would be used. On it there were nails which were poisoned. The arrows were fastened with a piece of cloth covered with gunpowder. It could hurt the soldiers and horses, burn the army provisions and the sail of the warship. The arrows were in the shape of three prism with hooks, which made them harder to be pulled out. This weapon were regular ones, but were much lethal.

第4节

火铳

火铳是中国元朝和明朝前期对金属管形射击火器的通称，有时又称"火筒"。火铳是依据突火枪的发射原理制成的，通常用铜或铁铸成，由前膛、药室和尾銎三部分构成。火铳以火药发射石弹、铅弹和铁弹，发射时，将火药从铳口装入药室，再将散状弹丸置于前膛，用火绳做引子，通过火门点火引燃火药，射出弹丸。

火铳是中国古代第一代金属管形射击火器，它的出现使热兵器的发展进入一个新的阶段，也为后来的战争形式和军事技术的发展开启了新的篇章。

火铳通常分为单兵用的手铳、城防与水战用的大碗口铳和多管铳等。手铳口径较小，铳身细长，药室呈球形隆起，尾銎中空，为单兵手持使用，相当于枪。碗口铳为重型火器之一，口径较大，形体短粗，铳口呈碗形，"碗"口中可放置一枚大弹，发射时置于发射架上，是后来的炮的雏形。三眼铳由三支单铳绕柄平行箍合成"品"字形，枪头突出，共用一个尾部，可依次点燃连续发射；或是将三个铳的药室做通，一次点火，三管齐发，火药发射完毕后可当锤击敌。嘉靖年间，军器局还据此生产过四眼铜炮、十眼铜铳等。

元代火铳主要是手铳和碗口铳两种。明朝火铳制造较精细，在火铳的结构、质量、品种、性能、威力等方面均做了大量的改进和提高，如口径减小，身管加长，自药室至铳口壁厚逐渐递减。铳炮也有大有小，大的用车载发射，用于守城；小的用支架托桩发射，用于冲锋陷阵。明后期火铳已可连发10次，最远达700步。

迄今为止，世界上发现最早的火铳是中国"元大德二年"的火铳，现存于内蒙古蒙元文化博物馆。这个铳为铜质，铸造而成，铜色紫，表面略有绿锈，铳体坚固，重6210克，全长34.7厘米，保存完好。

图 7–13　　　　　　　　　　　**青铜火铳**[①]（元）
Bronze Musket (Yuan Dynasty)

---

　①青铜火铳：元至顺三年（1332）造，这是目前所知世界上最早的有纪年的青铜火铳。
　Bronze Musket: It was made in 1332, which was the earliest recorded bronze cannon all over the world.

图 7-14

"元大德二年"火铳（元）

Hand Musket from the Mongol
[Yuan Dynasty (1271—1368)]

图 7-15

铜火铳[1]**（明）**

Bronze Musket (Ming Dynasty)

---

① 铜火铳：明景泰元年（1450）制，长 26.1 厘米，口径 10 厘米，底径 9.1 厘米，由前膛、药室和尾銎组成，药室有小孔，用于放置导火线。

Bronze Musket: It was made in 1450, 26.1 cm in length, 10 cm in muzzle bore diameter, 9.1 cm in diameter at the bottom, composed of a barrel, a gunpowder case and a hole. There was a small hole on the gunpowder case, for inlaying a fuse.

图 7-16　　　　　　　英字铜手铳①（明）
Bronze hand held Musket (Ming Dynasty)

图 7-17　　　　　　刘春造铜子母铳②（明）
Bronze Musket (Ming Dynasty)

① 英字铜手铳：1415 年制造，长 44 厘米，口径 5.2 厘米。
Bronze hand held Musket: It was made in 1415, 44 cm in length and 5.2 cm in muzzle bore diameter.
② 刘春造铜子母铳：明嘉靖二十四年（1545）造，中国火兵器史上后膛枪炮的开山之器。由 1 支母铳、4 枚子铳组成，母铳长 64 厘米、口径 2.8 厘米，子铳长 15.5 厘米、口径 1.6 厘米。母铳长口凹下呈半圆形，后沿两侧末端各有一个 2 厘米长、0.8 厘米宽的小口。尾銎内径 0.35 厘米，中空，口大里小。子铳由前膛、药室、尾冠三部分构成。前膛长 8 厘米，药室长 6 厘米，尾冠长 1.5 厘米，铳口内壁直径 15 毫米，口沿厚 5 毫米。药室中部上方有一小火线孔。铳身铸有七道加强箍。
Bronze Musket: It was made in 1545, which was regarded as the first firearm with the tube at the rear. There was a larger barrel and four smaller barrels. The larger one was 64 cm in diameter, 2.8 cm in muzzle bore diameter and the smaller ones were 15.5 cm in length, 1.6 cm in muzzle bore diameter

图 7-18

三眼铳（明）
Three-shot Musket (Ming Dynasty)

图 7-19

子母炮（清）
Hand Cannon (Qing Dynasty)

图 7-20

鸟枪①（清）
Gun (Qing Dynasty)

---

① 鸟枪：通长 153 厘米，口径 1.2 厘米，前装弹药、滑膛，火绳枪机，适合步兵、骑兵使用。

Gun: It was 153 cm in length, 1.2 cm in muzzle bore diameter. The pellets were loaded in the front of the barrel, with a fuse, serving as a trigger. This weapon was suitable for both infantry and cavalry.

第 **5** 节

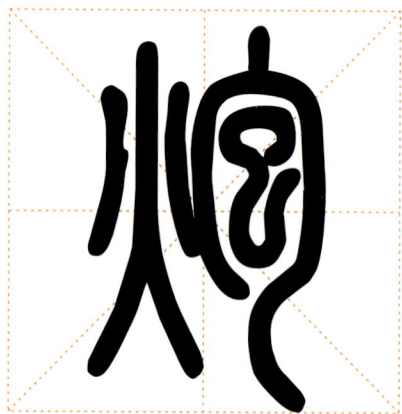

炮

中国古代一种口径和重量都较大的金属管形射击火器，由火铳发展演变而来，主要用于攻守城寨，也用于野战和水战。炮由身管、药室、炮尾等部分构成，滑膛多为前装，可发射石弹、铅弹、铁弹和爆炸弹等，大多配有专用炮架或炮车。

明朝丘濬撰《大学衍义补》中记载："今砲之制，用铜或铁为具，如筒状，中实以药，而以石子塞其口，旁通一线，用火发之。""亦谓之砲，又谓之铳。"自元朝以后，古代火炮开始成为中国军队的重要装备，主要用于攻城守寨，也用于野战和水战。

中国发明和使用火炮不迟于元朝，到明初已大批生产并用于装备部队。元末明初使用火铳作战的记载在《元史》《明史》及其他历史文献中已很常见，元朝和明洪武年间制造的火炮在中国各地博物馆中亦有收藏。

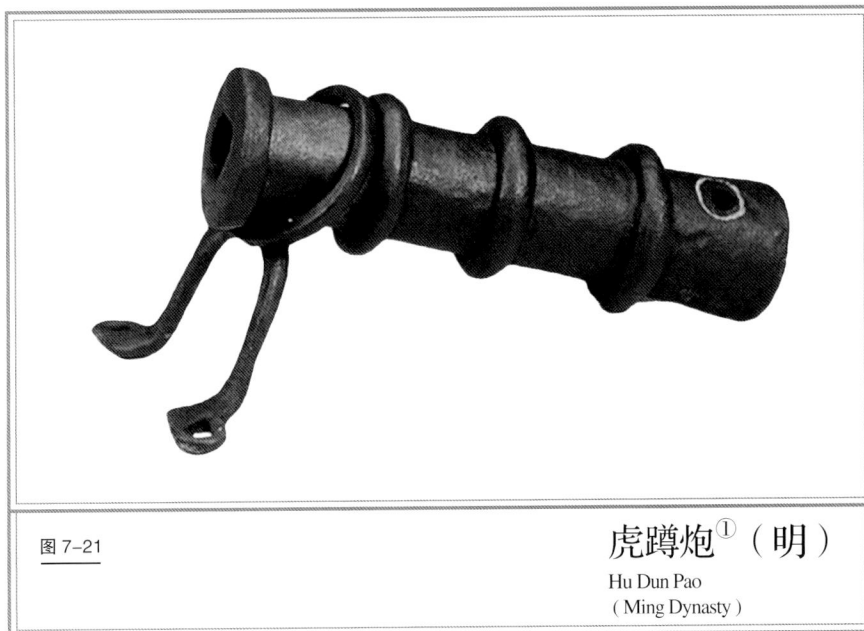

图 7-21

虎蹲炮[1]（明）
Hu Dun Pao
（Ming Dynasty）

---

[1] 虎蹲炮：明嘉靖年间制造，配有铁爪、铁绊，炮管薄，射程不远，一发能射上百枚小弹丸或 50 枚较大弹丸，散布面大。发射前可用大铁钉将炮身固定于地面，形似虎蹲，适用于山地作战、机动灵活，可以大仰角发射，克服了发射时后坐力大、跳动厉害的缺点。

Hu Dun Pao: It was known in English as Crouching Tiger Cannon. Made in Ming Dynasty, the "Crouching Tiger Cannon" was a small cannon that was propped up at the muzzle end and pinned to the ground to deaden the recoil. This setup supposedly resembles a crouching tiger, giving the cannon its name. The thin barrel could shoot 100 small pellets or 50 larger pellets. The shooting range was not long, but the coverage was large. It was suitable for battles in the mountains.

图 7-22　　　　天启癸亥年造安边神炮①（明）
An Bian Shen Pao
（ Ming Dynasty ）

图 7-23　　　　号炮②（明）
Signal Cannon
（ Ming Dynasty ）

---

① 天启癸亥年造安边神炮：铜质，属于没有耳轴及瞄准具的前装滑膛炮。炮为直筒形，炮身上铸箍7道，其中1~5道间为前膛；5~6道箍间为药室，上部开一直径1.6厘米的引信孔；6~7道箍间有阴文楷书"天启癸亥年造安边神炮"十字，其药室略粗，外形呈椭圆，尾部稍凹。

An Bian Shen Pao: Itwas known in English as Divine Cannon of Border Pacification. Made of bronze, this cannon had no aiming device, but the barrel was strengthened with seven cast-iron reinforce rings. The bore was from the first ring to the fifth ring. The gunpowder was loaded in the case between the fifth ring to the sixth ring, with a hole, 1.6 cm in diameter, to place a fuse. On the surface of the barrel between the sixth ring and the seventh ring, the Chinese characters, "Divine Cannon of Border Pacification", were inscribed. The gunpowder case part was a little thicker.

② 号炮：军中用来传递信息的火炮。

Signal Cannon: This cannon was used to transmit signals in the army.

图 7-24

神威无敌大将军炮^①（清）
Shen Wei Wu Di Da Jiang Jun Pao
(Qing Dynasty)

---

① 神威无敌大将军炮：1676 年制，铜质前膛炮，南怀仁督造。炮重 1137 千克，炮身长 2.48 米，口径 110 毫米，木制三轮（前二后一）炮车装运。炮管前细后粗，底如覆笠，有五道加强箍，两侧有耳，尾部有球冠。上有铭文"大清康熙十五年三月二日造"。炮口与底部正上方有"星""斗"供瞄准用。每次发射装填 1.5~2 千克火药，炮弹重 3~4 千克。此炮多用于攻城守寨和野战，在清朝与俄国的雅克萨之战中曾发挥巨大作用。

Shen Wei Wu Di Da Jiang Jun Pao: It was known in English as the Divine Invincible General Cannon, made in 1676. Made of Bronze, this cannon was 1137 kg in weight, 2.48 m in length, 110 mm in muzzle bore diameter, fixed with three wheels. The barrel tapers from the end to the mouth, fixed with five reinforce rings, with a knob at the end. There were Chinese characters, "made on March 2nd in the fifteenth year of Kangxi Emperor", inscribed on the barrel. There were aiming devices both at the mouth and the end. 1.5 – 2 kg weight gunpowder could be loaded in the barrel, with 3 – 4 kg weight shell. This weapon was suitable for besieging and defending cities, and played an important role in the Sino-Russian border conflicts of the Qing Dynasty.

图 7-25

威远将军炮[①]（清）
Weiyuan Generalissimo Cannon
(Qing Dynasty)

---

① 威远将军炮：清康熙二十九年（1690）制，戴梓发明。长 70 厘米、口径 21.2 厘米，火门铸铁，为一种大口径、短身管的前装火炮，重 280 千克；形如仰钟，炮筒粗短，有六圈加强箍，前粗后敛，炮中部置耳，用以支撑、平衡炮体和调整射击角度；以四轮木质炮车承载，发射铁弹。

Weiyuan Generalissimo Cannon: This cannon was made in 1690, 70 cm in length, 21.2 cm in muzzle bore diameter. Made of cast iron, it was muzzle-loading cannon, with a big muzzle mouth and short barrel, 280 kg in weight. The barrel tapered from the end to the mouth, strengthened by six reinforce rings. There was a rest in the middle for supporting and balancing the barrel and adjusting the shooting angle. It was fastened on a four wheel wooden camion, shooting iron balls.

第6节

地雷

　　地雷，一种埋入地表下或布设于地面的爆炸性火器，始创于明朝初年，以铁、石、陶制成，使用踏发、绊发、拉发、点发等引发方法。早期地雷构造简单，多为石壳，内装火药。明中期后，雷壳多为铁铸。明末，地雷种类更多，除单发雷之外，还有利用一条引信控制的群发雷、一个母雷引爆若干个子雷的子母雷等。

　　地雷在我国已有 500 多年的历史。明代兵器制造家发明了地雷，并大量用于战争。明代兵书《武备志》中记载了 10 多种地雷的形制及特性，并绘有地雷的构造图。地雷多是用石、陶、铁制成的，将它埋入地下，使用踏发、绊发、拉发、点发等方式引爆以杀伤敌人。早期的地雷多是用石头打制成圆形或方形，中间凿深孔，内装火药，然后杵实，留有小空隙插入细竹筒或苇管，里面牵出引信，再用纸浆泥密封药口，埋在敌人必经之处，当敌人将近时，点燃引信，引爆地雷。这种石雷又叫"石炸炮"，因构造简单，取材方便，广泛使用于战争，但也因贮药量小、爆炸力较小而渐被更新。后来地雷的形制，特别是发火装置得到不断改进，扩大了地雷的有效杀伤范围。

图 7-26

石雷（明）
Land Mine made of stone
（Ming Dynasty）

图 7-27

陶雷（明）
Land Mine made of pottery
（Ming Dynasty）

蒺藜陶弹（明）
Land Mine made of pottery inlaid with Iron Caltrop
(Ming Dynasty)

图 7-28

军用"国姓瓶" ①
Mine in the shape of bottle

图 7-29

① 军用"国姓瓶"：该瓶在闽南地区散布较广，大多是渔民从海里捞出，亦有从陆地挖土得到的。瓶中装火药、铁砂，引爆后杀伤力甚大。

Mine in the shape of bottle: These mines were discovered in Southern Fujian Province, most of which were netted by fishermen from the sea. Some were unearthed from ground. The mines were inlaid with gunpowder and pellets, and very destructive after triggered to explosion.

图 7-30　　　　**钢轮发火地雷**[①]（明）
Steel wheel triggering Land Mine
(Ming Dynasty)

① 钢轮发火地雷：明朝名将戚继光制，是世界上第一枚非人工引爆的触发式地雷，采用机械点火原理，生铁制作。将大小如碗的地雷炸炮装药后密封，在火药中插入一支小竹筒引出火线；再将几个炸炮的火线串联导出一条长线，顶端装置钢轮和火石，置于一个机械触发的钢轮发火槽内，选择敌人必经之路埋设。来敌触动引线，重锤下降，钢轮转动与火石急剧摩擦发火，引爆地雷。

Steel wheel triggering Land Mine: Invented by a famous general, called Qi Jiguang. It was the first land mine, which was not ignited by people. It comprised a complex system of a pin release, dropping weights, cords and axles to rotate a spinning "steel wheel" that acted as a flint to provide sparks that ignited the mines' fuses underground.

战车战船

从广义上说，中国古代战车是专供作战使用的各种战斗车辆的总称。它由原始社会晚期木板圆轮式陆上运载工具演变而来，除了辎重车和特种攻城车外，主要有商周车战时代用来乘载士兵作战的木质战斗车辆，以及宋代以后装备各种兵器的战斗车辆。

据文献记载，我国在远古时代已有车骑。随着社会生产力的发展和战争规模的扩大，战车的数量也越来越多。到春秋末期，有的诸侯国拥有战车达四千乘以上。春秋战国之际，虽然由于步骑战兴起，车战地位逐渐下降，但各诸侯国拥有战车的数量仍然相当可观。直到汉代初年，战车在战争中仍然发挥着一定的作用。

车战时代的战车在形制构造上大同小异。车战时代的马车由两马或四马驾挽，以四马为主。从殷墟出土的车马装具可知，大约在公元前13世纪的商代武丁时期，每乘四马战车的编制装备已经制式化。到西周时期，为适应作战的不同需要，战车的分类已经越来越明显。西汉以后，步骑兵逐渐取代了战车兵，战车便逐渐失去了它原有的地位。

宋代以后的战车同车战时代的战车作用不同，不是乘载士兵，而是装备各种冷兵器和火器，而且种类比较多，形制构造各有特点。如果说车战时代的战车主要是乘载甲士进行对阵作战和错毂拼杀的话，那么宋代以后的战车是兵器的毁杀作用和车辆的机动性相结合的攻击性战车，使用范围和战斗作用要宽广得多。

第 **1** 节

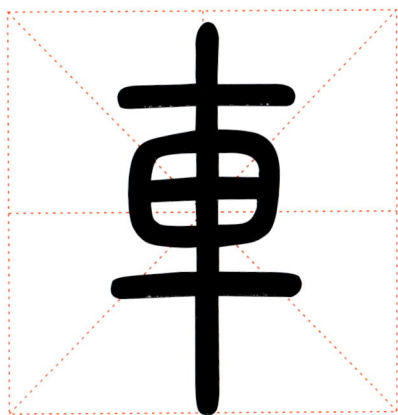

冷兵器战车

在《武经总要·器图》中绘制有车身小巧的独轮攻击型战车，包括运干粮车、巷战车、虎车。运干粮车、巷战车和虎车的基本构造相同。它们是在一辆独轮车上或车前安置挡板，两侧安置厢板；或在车上安一个虎形车厢，以掩护推车士兵。同时，在车的底座上和虎形大口中伸出多支枪尖，以便在作战时冲刺敌军。由于这种独轮车车身小巧，便于机动，所以士兵可以在狭窄的田埂、道路、街巷中推车冲进，同前来劫粮和进攻的敌军搏战；也可在旷野中排成车阵，由众多士兵拥推成百上千辆战车蜂拥向前，冲击敌军的前阵，配合步骑兵进攻。

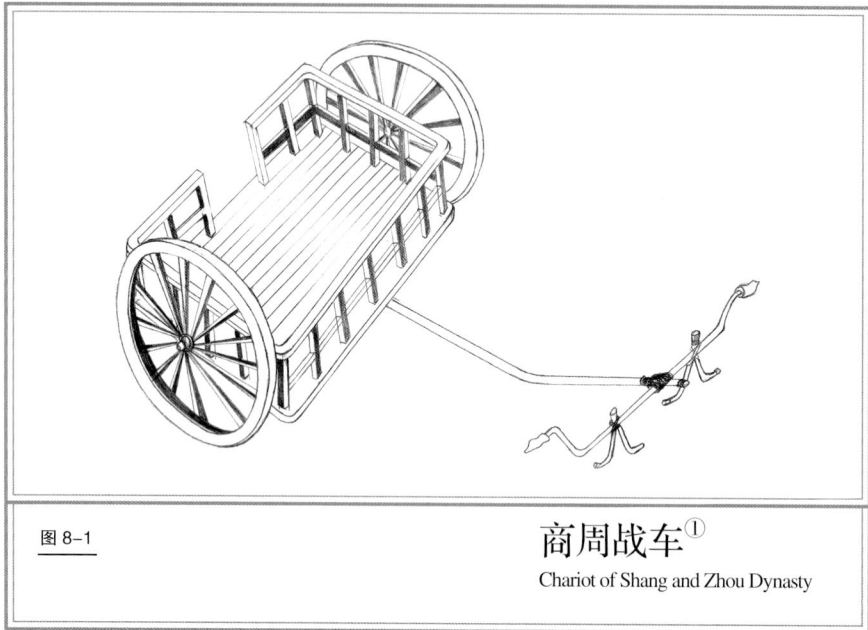

图 8-1

商周战车①

Chariot of Shang and Zhou Dynasty

① 商周战车：战车的使用可追溯到夏朝，车体为木质结构，在重要部位装有青铜部件，起到加固和装饰的作用。战车每车驾 2 匹或 4 匹马，4 匹马拉的车一辆为一乘。4 匹驾马中间的 2 匹称为"两服"，左右的 2 匹称"两骖"，四马以皮条系在车前，合称为"驷"。战车每车载甲士 3 名，按左、中、右排列。左方甲士持弓，主射，是一车之首，称"车左"，又称"甲首"；右方甲士执戈（或矛），主击刺，并有为战车排除障碍之责，称"车右"，又称"参乘"；居中的是驾驭战车的御者，佩带卫体兵器——短剑。除 3 名甲士随身佩持的兵器外，车上还备有若干有柄格斗兵器。据《考工记·庐人》记载，这些兵器是戈、殳、戟、酋矛、夷矛，合称"车之五兵"。从商经西周至春秋，战车一直是军队的主要装备，车战是主要作战方式，晋国和楚国拥有战车的数量多达 4000 乘以上。春秋战国之交，由于铁器的使用和弩的发展，也由于战车笨重、机动性差、难以驾驭等诸多不利因素，战车的使用开始大规模地减少，大约汉武帝时期逐渐退出了战争的舞台。

Chariot of Shang and Zhou Dynasty: The earliest archaeological evidence of chariots in China, dated to the Xia Dynasty (c. 2000 BC). Made of wood, the important parts of a chariot were reinforced and decorated with bronze. A chariot was often drawn by two or four horses, connected abreast by a special harness. The crew consisted of an archer on the left, a driver in the middle, and a third warrior on the right who was armed with a spear or dagger-ax. Massed-chariot warfare became all but obsolete after the Warring-States Period (476 - 221 BC). The main reasons were increased use of the crossbow, bulk of the chariots and poor mobility.

图 8-2

运干粮车①
Wheelbarrow for transporting
military supplies

图 8-3

虎车②
Tiger Wheelbarrow

①运干粮车：独轮车，主要用于粮草运输，同时也具备一定的攻击能力。

Wheelbarrow for transporting military supplies: The wheelbarrow also served as an attacking weapon against enemies.

②虎车：在独轮车上安一个虎形车厢，以掩护推车士兵。在车的底座上和虎形大口中，伸出多支枪尖，以便在作战时冲刺敌军。虎车车身小巧，快速机动，可排成车阵冲击敌军。

Tiger Wheelbarrow: A tiger shaped carriage was fixed on wheelbarrows to protect the soldiers behind. There were spears under the carriage or stretching out of the open mouth of the tiger, to impale enemies in battles. These wheelbarrows were small and maneuverable, which could be arrayed in formation to attack enemies.

图 8-4

象车①
Elephant Chariot

---

① 象车：形状似象，一般装有四轮，车身比较宽，车厢和挡板较大，象口处有多支枪尖用来刺敌，象身挡板也可掩护己方士兵；属中型战车，主要是在野战中排成车阵，用来冲击敌军的前阵，配合步骑兵进攻。

Elephant Chariot: This chariot took the shape of elephant, usually having four wheels and broader carriage. There were many spears projecting from the mouth of the elephant to impale enemies. The carriage could protect the soldiers marching behind. These chariots were usually arranged in formation to attack the vanguards of enemies and protect the infantry advance.

第 2 节

车

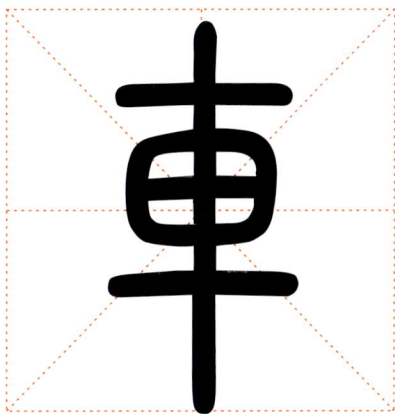

冷兵器和火器相结合的战车

明世宗嘉靖年间（1522—1566）以后，由于火器的大量制造和使用，装备火器和冷兵器的战车得到了长足的发展，种类繁多。适应各种不同作战用途的，首先是火器和冷兵器相结合的战车。这类战车有万全车、架火战车、破敌火风鼎等。它们的构造特点是在两轮或四轮车上安装大型木柜或木架，架置各种火器和冷兵器，杀伤敌军。有的木柜大到八尺见方，高达 1 丈多，顶部造成女墙形状，中藏折叠式望楼，可载乘 8 名士兵，形似活动式碉楼，具有攻守兼备的特点。

万全车是中国明朝后期创造的一处装备多种火器与冷兵器的攻守兼备的战车，设计巧妙，构造新颖，具有民族特色。车辕长 15 尺，阔 8 尺，下安 8 轮；车框上建有车厢，厢柱高 7 尺；前面与两侧都有厢板，顶部制成城垛型。全车似活动碉楼，内藏士兵 8 人，备有弩床、火弩、长杆刀枪、火铳、飞沙铁弹等兵器与器材。行军时用五马挽拽；冲击时用九马驾驰，冲入敌阵后各种兵器一起使用，发挥综合杀敌作用，使敌军难以抵挡。

破敌火风鼎是明代火器战车，为木制、柜形，内置火器，下设四轮，两人操纵，主要用于攻战。

架火战车是明代用来发射火箭的手推战车，是早期的多管火箭炮，它的发明比欧洲各国正式使用火箭炮早 500 多年。架火战车既有类似现代火箭炮的齐射火力和快速转移的机动性等特点，又具备现代战车在火力、机动性和防护方面的一些基本性能，因此在兵器发展史上占有重要地位，也是我国在火箭炮方面的杰出创造之一。

图 8-5

万全车^①（明）
Wan Quan Chariot
(Ming Dynasty)

---

① 万全车：明代后期创制，中载折叠望楼，内容八人，持火器、长枪、长刀，具备很强的杀伤力。

Wan Quan Chariot: This chariot was invented in the late Ming dynasty, which was equipped with firearms and cold weapons. This chariot was ingeniously designed for both attacking and defending. Eight soldiers could hide in the carriage, with bench crossbows, fire crossbows, spears, fire lances, iron balls. The chariot was driven by five horses in harness, but nine horses in warfare. All the weapons could be brought into use at the same time, which was invincible.

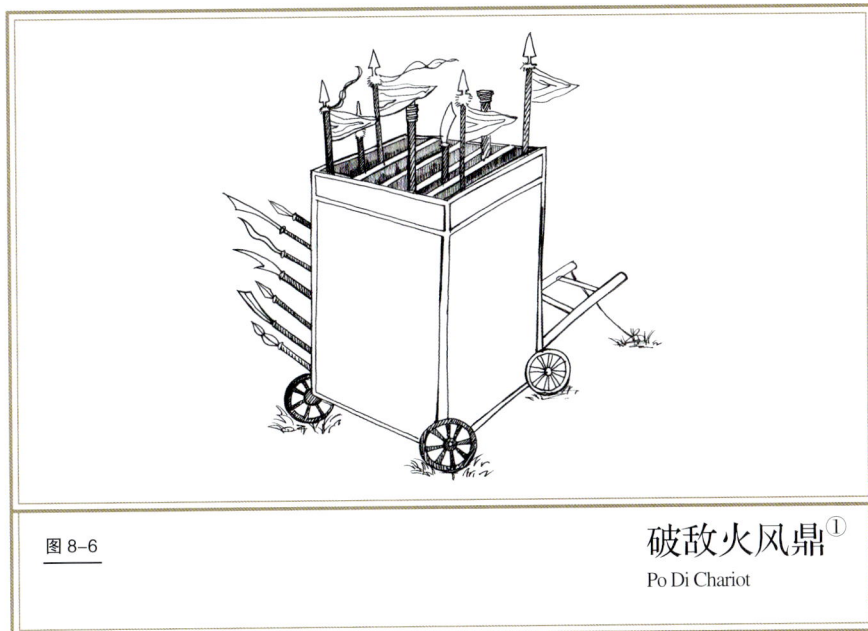

图 8-6

破敌火风鼎①
Po Di Chariot

---

① 破敌火风鼎：用大木制成方柜式车厢，内藏发射火药、火箭、鸟铳、飞弹等火器。每车编士兵 2 名，行军时推车前行；作战时，一人点火发射，一人准备装药。若多车排列阵前，一齐冲击，则敌军难以抵挡。

Po Di Chariot: This chariot was invented in Ming dynasty, made of wood, four-wheeled. There were projectile gunpowder, fire arrows, muskets, hand-thrown balls hidden in the square carriage. Two soldiers were arranged to take care of the chariot, who pushed the chariot in a march. But in war, one soldier loaded gunpowder and the other one ignited it. If many these chariots were arranged in formation to attack enemies, it was difficult to mount a defence against it.

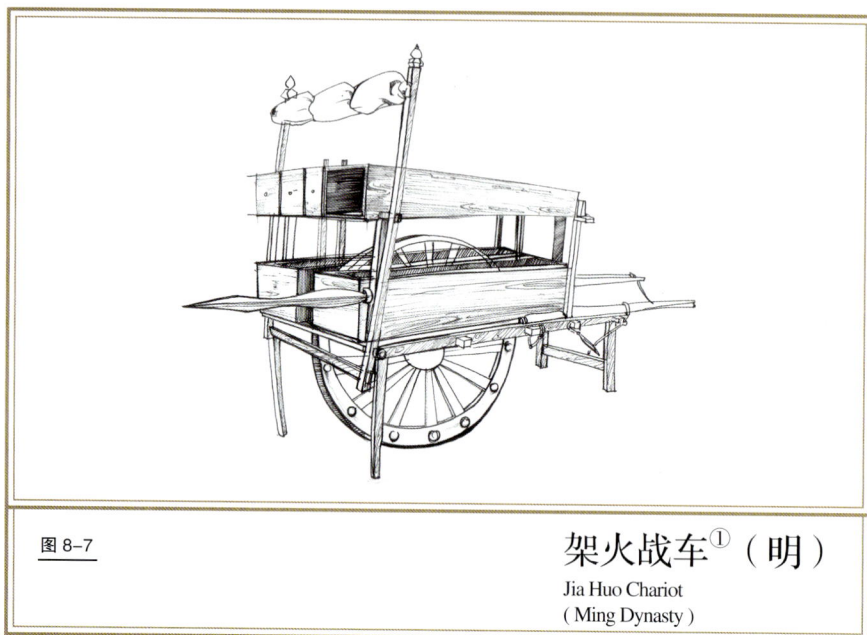

图8-7

架火战车[①]（明）
Jia Huo Chariot
（Ming Dynasty）

① 架火战车：明代装有火器的攻防两用战车，木质车身，以生牛皮和木板围护，车上装载火铳、火箭等火器，还安有刀、枪等冷兵器。冲锋时，用它来轰击或冲击敌阵；宿营或防御时，将它围在四周，成为阻挡敌人的障碍。

Jia Huo Chariot: This chariot was invented in the Ming dynasty, equipped with firearms, both for attack and defence. It was made of wood, covered with boards and ox hides. It was loaded with firearms, like fire lance and fire arrows, and personal weapons, like spears and axes. These weapons could be used bomb enemies during a charge. They could be arranged to block an enemies' attack in defense.

第 **3** 节

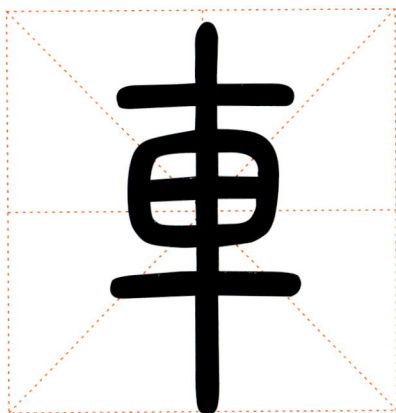

纵火战车

　　这类战车有火龙卷地飞车、铁汁神车、盛油引火车、行炉和扬风车等。它们是在一辆两轮或四轮车上装备各种燃烧性火药，或在锅内盛满烧沸的油和烧熔的铁汁，作战时，把它们迅速推到敌阵纵火，并用扬风车扇风催火，帮助燃烧。

　　火龙卷地飞车：兽形喷火战车，木质两轮，立有猛兽像，内藏火器24件，两旁设盾牌，车前有利刃，上有毒药。每车4人，轮流推车。作战时士兵推车冲进，并点火器药信，于是神火、毒火、法火、飞火、烈火从兽口喷出，毒杀敌军人马。

　　铁汁神车：中国古代创制的一种用于守城的战车。车身用坚木制造，下安四轮；车上安有一个冶铁炉，内熔铁汁；壁上开一孔，从孔中通出一个特制的竹槽，槽面涂泥浆，烤晒极干，不怕铁汁将其熔化。当敌军前来攻城时，即推车至城上，将铁汁从槽中倾注于城下，焦化和熔毁攻城器械。

图 8-8

火龙卷地飞车
Huolong Juandi Fei Chariot

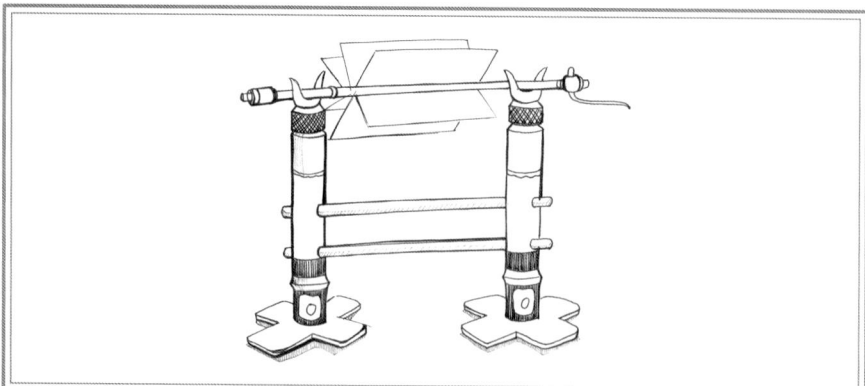

图 8-9

扬风车①
Yang Feng Chariot

---

① 扬风车：由架子、扇叶、手柄等部件组成，用人力转动风扇，扇风催火。

Yang Feng Chariot: It was known in English as the Wind Blowing Chariot, and was composed of a frame, fans, and a handle. The fans were propelled by human power to create a wind to enhance combustion.

图 8-10

铁汁神车①
Tiezhi Shen Chariot

---

① 铁汁神车：守城车具，上载冶炉，熔有铁汁，敌来攻城，则倾汁城下。

Tiezhi Shen Chariet: It was known in English as the Melting Iron Magic Chariot, invented to defend cities from a siege. Made of hard wood, the four-wheeled chariots were installed with a furnace, which heated a pot contained melting iron. There was a hole on the surface of the pot, connected with a specially-made bamboo tube. The tube was covered with mud which acted as insulation to the melting iron. When enemies besieged a city, this chariot was pushed onto the city wall. The melting iron was poured down to destroy the enemy's siege engines and kill attacking warriors.

第 **4** 节

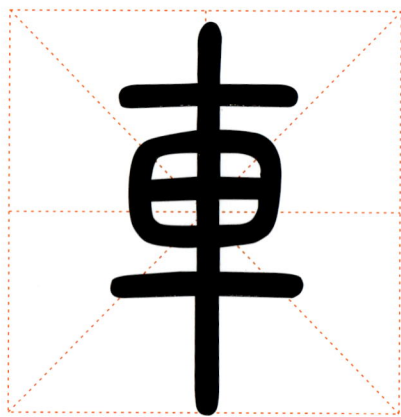

火箭战车

这类战车有冲虏藏轮车、火柜攻敌车等。它们是在独轮或两轮车上安置一个或几个大火箭筒,内装 40~100 支箭,用木柜或前挡板做屏障,以防敌军射来的矢石。作战时,士兵推车接敌,点燃火筋的火捻,使众箭齐飞,大量射杀敌军。戚继光在蓟镇练兵时编练的一个车营中,就有四辆火箭战车。

火柜攻敌车:冲击型战车。车厢长方形,两轮,轮高 2 尺 5 寸;辕长 1 丈,柜宽 2.8 尺,高 2 尺;车厢下架 5 杆尖枪,上有火箭 100 支,顶有油毡。战时由两名士兵点燃引信,百箭齐发,冲入敌阵,近战刺敌。

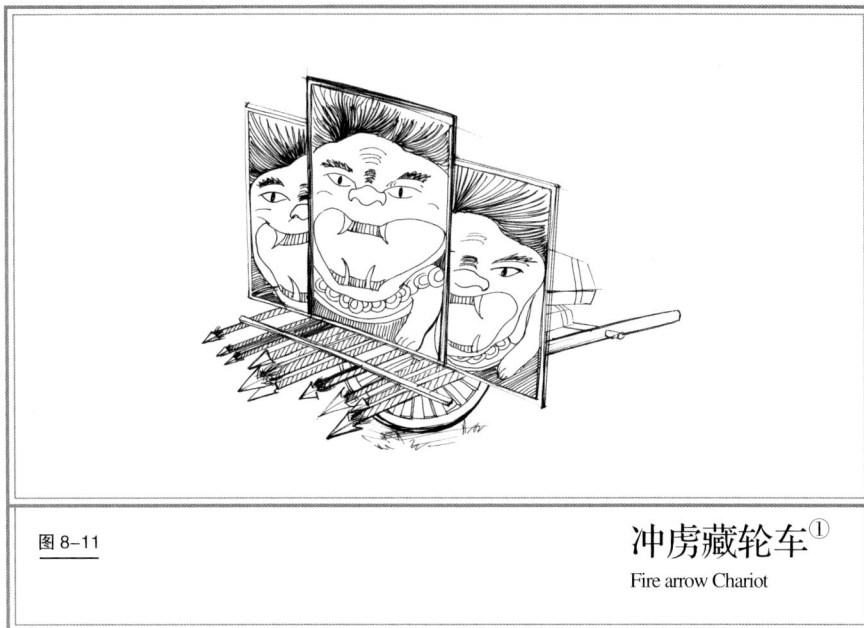

图 8-11

冲虏藏轮车①
Fire arrow Chariot

---

① 冲虏藏轮车：轻型战车。车辕长7尺，前安大盾，高5尺，面画猛兽，张大口；前辕2
层，架刀枪8杆，车厢中放有火箭匣，内有火箭40支，用士兵2人轮流推动射箭。
Fire arrow Chariot: It is a light chariot, with a shaft, about 2.33 m in length. The chariot was installed
with a big shield, about 1.67 m in height, painted with a ferocious animal, open-mouthed. Eight spears
were fixed on the shaft. There was a arrow case with 40 fire arrows inside in the cabinet. Two soldiers
pushed the chariot in turn to launch the arrows by means of a mechanical force.

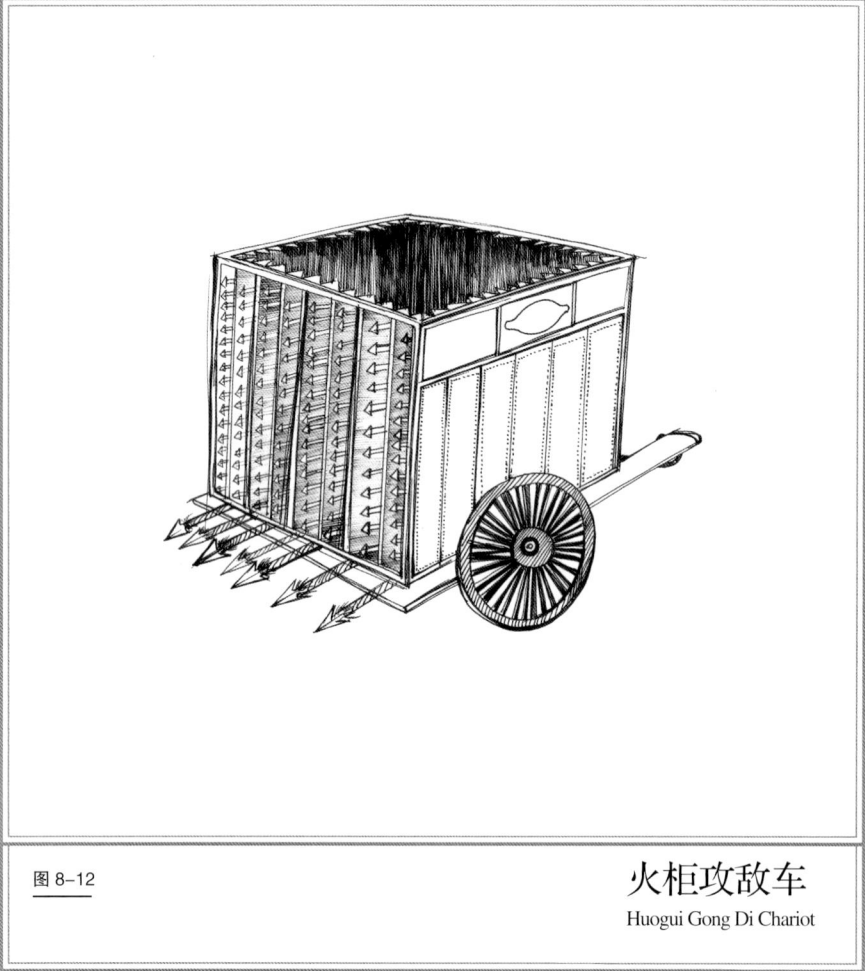

图 8-12

火柜攻敌车
Huogui Gong Di Chariot

第 **5** 节

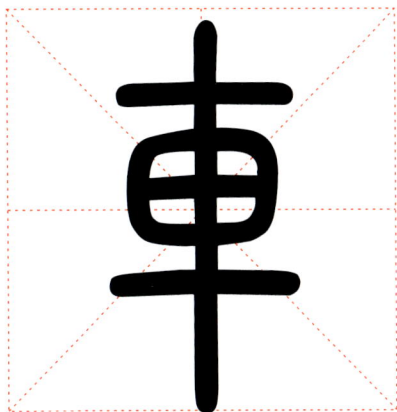

炮车

这类战车最多。明代后期的大型火炮都已安在车上，在戚继光编练的车营中，每营就有 128 辆炮车，载运 256 门佛朗机炮。其他如攻戎炮、千子雷炮、叶公神铳、灭虏炮、将军炮等，都由炮车载运。这类炮车把车的机动性和火炮的摧毁威力合二为一，提高了火炮的机动性、参战速度和毁杀威力。

图 8-13

攻戎炮[①]
Gong Rong Pao

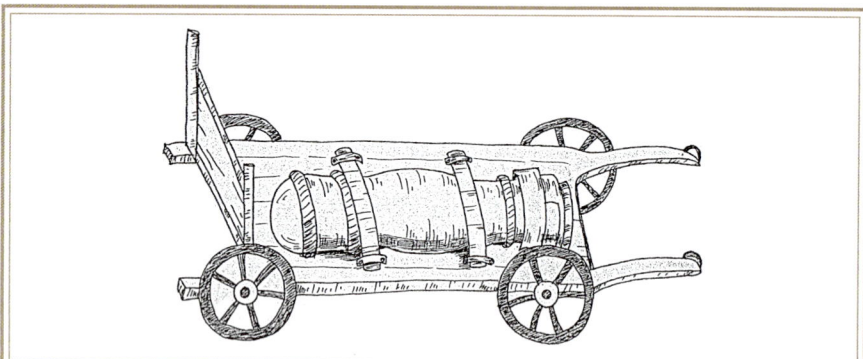

图 8-14

千子雷炮[②]
Qianzi Pao

[①] 攻戎炮：车载炮，下安两轮，上置车厢，炮身嵌安其中，加数道铁箍固定，车厢两侧各有铁锚2个。用时铁锚置地，用土压实，以减后坐力。用骡马拖曳，可随军机动。

Gong Rong Pao: It was known in English as the Attacking Nomadic Tribes Cannon, carried by a two-wheeled cart. A cabinet was installed on the cart, in which the cannon was mounted. The cannon was reinforced with several iron rings. There were two iron anchors on the two sides of the cabinet respectively. Before firing, the four iron anchors were tightly fastened to the ground to reduce recoil. The cart was pulled by mules or horses.

[②] 千子雷炮：车载炮，身用铜铸，口径5寸，管长1尺8寸，内装火药6成，后装细土2成，再装填铅弹二三升。炮身用铁箍固定于四轮车上，前有隔板，抵近敌军撤板而射。

Qianzi Pao: It was known in English as the Thousand Pellets Cannon, carried by a cart. The cannon was made of bronze, about 16.667 cm in muzzle bore diameter, 60 cm in length. The barrel was in-loaded with gunpowder, sand and lead pellets. The cannon was fastened on the four-wheeled cart by four iron rings. When soldiers pushed the cart near the enemy, a protective shield board was removed to shoot the cannon.

第6节

车

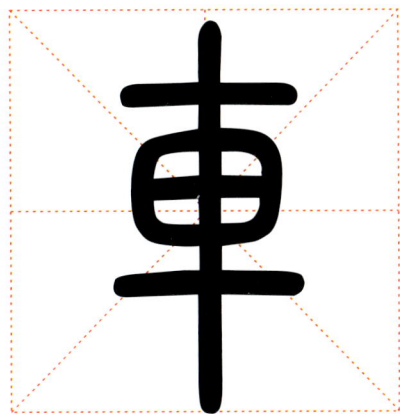

轻便火器战车

这类战车轻便灵活，如独轮屏风车，车前放置一个高于人体的屏板，两侧内折九十度角，使人体的三面受到保护；屏板上开有射孔，可对敌发射火箭和枪弹。每车编士兵三名，备干粮若干，供士兵食用。屏风车既可单车作战，也可多车并列射敌，并可在驻营时排列成临时军营的挡墙。

图 8-15

明代屏风车
Firearm Chariot with Screens in Ming Dynasty

第 **7** 节

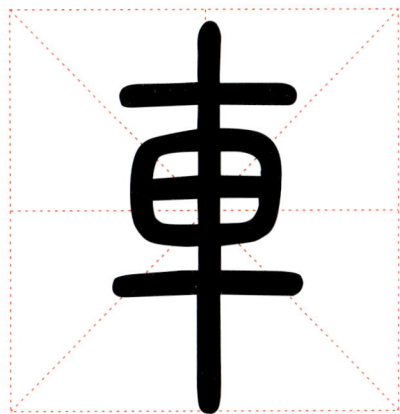

运输车

战争中还有一些运输车，如正厢车、偏厢车、联络战车、运干粮车、木牛流马等。

正厢车是指车体两侧都安厢板的战车。车下安两轮，车座上正面竖有较高的挡板，两侧都安有厢板，车上备有火铳、刀矛等兵器。

偏厢车是一种火器战车，双轮，车长1丈5尺，两头有辕都可以驾骡拉拽。车上或左或右一侧装有防护板，两头靠车辕处为可以开闭的活门，板上开有射孔。

木牛流马，为三国时期蜀汉丞相诸葛亮与妻子黄月英一同发明的运输工具，分为木牛与流马，建兴九年至十二年（231—234）诸葛亮在北伐时所使用，其载重量为"一岁粮"，大约400斤以上，每日行程为"特行者数十里，群行者二十里"，为蜀国十万大军提供粮食。另外，还有机关防止敌人夺取后使用。不过，确实的方式、样貌现在已不明，不同的人对其亦有不同的解释。

图 8-16

正厢车①
Zheng Xiang Che

图 8-17

偏厢车②
Pian Xiang Che

① 正厢车：出现于明代，传说为俞大猷所创，总体上利于进攻。车身两侧装有护板，平时用两头骡子拉动，战时靠车兵人力推进至发射阵地。车上装有火炮，每辆战车车兵定额24人，有佛朗机手、鸟铳手、火箭手、藤牌手等。作战时以战车为依托施放火器；扎营时将战车围绕营盘一圈，首尾相连，护卫营盘。因此，这种车兵实际上具有一定的炮兵性质。

Zheng Xiang Che: This cart was invented by Yu Dayou, a Chinese general and martial artist best known for countering the Japanese pirates along China's southeastern coast during the reign of the Jiajing Emperor in the Ming dynasty. It was suitable for attacking. This cart had two side boards. Usually, it was pulled by a mule. In the war, it was pushed to the battle field by soldiers. The cart was loaded with a cannon, fire lances, spears and allocated with 24 soldiers, such as musketeers, archers. Many carts could be parked head to tail, serving as a wall to protect the camp.

② 偏厢车：传说为戚继光所创，车身仅一侧有厢板，故称偏厢车；装备有各种火器，打仗时厢板在临敌一侧，具备相当的防守功能。

Pian Xiang Che: It is said that this cart was invented by General Qi Jiguang. There was a side board at either side. This cart was equipped with a variety of firearms.

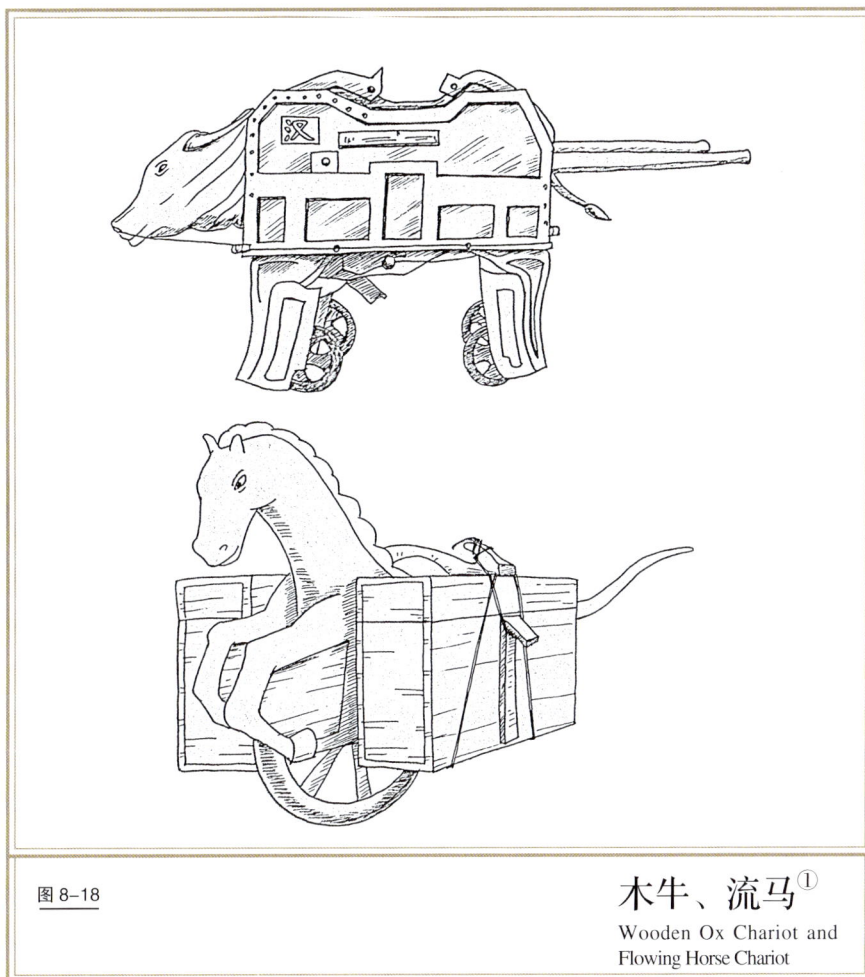

图 8-18

木牛、流马①
Wooden Ox Chariot and
Flowing Horse Chariot

① 木牛、流马：由于没有任何实物与图形存留于世，故众说纷纭。一种说法为诸葛亮改进了汉代的独轮小车——鹿车，改进后的独轮车被称为木牛、流马；一种说法认为木牛、流马是四轮车和独轮车；还有一种说法认为木牛、流马是新颖的自动机械。

Wooden Ox Chariot and Flowing Horse Chariot: It was created by Zhuge Liang. It was a thought to be either a mechanical, walking replica of an ox whose main purpose was to carry supplies such as grain to an army that was running low on supplies, or a sort of wheelbarrow that had 2 booms on which it was pulled (this was later reversed with the "gliding horse"). The correct English name should be "wooden galloper with a free-standing cargo box" since said device walks in a gallop form. It was equipped with two handles to make it walk by manpower. The swing cargo box was used to store useless work caused by the up-and-down motion of the walking machine. When the cargo box swung forward, the walking machine steps forward at the same time to raise efficiency.

第8节

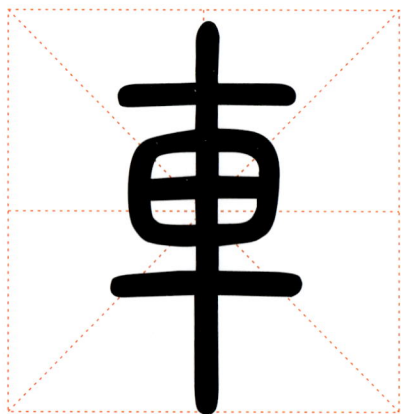

指南车

　　指南车是古代一种指示方向的车辆，也是古代帝王出门时作为仪仗的车辆之一，以显示皇权的尊崇。相传早在5000年前的黄帝时代就已经发明了指南车，当时黄帝曾凭借它在大雾弥漫的战场上指示方向，战胜了蚩尤。西周初期，南方的越棠氏使臣因回国迷路，周公就用指南车护送越棠氏使臣回国。三国时马钧所造的指南车除用齿轮传动外，还有自动离合装置，利用齿轮传动系统和离合装置来指示方向，在特定条件下，车子转向时木人手臂仍指南，在技术上又胜记里鼓车一筹。

　　指南车起源很早，历代曾几度重制，但均未留下资料，直至宋代才有完整的资料。

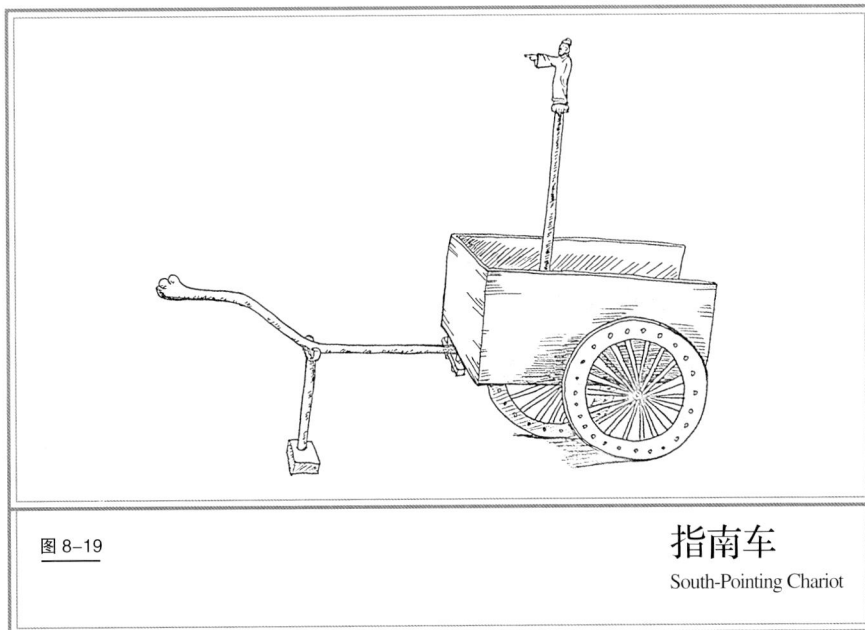

图 8-19

指南车
South-Pointing Chariot

第9节

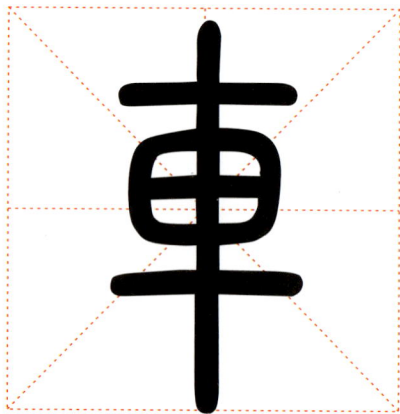

记里鼓车

　　记里鼓车是中国古代用于计算道路里程的车，又有"记里车"、"司里车"、"大章车"等别名。从三国开始，出现了很多对记里鼓车的记载，如《古今注》《晋书·舆服志》《宋书·礼志》《西京杂记》《旧唐书·穆宗本纪》等。据宋内侍省吴德仁记载，记里鼓车由两个车轮和六个齿轮组合的一套减速齿轮系构成，齿轮与车轮同时转动，其最后一根轴在车行一里或十里时才回转一圈，再经过传动机构，令木人击鼓击镯以计所行里程。

图 8-20

记里鼓车
Ji Li Gu Chariot

第 **10** 节

战船

商末周武王伐纣时，已经使用船只运送军队和战具渡过黄河去作战。到春秋时期，吴、楚、越三国争霸于长江流域，经常用船只运载军队进行水战。据《左传》记载，鲁襄公二十四年（前549），"楚子为舟师以伐吴"，这是关于水军和专为水战而建造船只的最早文献记载。随着水战的发展，各种用途的战船不断涌现。公元前6世纪末，伍子胥（？—前484）在吴国训练水军时，把大中小各型战船按作战用途分成大翼、小翼、突冒、楼船、桥船等，并以战车做比喻，说大翼相当于重车，小翼相当于轻车，突冒相当于冲车，楼船相当于行楼车（指挥车），桥船相当于轻足骠骑（据《越绝书》）。这些战船在水战中相互配合，发挥综合战斗作用。同时期的越国和秦国也建造了各型战船。

汉朝水军的规模更加巨大，战船更趋完备。南北朝时，人们认识到水战时风力大小无常，不可恃以作战，因而重视发展人力推进的战船，出现多桨快艇。到了宋朝，车船在战争中有很大发展，都料匠高宣所制巨型作战车船长 20~30 丈（合 60~90 米），有 23~24 个车轮桨。在其所制的十几种车船中，双车船和四车船是常用的中小型作战车船。

从秦汉到明代，战船的发展有以下几个特点：首先是水军战船数量多，舰队规模大。其次是大型主力战舰屡有创新，战船分类越来越科学，使战船将士既能明确自己的职责，又利于协同作战。再次是兵器装备逐渐更新。早期战船只装备刀、矛、弓、剑、戈；秦汉时期增加了弩；东晋（一说隋代）的战船已经安有拍杆；宋代的战船开始配备火球、火药箭、火枪，水军也进入冷兵器和火器并用的时期；元末明初的战船上开始装备金属管形射击火器——火铳。嘉靖年间，戚继光所编水军营的大型福船、中型海沧船、小型苍山船，都增加了大发贡（一种大型火炮，"贡"也作"熕"）、佛朗机炮、鸟铳等火绳枪炮，加上火箭、火砖、喷筒等火器，战船上使用火器的士兵已占编制总数的一半左右；同时，还创造了子母舟、连环舟、火龙船、赤龙舟等各种专门装备火器用于火攻的小型战船。此外，新创制的水雷和古代二级火箭——"火龙出水"已在水战中使用。

进入明清时期，中国古代战船的发展有两个显著的特点：一是隋唐五代两宋时期多用于锤击敌船的拍杆已经消失，而改以战船本身犁沉敌船，这说明船舶制造和驾驶技术的进步；二是从明初起，战船上配备了火炮。

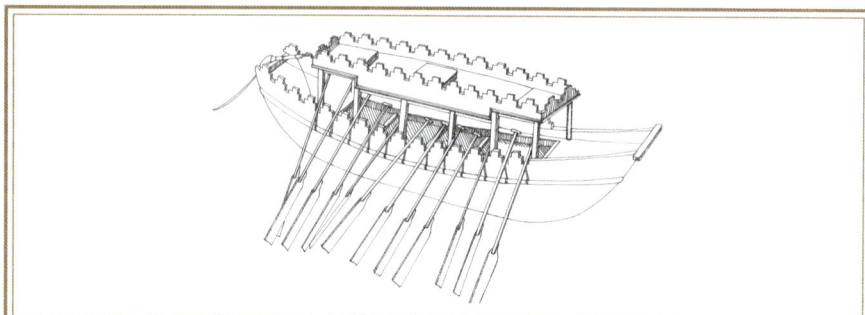

图 8-21　　　　　　　　　　**"大翼"战船**①（春秋时期）
Big-Size Warship
(The Spring and Autumn Period)

图 8-22　　　　　　　　　　**楼船**②（春秋晚期）
Lou Warship
(The Spring and Autumn Period)

---

①　"大翼"战船：最早出现于春秋时代的吴国，中国最早的战船，也是春秋时代体积最大的战船。它与中翼、小翼配合使用，能在水战中产生大中小型战船综合杀敌的作用，对后世水师船队采用大中小型战船按比例混合编配产生了重要影响。

Big-Size Warship: These warships were invented in the State of Wu in the Spring and Autumn Period, which were the earliest and biggest warships in China at that time. They were used with medium-sized and small-sized warships, which had an impact on the later arrangement in navy.

②　楼船：中国古代的一种巨型战船，最早出现于春秋晚期，因船上建有重楼而得名。这种船装备有大型战具，并可装载士卒千余人。在水战中，楼船远发炮石、弓弩，近以拍杆对敌，甚至可凭借自身重力使敌船倾覆。

Lou Warship: It is known as the Tower Ship in English, a kind of giant warships invented in the Spring and Autumn Period. These ships had three decks equipped with towers for the fighting lines, hence the name. They were equipped with heavy weapons and could accommodate more than 1,000 soldiers. In naval wars, crossbows and trebuchets were used for ranged combat.

图 8-23

车轮舸①（南北朝时期）

Che Lun Warship
(The Northern and Southern Dynasty)

图 8-24

苍山船②

Cang Shan Warship

---

① 车轮舸：又名“车船”，早在南北朝已有车船的记载。船舷两侧装有带叶片的转轮，中以转轴相连，轴上装踏板，水手用力踩踏，转轮转动，叶片击水推进。在船舶的推进主要仰仗风力和人力的时代，通过车轮转动原理加速船只前进的设计是一种新的尝试。

Che Lun Warship: It was known as the Wheel Warship in English, also called Paddle-Wheel Driven Warship. The first use of a paddle-wheel ship is in the Northern and Southern Dynasty. Both sides of these ships were installed with paddle wheels, which were linked by hinges. When sailors paddled, the wheels rotates in the water, which propelled the ships forwards. In the times when people took use of wind, the invention of paddle-wheel ships was a new trial.

② 苍山船：船身长七丈，艋梢长八尺五寸，舱深七尺五寸，底板厚二寸五分。分为三层：下层装填压船用的土石，中层供兵士寝息，上层为战斗场所。

Cang Shan Warship: These ships were 26.67 meters in length, 2. 5 meters in depth, which was divided into upper, middle and lower layers. The lower lay was loaded with stones and sand to stabilize the ship, the middle layer to accommodate soldiers and the upper layer for fighting.

图 8-25

沙船① (唐)
Sha Warship
(Tang Dynasty)

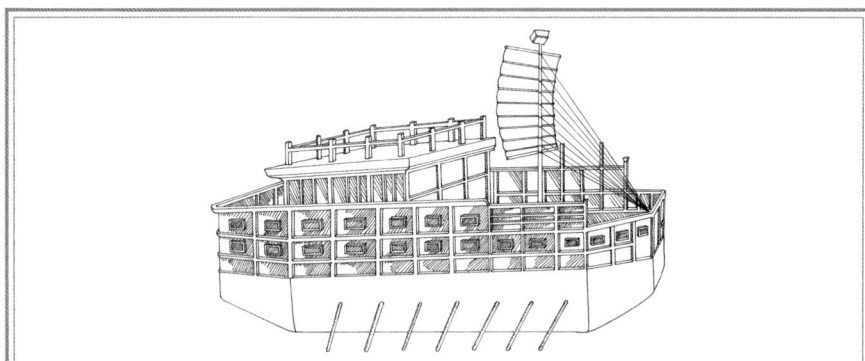

图 8-26

斗舰② (唐)
Dou Jian
(Tang Dynasty)

---

① 沙船：中国古代近海运输的海船中的一种优秀船型，也叫"防沙平底船"，是中国"四大古船"之一，因其适于在水浅多沙滩的航道上航行，所以被命名为沙船。在唐宋时期，它已经成型，成为我国北方海区航行的主要海船。

Sha Warship: It was known as the Sand Ship in English, suitable for near sea transportation, also called "Sandproof Flat Bottom Ship". The ships were commonly used in the shallow waters.

② 斗舰：一种双层的中型战船，出现于唐代，是古代水上作战的主要舰艇，其尺寸比艨艟稍大些。舰舷两侧设有垛墙，可以使士兵躲在墙后向敌舰发射箭石。垛墙下开有孔穴，便于士兵操桨行船。

Dou Jian: It was known as the Battlement Ship in English, a double-decked medium warship. It was invented in Tang Dynasty. On both sides of the warship, battlements were built for soldiers to hide behind while shooting arrows and throwing stones.

图 8-27

艨艟^①（宋）

Meng Chong

(Song Dynasty)

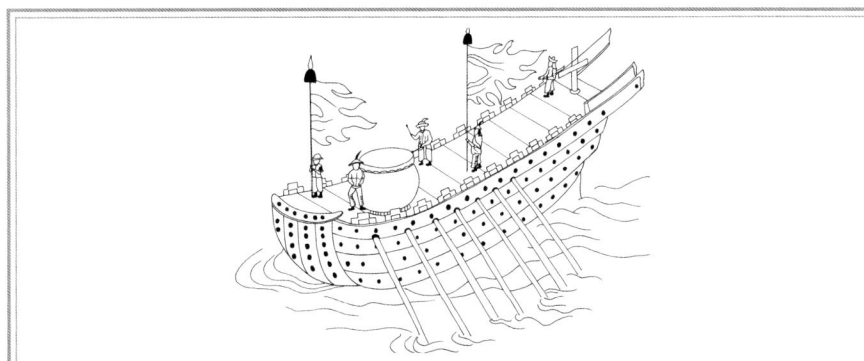

图 8-28

走舸^②（宋）

Zou Ge

(Song Dynasty)

---

① 艨艟：也叫"蒙冲"，是中国古代一种以速度著称的轻型战船，因为船背上蒙着生牛皮，可冲击近处的敌船而得名。艨艟以生牛皮蒙背，利于乘风破浪，具有良好的防御性能。

Meng Chong: It was known as the Covered Swooper in English, a kind of light warships in China. These are ships which have their backs roofed over and (armored with) a covering of buffalo hide. This arrangement was not adopted for large vessels because higher speed and mobility were preferable, in order to be able to swoop suddenly on the unprepared enemy.

② 走舸：一种轻便的快船，结构较为简单，船上桨手多、兵卒少，故能灵活机动、往返如飞。走舸上兵卒虽少，但都是精锐勇猛之人，可乘敌不备突袭敌船，斩将夺旗。

Zou Ge: It was known as the Quick Boat in English, whose structure was very simple. There were more sailors but less soldiers on board, so it could move swiftly. Although soldiers were limited on board, they were brave and aggressive, and could attack enemies unexpectedly.

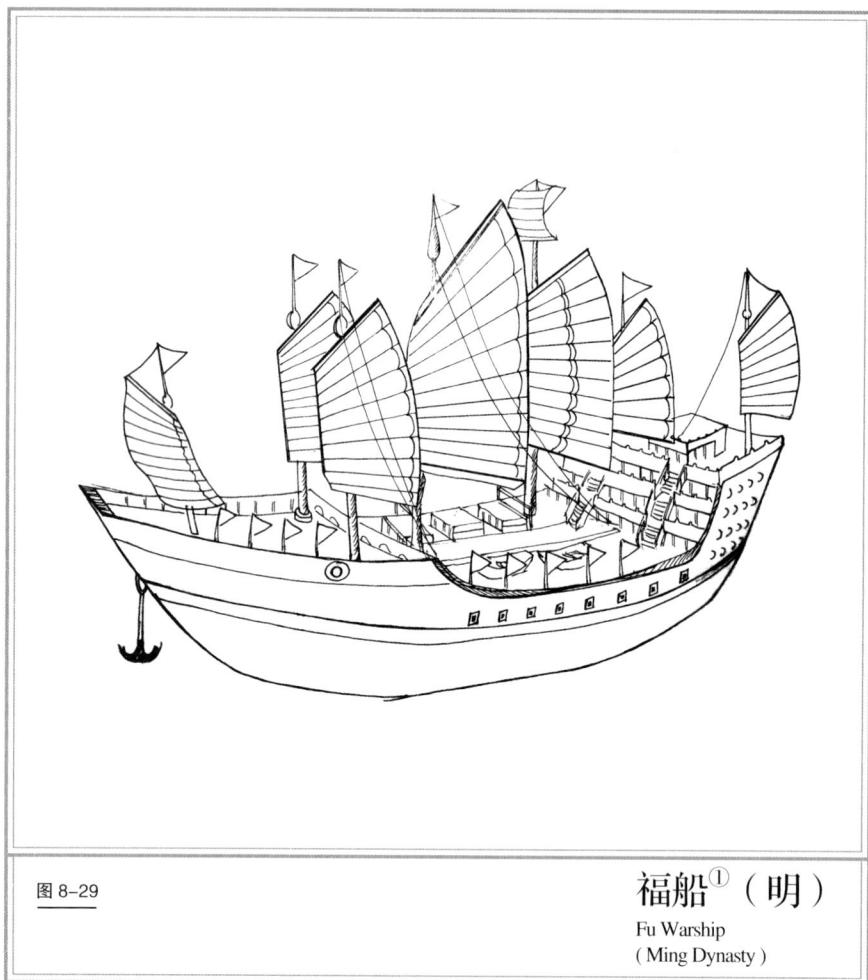

图 8-29

福船[①] （明）
Fu Warship
(Ming Dynasty)

---

① 福船：福船高大如楼，可容百人。共有四层，下层装压舱石；第三层放置淡水柜；第二层为士兵居住的地方；最上一层为露台，需从第三层的梯爬上，两旁用板翼做栏，人靠在上面作战，矢石火炮皆俯瞰而发，实为海战利器。

Fu Warship: These ships were as high as towers, and could accommodate 100 people. The cabin was composed of four layers. The lowest layer was loaded with stones and sand to stabilize the ship. The fresh water was put in the third layer. The second layer was used to accommodate soldiers. The upper layer served as platform for soldiers to fight on. Soldiers threw stones or shot arrows, fire lances from above, which increased the combat effectiveness.

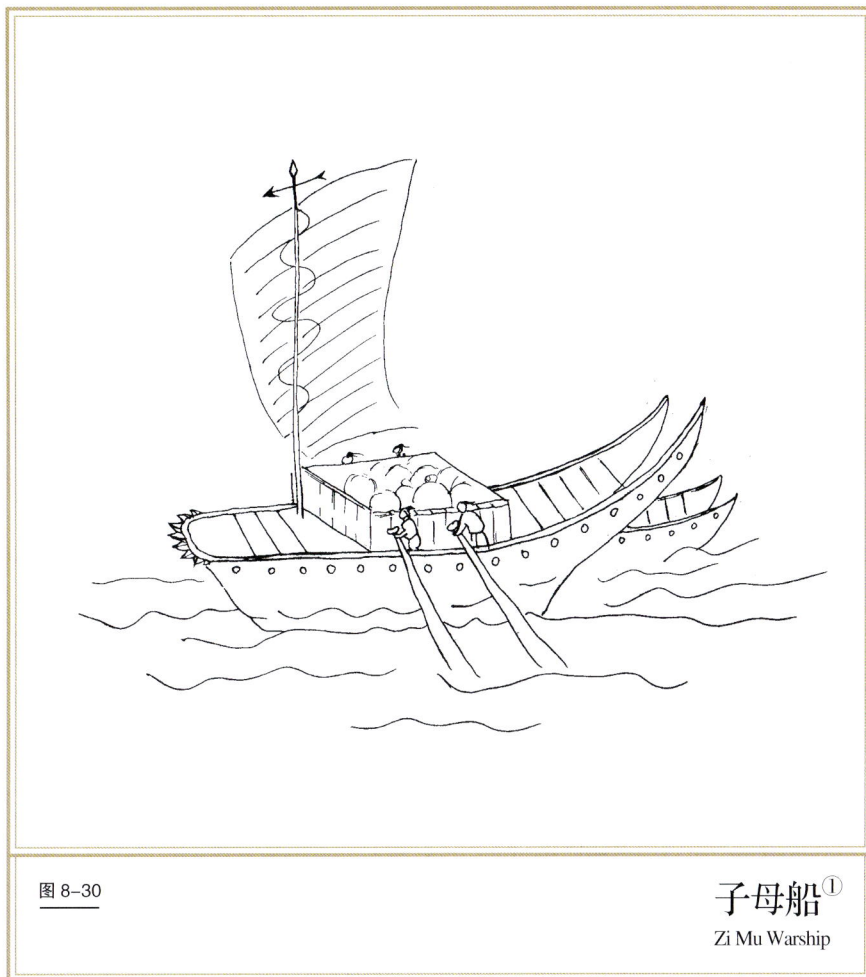

图 8-30

子母船①
Zi Mu Warship

---

① 子母船：母船长三丈五，前两丈，后一丈五，只有两边舷板，内空；有一小船，上有盖板，有四桨可划，用绳索与母船绑；母船有柴火猛油、火药火线。战时母船迅速抵近敌船，钉在一起，点燃母船后人乘子船而返。

Zi Mu Warship: It was known as the Mother-and-Son Ship. The carrier, the Mother Ship, was 11.67 meters in length, two sides of which were tied with the Son Ships. The Mother Ship was loaded with gunpowder, oil and firewood while the two Son Ships had paddles. In wars, the Mother Ship approached enemy ship quickly. After the Mother Ship was ignited, soldiers took to the Son Ship to escape.

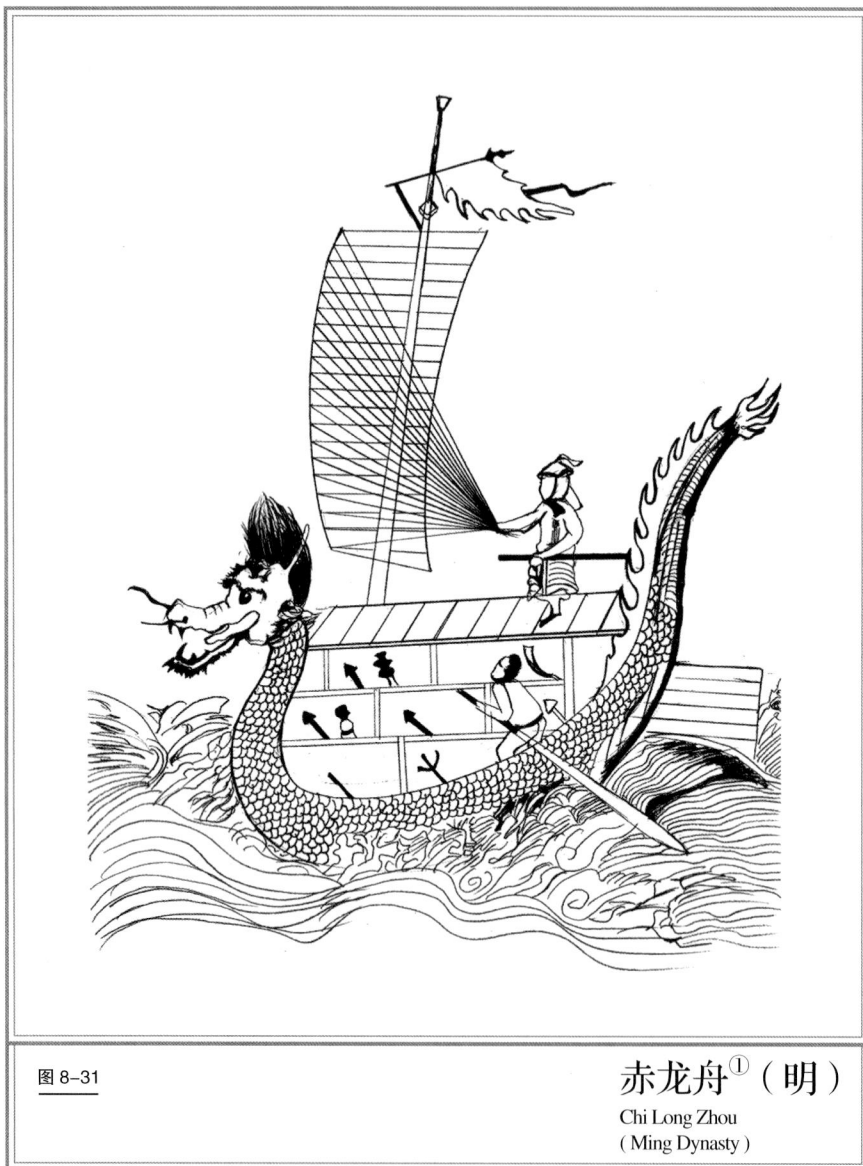

图 8-31

赤龙舟[1]（明）
Chi Long Zhou
(Ming Dynasty)

---

[1] 赤龙舟：《武备志》中对赤龙舟的描述："舟形像龙，分作三层，内藏器械火具。盖头做成龙首，口开，容兵一人，窥贼动确为最上。"

Chi Long Zhou: It was known as the Red Dragon Boat in English. Historical records mentioned this boat，"The boat takes the shape of a dragon, three layered, loaded with firearms. The mouth of the dragon was open to accommodate a soldier to keep watch on enemies."

攻守城器械

攻守城作战是中国古代战争的重要形式。城市是国家的政治、经济、文化中心，是国家各级政权所在地，有些城市还在战争中有着重要的战略地位，故城市的得失，特别是重要城市的得失，常常关系到战争胜败以至国家存亡。在中国古代频繁的攻城和守城作战中，除使用常规兵器外，还创制了一批专门用于攻城和守城的兵器，形成了冷兵器中的一个系列——攻守城器械。古代筑城体系到宋代已日趋完善，并形成了多层次、立体设防的筑城。城池防御体系的完善和城战的发展，促进了攻守城器械的发展。北宋时已经形成了比较完整的攻守城器械系列。

在攻守城战中，双方都要综合使用各

种兵器和器械，才能夺取胜利。在通常情况下，攻城部队携带各种攻城器械蜂拥而来，在距城数十丈处围城驻营，迅速架设远距离攻击器械，摧击城防设施；架设望楼、巢车，侦察瞭望城内军情；准备铺架壕桥，让部队通过护城河。守城部队在早已构筑坚固、设防充分的城防体系中，以羊马墙为第一道防线，利用反击式器械，摧击攻城部队的人马和器械，击砸敌军设置的抛石机、床弩阵地和望楼、巢车；同时抽起吊桥，阻止敌军通过护城河，消减攻城敌军的兵力。如果第一道防线没有守住，那么攻城部队就可能迅速铺架壕桥，让士兵和攻城器械通过壕桥，向城墙靠近。守城部队则以瓮城和城墙为第二道防线，利用弓弩和抛石机向攻城敌军发射箭镞、石弹，击砸敌军人马，摧毁敌军各种攻城器械；同时以重兵坚守城门，并利用地听侦听敌军是否在挖掘地道，以做好反击准备。如果守城部队未能阻止敌军接近城墙，则攻城部队便在轒辒（fén wēn）车和各种活动掩体遮挡下挖掘城基、钻凿城壁，利用撞木撞击城门，架设各种云梯攀登城墙，利用吕公车和对楼车等高层攻城车塔直接登城，选择要点挖掘地道攻入城内。守城部队在此紧急情况下，便从城上推出托杆、抵篙，托阻云梯、对楼车，使其不得贴附城墙；向城下击砸滚木礌石、喷浇烈焰铁汁，杀伤攻城士兵，烧毁攻城器械；通过竖井向地道内簸扇烟焰，熏灼从地道内攻入的敌军。如果守城部队坚守无效，又无救援部队，那么攻城者便能攻占坚城；如果守城者反击得力，又有救援部队从外围赶来，对攻城部队形成内外夹击之势，那么攻城者便会撤围而去，弄不好还有全军被歼的危险。

古代利用各种攻守城器械进行攻守城战的精彩战例甚多，其中尤以蜀魏攻守陈仓之战、东西魏攻守玉璧之战、蒙金攻守居庸关之战、常遇春攻取衢州之战最为脍炙人口。

蜀魏攻守陈仓（今陕西宝鸡东）之战，发生于蜀汉建兴六年（228）。是年十二月，诸葛亮得知魏军主力在石亭（今安徽潜山东北）败于东吴大将陆逊，陈仓守军仅有数千人的消息后，即率数万人复出祁山（今甘肃礼县东），围攻陈仓。陈仓守将郝昭率部坚守。诸葛亮劝降不成，便用云梯攻城；郝昭命魏军用火箭齐射云梯，烧死攀梯攻城的蜀兵。诸葛亮又用冲车攻城，魏军用绳索扣系大如磨盘的巨石将冲车砸毁。蜀军再用高达百尺的临车攻城，魏军构筑双重女墙阻挡蜀军。诸葛亮又命蜀军挖地道攻城，魏军则在城内挖竖井击退蜀军。蜀军猛攻20多个昼夜，未能成功，诸葛亮被迫撤军。此战，攻城者虽猛，但守城者更坚，最终守住了城。

蒙金攻守居庸关之战发生于金至宁元年（1213）七月。其时，蒙军由野狐岭突入，克怀来（今属河北）、缙山（今北京延庆），直抵居庸关北口（今北京八达岭）。金军精锐据关坚守，冶铁封固关门，布铁蒺藜百余里。成吉思汗见金军守备坚固，只留少数兵力在古北口牵制金军，自率主力由林中间道迂回南下，袭取紫荆关（今河北易县西南），攻克涿州（今河北涿州市）；另派哲别率部从小道袭取南口；而后南北夹击，夺取居庸关。这是避实击虚攻克坚城的著名战例。

明代后期，由于枪炮等火器在攻守城战中的大量使用，上述许多笨重的攻守城器械便逐渐在战场上消失了。

第 **1** 节

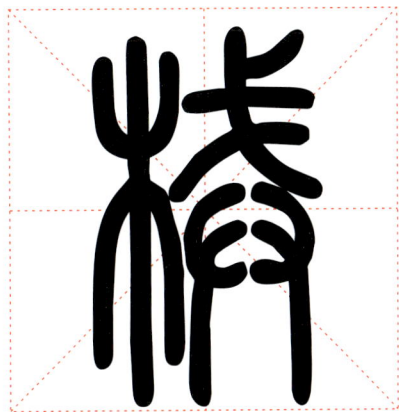

攻城器械

古代攻城器械虽然名目繁多，但是就其作用而言，可分为远距离攻击式、侦察瞭望式、接通式、遮挡式、抵近摧毁式、攀登式等六大类。

远距离攻击式器械有抛石机、床弩与火攻器具等。它们可以在较远的距离上抛射石块、发射箭镞、放纵带有火攻之物的火禽和火兽，杀伤守城士兵，摧毁和焚烧城防设施，为攻城士兵打开通路，在攻城战中发挥重要的作用。

侦察瞭望式攻城器械有巢车、楼车、望楼及望杆车。据唐朝杜佑《通典·兵典》记载，巢车是在一种底框安有八轮的车上竖立两根长竿，"竿上安辘轳，以绳挽板屋止竿首，以窥城中。板屋方四尺，高五尺，有十二孔，四方别布，车可进退，环城而行"。因高竿上吊悬的板屋"如鸟之巢"，故有其名。最早使用巢车的记载见于《左传·成公十六年》。是年，晋楚两军战于鄢陵（今河南鄢陵西北），楚共王与太宰伯州犁曾一起登上巢车观看晋军动向。楼车之名首见于《左传·宣公十五年》，其时，楚军曾强迫俘获的晋使解扬登上楼车，劝降被围的宋人。据晋杜预注称，楼车是"车上望橹"，巢车是"车上为橹"，"橹"就是"楼"。由此可见，在春秋战国时期，巢车和楼车实际上是同一类侦察瞭望器械的不同名称而已。

北宋庆历四年(1044)刊行的《武经总要》绘有巢车和楼车的图形，同时有文字说明，并将楼车称作"望楼车"，简称"望楼"。望楼是在一个长方形大木框下安置四轮，车上竖望竿，竿上置望楼，竿下装转轴，并以六条绳索分作三层，从六面将望竿固定，绳索底部用带环铁橛揳入地下。由此可见，宋代的望楼较巢车更为完备。

明人刘效祖在《四镇三关志》中记载了一种新型望杆车：车座下安四轮，车座前端挡板上有两支枪伸出车外；车座中央竖立一根大木柱，其上部用八根粗绳分扣于车座四角，用以固定。大木柱的顶部附近设有一个皮制的筒袋，可容一名士兵站立，士兵手执小旗，旗上有飘带。士兵在筒袋中可四向瞭望，观察敌情，并可挥动小旗向军中传递信号。这是迄今所见的第三种侦察瞭望器械。

接通式攻城器械有单面和双面壕桥车。攻城时，士兵将其推至城壕中，以车轮做架，支撑桥面，接通城壕的两岸，供攻城士兵和器械通过。桥长视壕阔而定，城壕过阔则加长桥面或将两座壕桥连接起来。

遮挡式攻城器械有大中小三种。大型的有木牛车、轒辒车、尖头木驴、狗脊洞子、牛皮洞子等。它们是在长方形的车座上建有长方形或山脊形木屋，外蒙牛皮，下安四轮，形同活动掩体。使用时，士兵将其推至城下，或者多车相连成地面通道，掩护士兵抵近城墙，进行攻城作战。中小型遮挡式器械有厚竹圈篷、半截船、木立牌、竹立牌、木幔、皮帘等，它们轻巧灵便，可掩护四五名士兵或单兵抵近城墙，进行攻城作战。

攀登式攻城器械有飞梯、蹑头飞梯、避檑木飞梯等轻便云梯，以及供多名士兵同时攀登的复合式车梯。单梯梯身狭窄，仅容单人鱼贯而上，士兵既要注意登梯，又要持械作战，容易失足坠地。车梯是车座与宽面梯组合的云梯，可供多名士兵同时攀登，增强了仰攻能力。车梯的样式很多，有行天桥、行女墙、翻梯云车、搭天桥等，它们的构造类似于现在飞机场上登机用的舷梯。

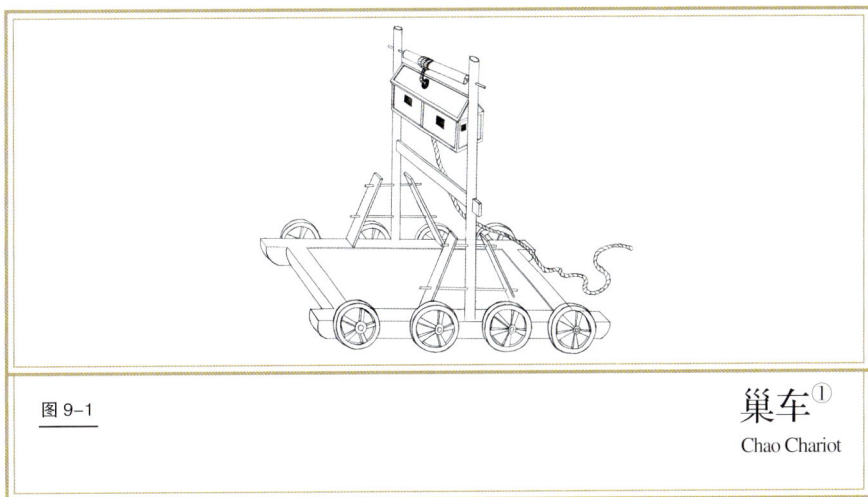

图 9-1

巢车①
Chao Chariot

---

① 巢车：一种专供观察敌情用的瞭望车。车下装有 8 个轮子，可以推动。车上竖立两根长柱，柱的长度以城的高低而定，柱的上端设一辘轳，用绳子把一小木板屋系在辘轳上。小板屋高 5 尺、方 4 尺，四面都有展望孔，外面蒙上生牛皮，以防敌人矢石破坏，屋里可容纳一两个人。人藏在屋里，用滑车升上去，就可以居高观察敌人的行动。在公元前 575 年，晋楚鄢陵之战时，楚共王就曾亲自登上巢车以望晋军。

Chao Chariot: It was known as the Nest Cart in English. It was a huge eight-wheeled cart mounted with two tall wooden poles. A small wooden house, about 1.67 m in length and 1.33 m in width, was attached between the poles, and it served as a belvedere. A pulley would pull the house up and down. The house, covered with ox hide, could contain two soldiers, and these soldiers would hide in this house to observe the situation inside the enemy city, hence this reconnoiter cart had to be taller than the walls of ancient Chinese cities.

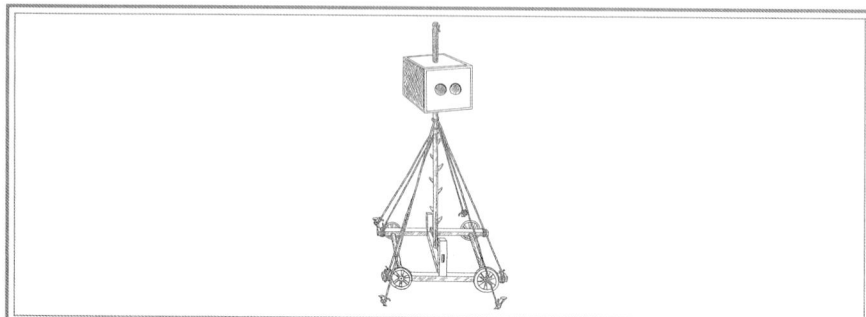

图 9-2 　望楼①
Wang Lou

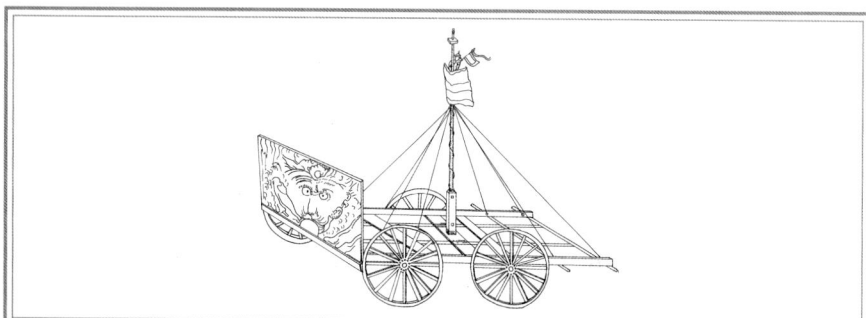

图 9-3 　望杆车②（明）
Wang Gan Chariot
（Ming Dynasty）

① 望楼：又名楼车，是用以登高观察敌情的车辆。根据《通典·兵典》的记载，其车体为木质，底部有四轮，可推动。车上竖望竿，竿由上向下设有很多脚踏板，可供哨兵上下攀登。竿上还系有六条绳索，绳索没有绕过望楼顶端，仅起加固作用，其下端以带环铁概揳入地下。竿顶设置望楼，楼下装转轴，可四面旋转观察。

Wang Lou: It was known as the Watch Tower in English, which was used to observe the situation inside the enemy city. It was a four-wheeled wooden cart mounted with a tall wooden pole. There were many rungs on the pole for soldiers to climb up and down. Six ropes, the ends of which were fixed on the ground, were tied to the pole to reinforce it. The wooden watch cabin, with a rotating bearing, was fixed on the upper part of the pole.

② 望杆车：明朝后期创制的一种新型随军瞭望车。车座较大，中竖大木杆，上设皮制望斗，士兵在其中瞭望敌情，车座前有挡板和外伸枪，起保护和冲击作用。

Wang Gan Chariot: Literally Watching Pole Cart in English, a new watchtower cart after the Ming Dynasty. It was a four-wheeled wooden cart mounted with a tall wooden pole. A small wooden house, covered with ox hide, was attached to the pole, and it served as a belvedere for soldiers to observe the situation inside the enemy city. A shield was fixed to protect the cart.

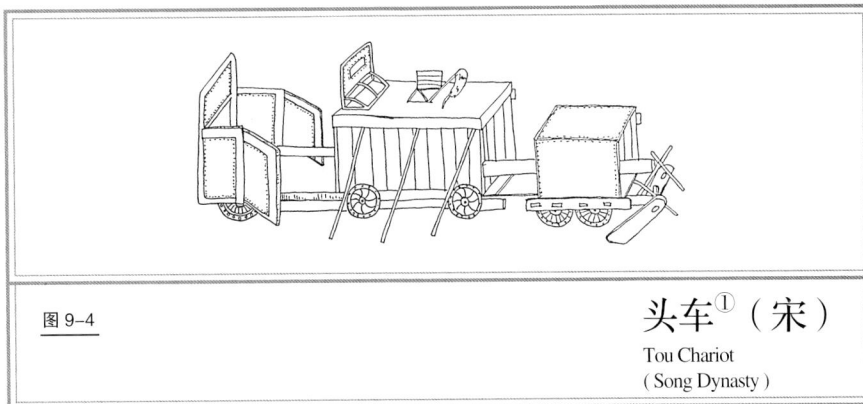

图 9-4

头车①（宋）
Tou Chariot
(Song Dynasty)

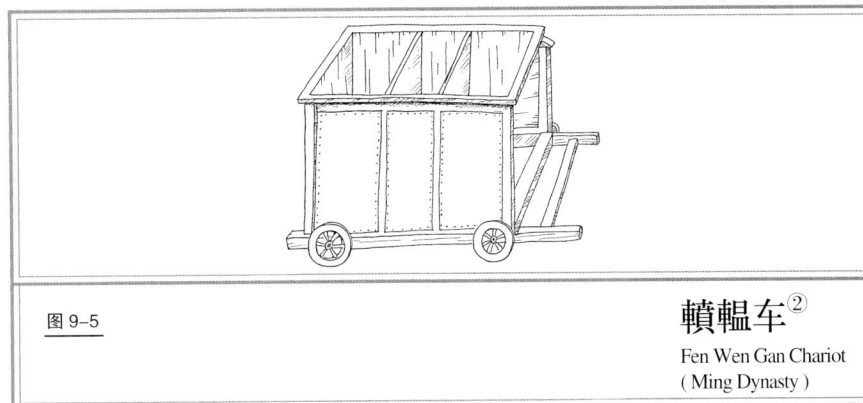

图 9-5

轒辒车②
Fen Wen Gan Chariot
(Ming Dynasty)

① 头车：一种专门用于挖掘地道的车辆，发明于宋代。头车的结构很复杂，共分为三个部分：屏风牌、头车及绪棚。屏风牌在车列的最前端，车前及两侧设有防护，等于是整组头车的出口。在出现敌情时，屏风牌和头车紧接，给攻城部队提供良好的防护。等到地道挖掘得差不多时，攻城部队会在车内集结；待地道挖通后，迅速地将屏风牌推开，部队就可鱼贯而出，进行攻击。

Tou Chariot: A specialized tunnel boring equipment, invented in Song Dynasty. This cart was complicated, composed of three parts. The front part served as shield to protect the middle and rear parts. The soldiers hid themselves in the middle part. The rear part served as tunnel boring.

② 轒辒车：轒辒车是用以掩护攻城人员抵近城池的攻城器械，早在春秋战国时代便已出现。唐代杜佑《通典·兵典》描述轒辒车是一种四轮车，用绳索作为上面的脊梁，以生牛皮蒙覆，下面容纳十个人，底部是空的，士兵可以在里头推车前进，在掘城墙、挖地道、运土填沟时免遭敌人矢石、纵火、檑木伤害。

Fen Wen Chariont: This cart was a city attacking equipment for covering soldiers to approach city walls, which was invented in the Spring and Autumn Period. According to historical record, "It is a four-wheeled cart, covered with ox hide. It can contain ten soldiers. The cabin is bottomless, and soldiers in it can push the cart forward. It can protect soldiers from being hurt by stones, arrows, logs from the top of city walls when soldiers are digging tunnels or approaching cities.

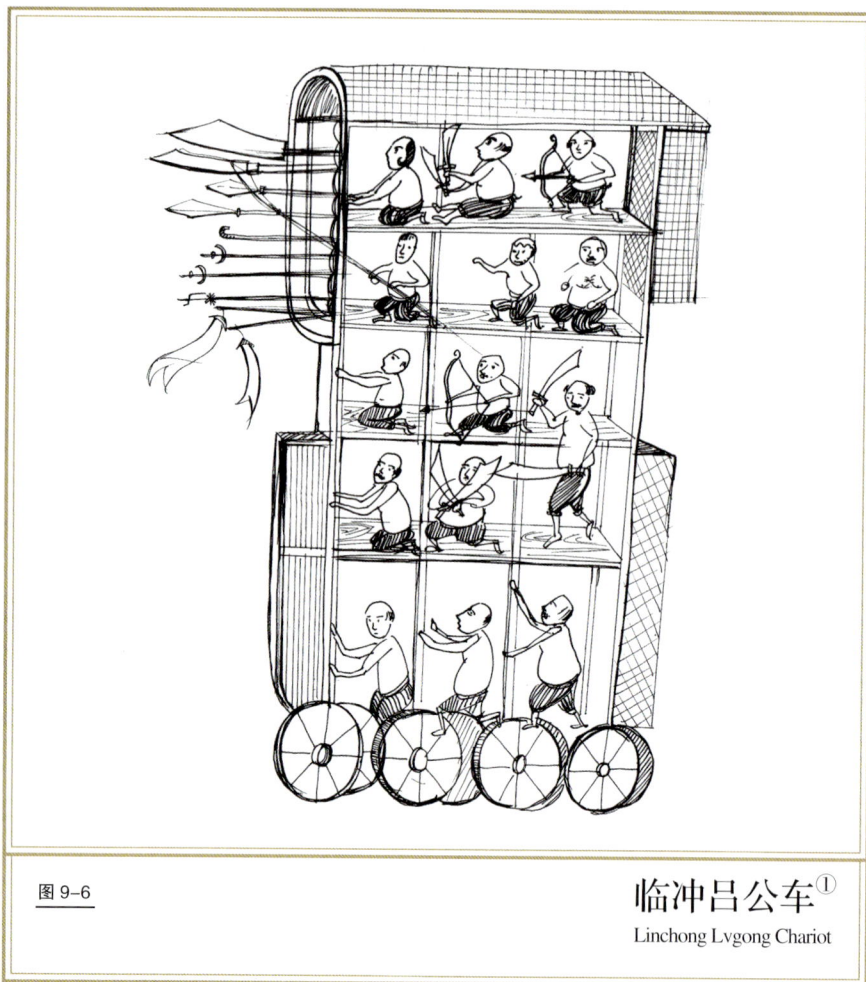

图 9-6

临冲吕公车[1]
Linchong Lvgong Chariot

---

[1] 临冲吕公车：古代一种巨型攻城战车，也是世界上最大的战车。车高数丈，长数十丈，车内分上下五层，每层有梯子可供上下，车中可载几百名武士，配有机弩毒矢、枪戟刀矛等兵器和破坏城墙设施的器械。进攻时众人将车推到城脚，车顶可与城墙齐，兵士们通过天桥冲到城上与敌人拼杀，车下面用撞木等工具破坏城墙。

Linchong Lvgong Chariot: This cart was a kind of giant city attacking chariot, and the largest chariot in the world as well. This cart is about 20 m in height, 30 m in length, having five layers. Soldiers went upstairs or downstairs by means of ladders. This cart can accommodate several hundred soldiers and is equipped with bows, crossbows, poisonous arrows, spears, dagger-axes, falchions and city-destroying equipment. In an attack, the cart was pushed to a city. The top of the cart was as height as the city wall. Soldiers were able to rush onto the city wall to confront the defending army. Meanwhile, soldiers on the lowest layer could use battering ram to break open the masonry walls or city gate.

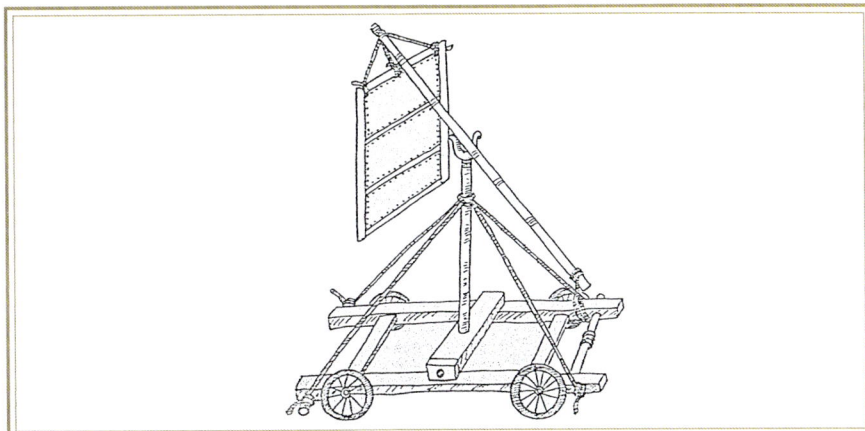

图 9-7

木幔①
Mu Man

图 9-8

行女墙②
Xing Nv Qiang

① 木幔：为一面活动的盾墙，木质结构，有四轮，中间立一杆，支撑木幔，似杠杆活动自如，进攻时可抵挡矢石、檑木及火器的袭击。

Mu Man: It was known as the Wooden Screen in English. It was a four-wheeled wooden cart mounted with a tall wooden pole, hung with a wooden screen, which was able to move freely. The wooden screen was effective to block stones, arrows.

② 行女墙：上施尖顶，车内蔽士兵，可掩护士兵作战。

Xing Nv Qiang: It was known as the Walking Parapet Wall, hiding soldiers inside and protecting them from military attack.

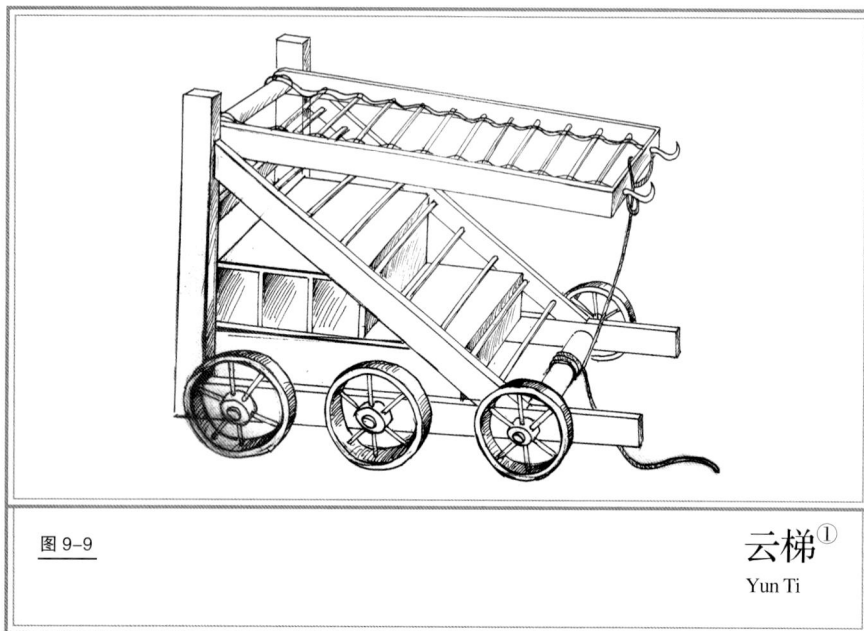

图 9-9

云梯①
Yun Ti

---

① 云梯：专门为了攀登高耸的城墙而发明的攻城兵器。我国古代的云梯下带有轮子，可以推动行驶，故也被称为"云梯车"，配备有防盾、绞车、抓钩等器具，有的带有滑轮升降设备。在云梯的末端绑着一条很长的绳子，通过拉动这根绳子，能够调节云梯的角度和高度。梯子的长度会根据目标城池的不同进行调整，甚至有高达十几米的长梯。

Yun Ti: It was known as the Cloud Ladder in English. It was invented to climb tall city walls. In ancient China, the scaling ladders were loaded on cart, hence the name, the Cloud Ladder Carts. A pulley would pull the ladders up and down. By pulling a long rope at the top of the ladder, soldiers could adjust the height an angles of the ladder. The length of the rope could be adjusted according to the target city walls. Some ropes could be longer than 10 meters.

第2节

守城器械

　　守城器械是指在通用的兵器外，专门用于守备城池的器械。这些器械虽然种类繁多，但是就它们在守城战中的作用而言，大致可以分为反击式、侦听式、抵御式、撞击砸打式、烧灼式、灭火式等六大类。

　　反击式守城器械主要有抛石机、床弩。

　　侦听式守城器械在宋代称瓮听，在明代称地听。中国古代战争中用于侦听声源方位的军用器具，战国时已有使用记载。据《墨子·备穴》记述：当守城者发现敌军开掘地道时，立即在城内墙下挖井，井中放置一口新缸，缸口蒙一层薄牛皮，令听力聪敏的人伏在缸上，监听敌方的动静。此种方法也被用于地面战斗，据唐《太白阴经》记载：夜间战斗时，令少睡者伏地枕在空葫芦上，可听到几十里外的人马脚步声。瓮听在古代主要用于防备敌人偷挖地道入城。

抵御式守城器械甚多，其中有张挂于垛口外侧的木幔、布幔、皮帘等，竖立于城墙上的竹立牌、木立牌、篦篱笆、皮竹笆、护城遮架等遮挡器械，以遮挡攻城敌军射来的箭镞和击砸的石块；有加强城门和城垛防御的插板、暗门、槎牌、塞门刀车、木女头和木女墙等，以便在城门、女墙被摧毁时，使用这些器械进行应急性补救，阻止敌军从突破口冲入城内；还有阻碍敌军云梯近城的叉杆、抵篙等。

撞击砸打式守城器械有撞毁敌军云梯和尖头木驴的撞车和铁撞木，有击砸敌军人马和攻城器械的各种檑木（包括夜叉檑、砖檑、泥檑、木檑、车脚檑）、奈何木、坠石、狼牙拍等。

烧灼式守城器械有铁火床、游火铁箱、行炉、猛火油柜、燕尾炬、飞炬、金火罐等，它们或以猛烈火焰或以烧熔的铁汁烧灼敌军的人马和攻城器械。

灭火式守城器械有水囊、水袋、麻搭、唧筒、溜筒等，它们的作用是在敌军焚烧城门、城楼时将火浇灭。

此外，还有一些特殊用途的守城器械，如钩取敌军士兵和器械的飞钩、铁提钩、绞车，供守城士兵上下城墙用的吊机、吊车、绳梯，抵御敌军从地道中攻城的风扇车、土色毡帘等。

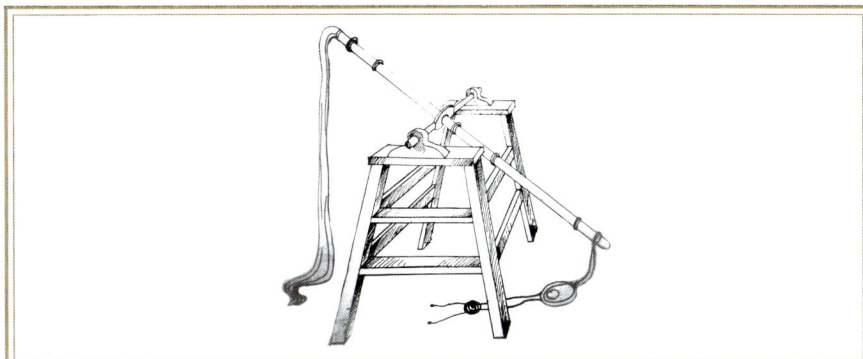

图 9-10

抛石机①
Trebuchet

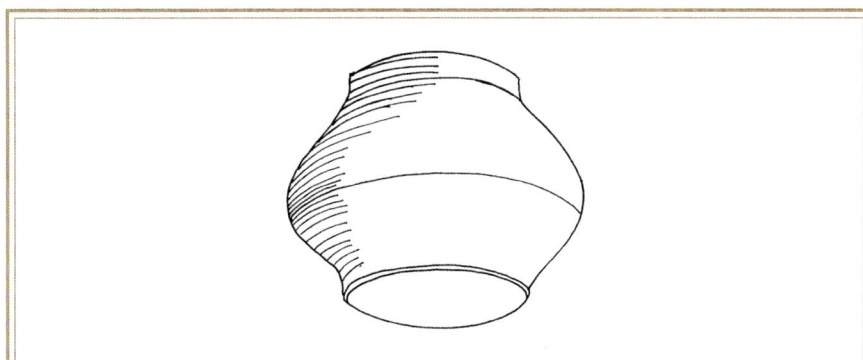

图 9-11

瓮听②
Weng Ting

① 抛石机：又称石炮，是利用杠杆原理抛射石弹的远程攻击性武器。春秋末期抛石机便已经出现，汉唐时期屡有使用，到了宋代有了很大发展，品种日多，威力增大。防御使用时，不设置在城墙上，而是在城中，由城墙上的观测手校订坐标瞄准进行发射，可压制和摧毁敌人的大型攻城兵器和攻城设施。

Trebuchet: The trebuchet, was a long range attacking weapon, making use of the mechanical advantage of a lever. It was invented in the Spring and Autumn Period, commonly-used in the Han Dynasty and the Tang Dynasty, and was greatly improved in the Song Dynasty. When used as a defending device, it was not put on the city wall, but inside the city. It could block enemy's attack and destroy city attacking devices.

② 瓮听：《武经总要》中记载，将瓮置于地面或地下室中，地面声波在瓮内增大混响，可听到远处人马声。

Weng Ting: It was known as the Urn Monitoring in English. When used, it was put above the ground. The sound wave could be magnified by the urn to identify the steps of soldiers and horse far away.

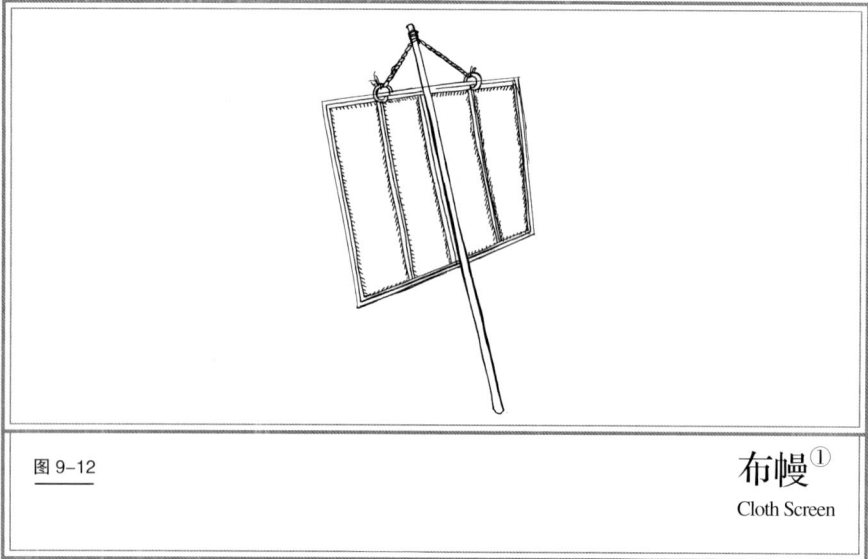

图 9-12

布幔①
Cloth Screen

图 9-13

护城遮箭架②（明）
Hucheng Zhejian Frame
（Ming Dynasty）

① 布幔：以麻绳等材料密集编织而成的幔称为布幔。布幔多用于守城，不仅能够防御箭矢的攻击，有的甚至能够抵挡投石机和床弩的攻击。

Cloth Screen: The Cloth Screen was made of intensely woven jute, mainly used to defend cities. The Cloth Screen could block arrows and stones.

② 护城遮箭架：护城遮箭设置，以木架置两垛口间，上垂湿毡被褥，箭不能入。

Hucheng Zhejian Frame: Literally the Defending City and Blocking Arrow Frame. The frames were installed within crenels, on which wet blankets and quilts were hung to block arrows.

图 9-14

木女头① （宋）
Mu Nv Tou
（ Ming Dynasty ）

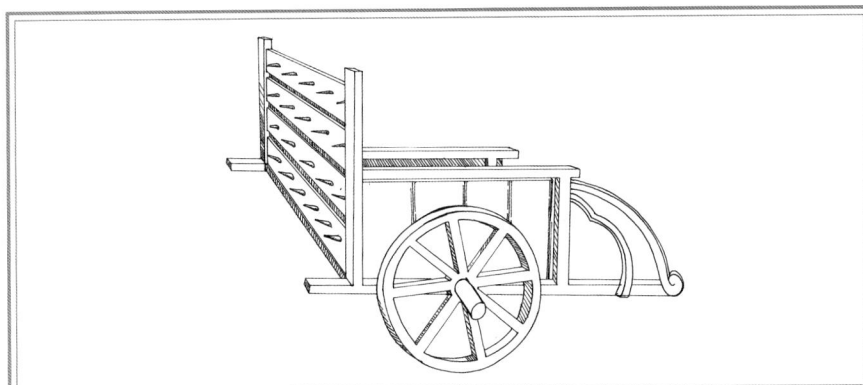

图 9-15

塞门刀车② （宋）
Saimen Dao Chariot
（ Song Dynasty ）

① 木女头：流行于宋代的防御器械，其形如城垛，用木板制成，高六尺，宽五尺，下设两轮，用以堵塞被破坏的城垛或城墙缺口。

Mu Nv Tou: This was a wooden wall, usually 2 m in length and 1.67 m in width, mounted on a cart. When the brick walls were breached by the enemies, this mobile wooden wall could be pulled into place and serve as a temporary defence.

② 塞门刀车：流行于宋代，其车双轮，车之前侧装设诸多枪刃。若城门被敌破坏，则由士兵推车堵塞城门，枪刃朝外以御敌。

Saimen Dao Chariat: This was commonly used in Song Dynasty, mounted on a two- wheeled cart. The front board was fitted with knives. When the city gates or city walls were breached by the enemies, these knife carts would be rolled into place to block up the breaks.

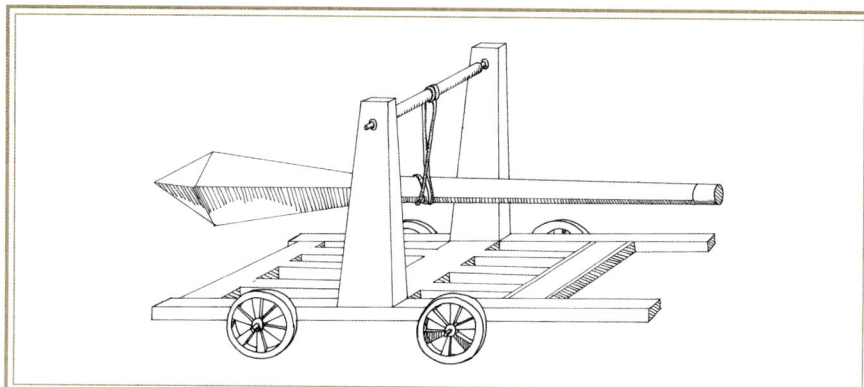

图 9-16

撞车①
Battering Ram

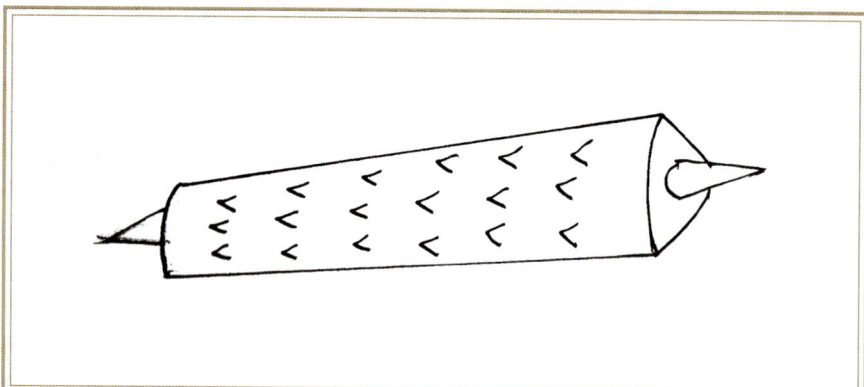

图 9-17

木檑②
Mu Lei

---

① 撞车：由撞锤、锤柄、支架等几部分构成，撞锤多为铁制。撞车在守城时是对付云梯的有效武器，攻城时可用其撞击城门或城墙，以便打开缺口，攻入城中。

Battering Ram: This was composed of the head of a ram, a shaft and a holder. The head of a ram was mainly made of iron. The battering ram was effective against scaling ladders when a city was defended. When a city was attacked, the battering ram was used to break open the masonry walls or splinter their wooden gates.

② 木檑：木质檑木。檑木是用于城上的防御武器，其形如同一段木柱，当敌方攻城士兵向城上攀爬时，将檑木顺城滚下，将敌人撞落。由于材质的不同，檑木可分为木檑、砖檑、泥檑等。

Mu Lei: It was a wooden log swung from city wall to attack the enemy below. Mu means wood. This is part of a city defence equipment. The logs were divided into wood logs, brick logs and mud logs.

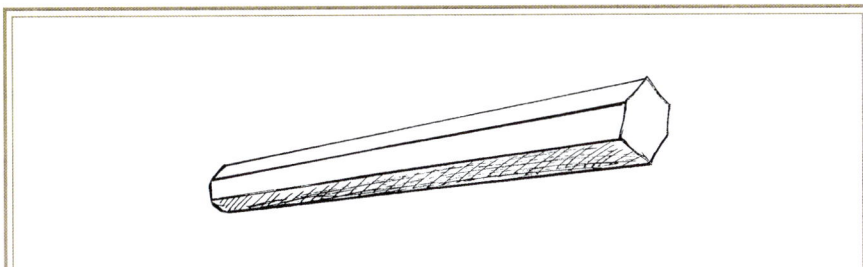

图 9-18

砖檑
Brick Log

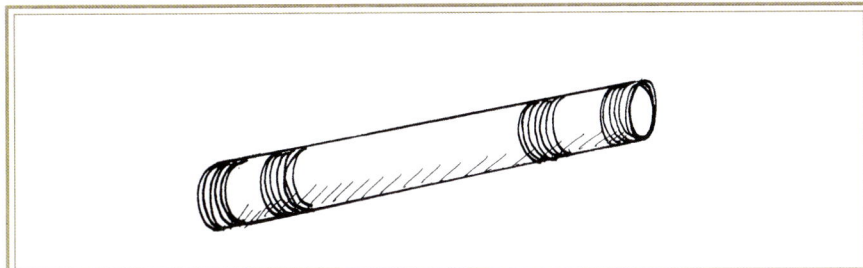

图 9-19

泥檑
Mud Log

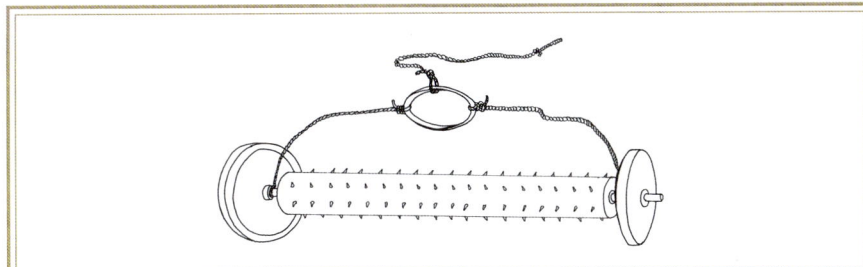

图 9-20

夜叉檑①
Yecha Lei

---

① 夜叉檑：用直径 1 尺、长 1 丈多的湿榆木为滚柱，周围密钉"逆须钉"，钉头露出木面 5 寸，滚木两端安设直径 2 尺的轮子，系以铁索，连接于绞车上，当敌兵聚集城脚时，投入敌群中，绞动绞车可将敌人碾压致死。

Yecha Lei: Yecha means a yakkha in Buddhism. This is a large cylindrical hardwood with many spikes on its sides. The hardwood was over 3.3 meters long with a diameter of 1.3 meters. There were two wheels on the both end of the hardwood, which was attached to a winch with iron chains. It could be thrown into the enemy groups who would be ground to death.

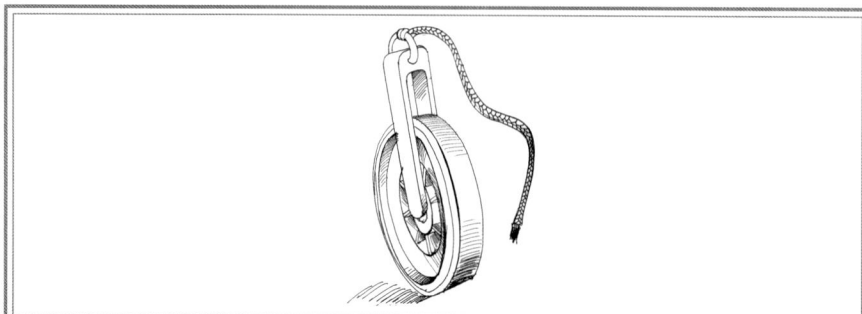

图 9-21

车脚檑
Che Jiao Lei

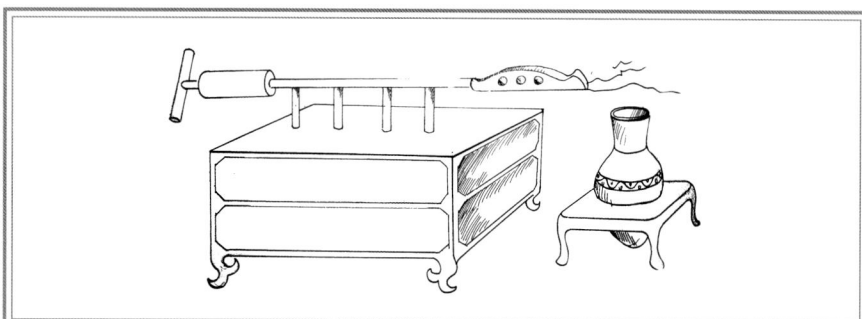

图 9-22

猛火油柜①
Meng Huo You Gui

① 猛火油柜：出现于宋代前后，是中国古代利用石油作为燃料的一种火焰喷射器。其构造原理与现代火焰喷射器相似，喷射火焰时，先把火药填入"火楼"，然后用热的烙锥点火。点着火后，拉出塞棒，把猛火油从燃料箱中抽吸上来，再依靠塞棒的推压使油喷射出去。油通过火楼时被点燃，把火焰喷向敌人。形制大而笨重，这种火器可设在城墙上，作为一种守城的重要兵器。

Meng Huo You Gui: It was known as the Fierce-Fire Oil Tank in English. It is a Chinese piston flamethrower that used a substance similar to gasoline, invented in the late Song Dynasty. The double-piston pump flamethrower comprised of a rectangular container and a brass tube on top of the container. The soldier would pull the piston back and forth to spray a continuous stream of flame. The piston-bellows inside the container would pump the flammable liquid up to the brass tube where a gunpowder spark would ignite the liquid before sending it to the enemy. The container was probably filled with something like petrol or naphtha. The Song Dynasty soldiers would probably put these flamethrowers on top of city walls so that they could use the flamethrowers to repel enemy sieges.

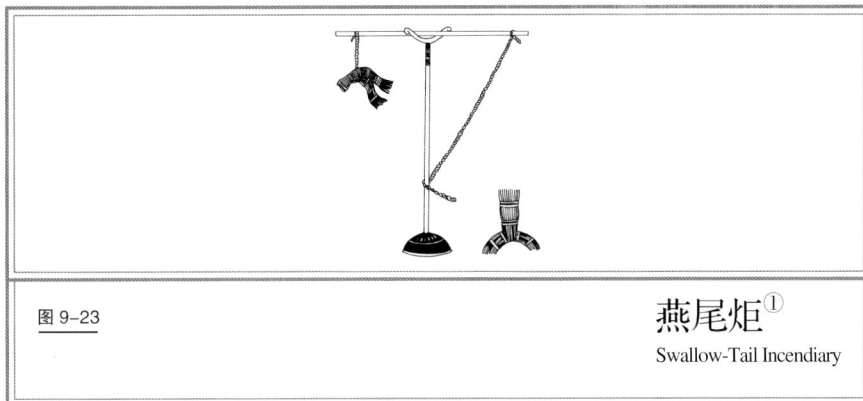

| 图 9-23 | 燕尾炬[①]
Swallow-Tail Incendiary |

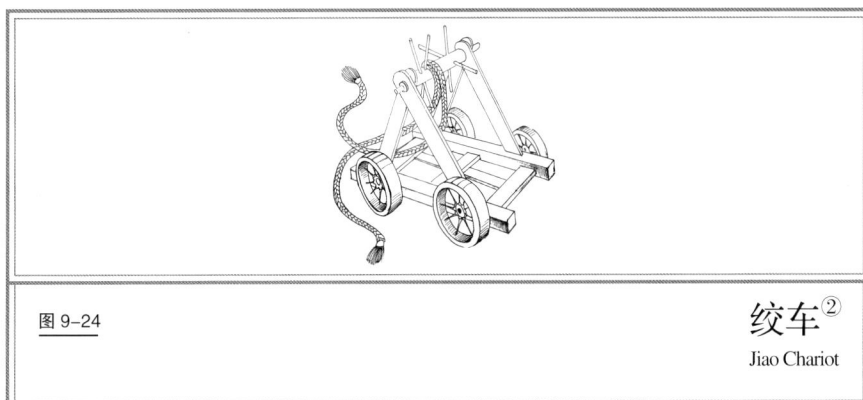

| 图 9-24 | 绞车[②]
Jiao Chariot |

---

① 燕尾炬：束菁草，下分两歧如燕尾，以脂油灌之，发火自城上掷下，因其分叉，可骑木驴等攻城器械上，以烧之。亦有城上设桔槔以铁索系燕尾炬者，称飞炬，垂城以上下，烧攻城蚁附者。

Swallow-Tail Incendiary: The swallow-tail incendiary was made of straw that had been tied together and dipped in fat or oil. Chinese soldiers defending a city under siege would light the incendiary and lower it onto any wooden structure of the invading army to engulf it in fire.

② 绞车：古代军队在守城战中使用的一种钩毁器械。长方形车座用方木制成，下安四轮，车座上用四根阔厚的大木建成一个叉手形柱架，架端用可转横轴相连，横轴两端安绞木，中央缠两根粗大绳索，索端系一个大铁钩。当敌军拥飞梯、木幔、尖头木驴等攻城器械逼近城墙时，守城士兵即抛下横轴上的索钩，钩住上述攻城器械，而后转动绞木，将其绞入城中，既得其器，又俘其人。

Jiao Chariot: It was known as the Twisting Chart in English, a city defence weapon in ancient Chinese wars. The frame was mounted on a four-wheeled wooden cart. A rope, tied with a large iron hook the one end, was tied on a shaft. When attacking soldiers approached the city, with scaling ladders or wooden screens, the defending soldiers threw down the iron hook onto the attacking equipment and wound up the rope to remove the enemy scaling ladders.

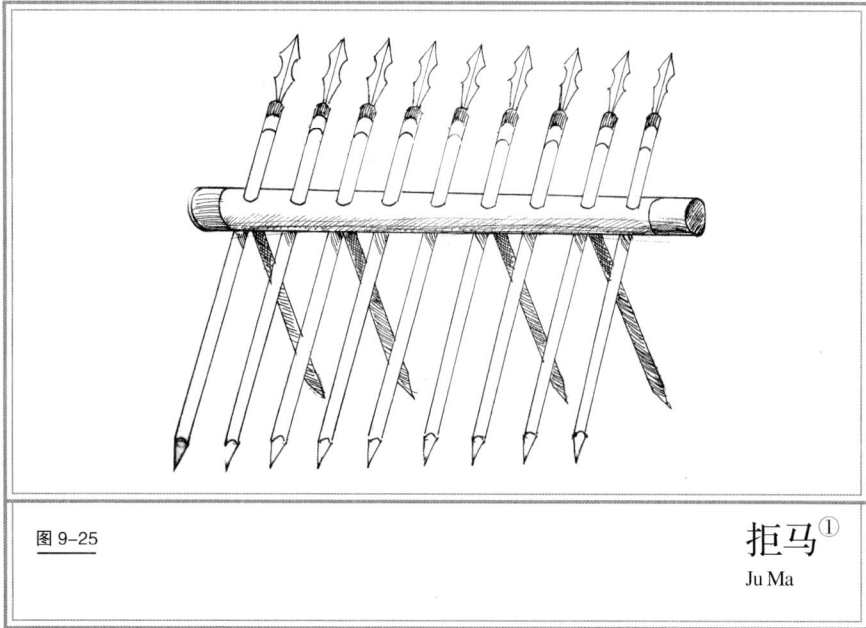

图 9-25

拒马①
Ju Ma

---

① 拒马：古代作战时用的障碍物，唐宋称拒马枪，以圆木为杆，穿杆插枪。明戚继光《练兵实纪》杂集卷 5："拒马每根长九尺二寸，重三斤十二两；铁锤一把，重二斤六两；铁钉一根，重十二两；皮条一根，长四尺。"用时串起钉牢，插入土中，合许多具成为防线。

Ju Ma: Literally, the Anti-Cavalry Pikes, was an array of pikes or spears which were put up together on a wooden rack in order to repel enemy cavalries. The ancient Chinese soldiers would put the Anti-Cavalry Pikes in front of gates, on streets, on paths, and around their military camp in order to stop the advancing cavalries.

参考文献

1.《武经总要》，（北宋）曾公亮、丁度；

2.《武备志》，（明）茅元仪；

3.《考工记》，春秋末年至战国初成书，作者不详；

4.《释名》，（汉）刘熙；

5.《三才图会》，（明）王圻、王思义；

6.《左传》，（春秋末）左丘明；

7.《六韬》，战国时代成书，作者不详；

8.《练兵实纪》，（明）戚继光；

9.《智囊补·兵智·鸳鸯阵》，（明）冯梦龙；

10.《武编》，（明）唐顺之；

11.《大学衍义补》，（明）丘濬；

12.《四镇三关志》，（明）刘效祖；

13.《通典》，（唐）杜佑；

14.《墨子》，（春秋末年）墨翟；

15.《中国古兵器集成》，沈融编著，上海辞书出版社 2015 年 8 月版；

16.《中国兵器收藏与鉴赏全书》，韩欣主编，天津古籍出版社 2008 年 8 月版；

17.《文物藏品定级标准图例：兵器卷》，国家文物局、国家文物鉴定委员会，文物出版社 2011 年 12 月版；

18.《中国古代兵器》，《中国古代兵器》编纂委员会，陕西人民出版社

1995 年 6 月版；

19.《中国古代兵器鉴赏》，谢宇、唐文立编纂，华龄出版社 2008 年 10
月版；

20.《兵器读本》，（日）青木保著，日本评论社昭和十二年十月版；

21.《中国古代兵器图说》，刘秋霖、刘健、王亚新、关琦编，天津古籍
出版社 2003 年 1 月版；

22.《中国青铜器全集》，文物出版社 1995 年 8 月版；

23.《中国兵器甲胄图典》，魏兵著，中华书局 2011 年 9 月版；

24.《中国传统兵器图鉴》，伯仲编著，东方出版社 2010 年 1 月版；

25.《中国古兵器大全》，（日）筱田耕一著，万里机构·万里书店 1996
年 2 月版；

26.《中国古代兵器图集》，成东、钟少异编著，解放军出版社 1990 年 9
月版；

27.《图说中国古代战争战具》，陆敬严著，同济大学出版社 2001 年 1 月
版；

28.《图说中国古代兵器与兵书》，杜文玉、王颜等编著，世界图书出版
公司 2007 年 2 月版。

后　记

　　五千年中华文明，五千年华夏战争史，先人们的智慧幻化出浩如烟海的古兵器形态。经过近两年的调研拍摄、图片收集和文献整理，《中国古代兵器图鉴》终于接近完成，但其中仍不乏遗憾之处。碍于篇幅和种种现实性问题所限，此书所收录讲述的近400幅图片仅能作为路引掀开中国古兵器多彩世界的一角，希望能借此窥见广博深邃的中国古代战争文化之一面。

　　在全书的编纂过程中，于孟晨负责整体的统稿和编审工作，刘磊负责具体分工实施并走访拍摄了其中半数左右的实物照片，组织绘制了一批未能保留实物的古兵器与器械式样。其间特别感谢中国国家博物馆、首都博物馆、陕西历史博物馆、河南博物院、湖北省博物馆、河北博物院、山西博物院、西藏博物馆、新疆维吾尔自治区博物馆、广东省博物馆、宝鸡青铜器博物馆、洛阳博物馆、长沙市博物馆、泸沽湖摩梭民俗博物馆等近20家文物保护单位对信息采集提供的支持，以及参与复原绘图工作的专业人士的协助。

　　在全书各章的写作中，陈红负责第一章（长兵器）、第四章（软兵器）、第五章（暗器）的编写和图说；王祖基负责第三章（远射兵器）、第八章（战车战船）、第九章（攻守城器械）的编写和图说；李亦宁负责第七章（火器）的编著；王嘉负责第二章（短兵器）的编写和图说；牛芳负责第六章（防护具）的编写和图说。随后，张华、杨静又对图鉴中的图片说明文字进行了英文翻译，其中张华翻译了第一章至第三章，杨静翻译了第四章至第九章。另外，澳大利亚的 Rob Collins 先生受邀进行了英文校对。

胡记武、温潇、李金芳、田梦、何之、苏倩等研究生同学也积极参与了本书的编写，其中胡记武、温潇精心修复处理了大量图片；李金芳、田梦同学负责了全本的校对和格式规范；何之、苏倩、胡记武同学分别参与了第四、第五、第六章的部分文字工作。

可考的历史遗存与此前的研究成果为本书提供了宝贵的参考和佐证，许多未能寻到实物的古兵器种类与式样便借鉴了前辈研究者们的成果；发达的互联网信息技术则为影像的拾遗补缺起到了至关重要的作用。本书能够顺利问世，得益于丛书策划者的高瞻远瞩、编写团队的不懈努力与精益求精，以及出版社同仁的悉心指导和大力支持，在此特别向所有支持帮助《中国古代兵器图鉴》的人表示由衷感谢。

于孟晨　刘磊